Advocacy and Learning Disability

Advocacy and Learning Disability

Edited by Barry Gray and Robin Jackson

Jessica Kingsley Publishers
London and Philadelphia

First published in the United Kingdom in 2002 by
Jessica Kingsley Publishers Ltd,
116 Pentonville Road, London
N1 9JB, England
and
325 Chestnut Street,
Philadelphia PA 19106, USA.

www.jkp.com

Library of Congress Cataloging in Publication Data
A CIP catalog record for this book is available from the Library of Congress

British Library Cataloguing in Publication Data
A CIP catalogue record for this book is available from the British Library

ISBN 1 85302 942 4

Printed and Bound in Great Britain by
Athenaeum Press, Gateshead, Tyne and Wear

Contents

CHAPTER ONE

Introduction
Advocacy and Learning Disability

Barry Gray and Robin Jackson

For them we are a bother, an obstacle that must be eliminated, silently. Their cruelty today is seen as a form of charity; death looks for silent paths; it looks for the complicit darkness and the silence that hides. They have already tried to exterminate us. Different doctrines and many different ideas have been used to cover ethnocide with rationality. (Marcos 2001, p.83)

The 'right' to a voice throughout history has been bestowed according to fluctuating perceptions of an individual's ability to benefit from that right. It is only in more recent times that the essential personhood of people with learning disabilities has been more widely acknowledged, and with it their entitlement to support. Many marginalised groups, which by definition are excluded from society, usually find a 'voice' to represent their cause, for it is believed that by removing the 'excluding' quality, the 'whole' human being underneath will be revealed (e.g. homeless people, alcoholics, and so on). These groups who are portrayed as 'less than human' (e.g. 'criminally insane', people with learning disabilities) have suffered throughout history from society's tendency to question their essential humanity and, therefore, their right to a voice.

Boddington and Podpadec (1991) have suggested that philosophers and psychologists view people with learning disabilities from different stances. Psychologists, and particularly those working in clinical settings, assume people with learning disabilities are people first with the same human value and rights as any other person (Firth and Firth 1982). Philosophers, however, engage in debate as to what constitutes humanness, and for some, this leads to a position where some people with learning disabilities are seen as failing to meet the criteria which merit classification as a person (Kuhse and Singer 1985). Classed as a person is clearly a prerequisite to being seen as benefiting from 'having a voice' but for some philosophers, people with learning disabilities do not reach the starting gate in the 'advocacy stakes'.

The UK government's White Paper, *Valuing People* (Department of Health 2001), defines learning disability in the following way:

> people with learning disabilities are people first. We focus throughout on what people can do, with support where necessary, rather than on what they cannot do. Learning disability includes the presence of:
>
> > a significantly reduced ability to understand new or complex information, to learn new skills (impaired intelligence), with
> >
> > a reduced ability to cope independently (impaired social functioning)
> >
> > which started before adulthood, with a lasting effect on development. (Department of Health 2001, p.14)

Whatever the term or definition used, the characteristics listed above are usually associated with, or lead to, low status and a devalued role in society (Wolfensberger 1983). This has significance when examining the role of advocacy, both in terms of highlighting the need for and in explaining the lack of such services until fairly recently. From an examination of the skills which are required for successful advocacy, it would appear that a fairly high level of competence is needed. At first sight the Department of Health's (2001) definition suggests that this level of competence may be beyond a person with a learning disability.

However, one should be cautious about accepting such a generalisation without qualification, as there are people with learning disabilities who may well be very competent in specific areas of behaviour and/or cognitive functioning, although it remains probable that the person will have significant areas of 'incompetence' that make the skills needed for advocacy difficult to acquire. That is not to suggest that people with learning disabilities cannot advocate: the large number of self-advocacy groups – at least one for each medium-sized town in the UK – is testament to that fact. However, advocacy remains an activity that is, in the main, left to trained professionals.

It is possible to identify some of the activities involved in advocacy (Atkinson 1999; Booth and Booth 1998; Further Education Unit 1990; Wertheimer 1998) and these become pertinent when applying the advocacy concept to people with learning disabilities. At this point we propose to set the scene in relation to what may be referred to as 'formal' advocacy schemes and their historical development.

David Schwartz (1992, 1997) has referred to two types of caring. He compares the 'informal' care provided in natural communities with the 'formal' care provided by professional services. In a similar vein to John McKnight (1995), he suggests that professional care is in some sense less 'human' and reduces the natural caring capacity of the community.

Advocacy for people with learning disabilities can possibly be viewed in a similar fashion with informal and formal forms of advocacy, and that subsequent analysis will reveal similar processes of 'dehumanising' and 'deskilling'. However, the point needs to be stressed that the activities of caring and advocating are quite different. Informal caring indicates an acceptance of a (often mutually) dependent relationship. On the other hand, advocacy, because of the potential conflicts between needs, wants and rights, and the inevitable presence of challenge, may be a less comfortable and 'natural' human relationship.

Certainly from a historical perspective, it is possible to make a distinction between the human disposition towards standing up for oneself or others and the more formal advocacy that is part of a structured and regulated system. It is likely that advocacy behaviours have been a constituent part of the human repertoire since the earliest times. Whilst it is not being proposed that formal advocacy is more important, we will for the purposes of this chapter concentrate on the development of 'official' advocacy work with and by people with learning disabilities. Possibly the keenest advocates have been parents and we will see how their efforts to gain a stronger and louder voice have played a significant part in the growth and acceptance of advocacy services.

Jessing and Dean (1977) have suggested that the single most important factor in any advocacy system is the ideology held with respect to the people it is designed to serve. They describe five *components* along with *underlying assumptions* that they believe are essential for the delivery of quality services. First, it is assumed that *each person has value*, which is particularly important for individuals who historically have been devalued by society. Second, an acceptance of *developmental theory*, which assumes that every person has the capacity for growth and learning (Wolfensberger 1972). The *normalisation principle* is the third component: this system of beliefs holds that people with learning disabilities are marginalised members of society who are as a consequence 'devalued' and ascribed correspondingly devalued social roles. One of the major goals of any human service should be to enable and support individuals towards achieving more valued social roles. The fourth key component is *consumer participation*, which relates to the importance of making human service systems accountable to consumers and their representatives. The fifth component concerns *human and legal rights*: the principle that people with learning disabilities are citizens with the same rights and responsibilities as other citizens of the same country and the same age should be apparent from all activities undertaken by an advocacy service.

These five components can be found, in a slightly different form, in all advocacy schemes. For example, when Atkinson (1999) talks about *empowerment, autonomy, citizenship, and inclusion*, she is referring to aspects of these components. Whilst there are some cultural and language differences, the fundamental ideology is the same. In essence we are arguing that advocacy by and for people with learning disabilities is based on the belief that we are all citizens with the same rights, responsibilities and potential for growth, and that there is a need to combat the exclusion and discrimination experienced by some members of our society through enabling them to access their human and legal rights.

In an article on advocacy and learning disabilities, Mack (2001) focused on self-advocacy and the potential conflict between competent self-advocates and parent-dominated organisations such as Mencap. Mack (2001) looked at the ways in which the interests of people with more severe and profound learning disabilities, who are unlikely to have a 'voice', can be represented. For people with severe intellectual impairments, there continues to be a debate as to who best represents their views. Heal (1999) has posed the question whether the achievement of quality of life goals and the attainment of valued social roles are limited by competence. His conclusions are tentative but he, like other workers in the field, hopes that competence is not a limiting factor. However, given that our social systems intrinsically link value, competence and quality, it is difficult to see how a valued social role can be obtained, when a person is seen as having only limited personal competence. This interpretation lends support to what Marc Gold (1975) has termed 'the deviance-competence hypothesis'. Simply stated, the more competence one is perceived as having, then the more deviance one is allowed. So a professor who is perceived as having great competency is allowed, and even expected, to be deviant (i.e. eccentric) in several areas. The opposite is also true that the less competence one is perceived as possessing then the less deviance one is permitted.

Certainly the perceived inability of those with learning disabilities to advocate for themselves is a contributory factor to the nature of advocacy services that have developed over the years. Not only do self-advocacy services for people with *physical disabilities* have a longer history but also access to education, employment and other normal societal facilities are legally recognised for this group in most western societies (e.g. USA: Americans with Disabilities Act 1990; UK: Disability Discrimination Act 1995). Whilst this legislation is also intended to cover people with learning disabilities, there are often 'get-out' clauses that permit discrimination towards this group to continue. For example, under the UK's Disability Discrimination Act 1995, employers and services are required to make 'reasonable adjustment' in order to accommodate disabled applicants or customers. Provision of ramps to allow access for someone using a wheelchair would be seen as a 'reasonable adjustment'; however, providing a support worker for one year, so that a person with learning disabilities can be employed to learn a routine work task, is less likely to be viewed as 'reasonable' by either an employer or the law.

Given the limited evidence for any presence of advocacy for people with learning disabilities up until the twentieth century, when were its first stirrings? In the UK this can be traced to the formation of Mencap in 1946, when a group of parents of children with learning disabilities joined together to campaign for better education for their children. Since that time Mencap (originally the Royal Society for Mentally Handicapped Children) has fought for improved education, residential, leisure and employment services. Mencap has now become a major provider of services, which has increased the likelihood of conflicts of interest, given its role as campaigner, advocate and service provider. It is not altogether surprising that Mencap has found the rise of self-advocacy within its organisation such a challenge (Mack 2001).

A further conflict of interest can occur where an organisation moves from being run *by* a particular group to an organisation run *for* a particular group. This conflict has been well documented by Woodward (1995), who has described the development of Centres for Independent Living (CILs) in the USA. The original organisations founded *by* disabled people are now facing a take-over by non-disabled administrators who claim they can create a more effective organisation *for* disabled people. In some ways this development resonates with an argument put forward by Colin Low (2001) in which he has suggested that perhaps rights for 'the disabled' may have 'gone too far' and that the radical disability movement, as personified by Oliver (1990, 1995), can only ever achieve its aim of full inclusion, if there is a 'dulling' or 'toning down' of that movement's radicalism.

Whilst there is some way to go before self-advocacy organisations are seen as posing a threat, there are some signs they are making an impact. For example, the introduction of direct payments in the Community Care (Direct Payments) Act 1996 was originally heralded as a means of empowering people with impairments to obtain the support required to meet their social needs. Local authorities have been particularly slow in providing direct payments for people with learning disabilities. An unpublished survey (Downes 2001) has indicated that in the south of England less than 50 per cent of authorities have activated direct payments for people with learning disabilities and, where this has happened, it has often been in a form that is less empowering (e.g. the administration of the payments scheme through a trust). The self-advocacy organisation People First has produced easily accessible material drawing attention to the availability of direct payments, yet many of the local and county self-advocacy groups, which are supported by professionals, do not appear to see direct payments as an important issue.

Other organisations for people with learning disabilities claim to have developed a remit for advocacy. In 1973 the Association for Professions in Mental Handicap (APMH) was established. The following objectives were set out in its constitution:

> To promote the general welfare of mentally handicapped people and their families, by encouraging high standards of care and development of mentally handicapped people, by facilitating co-operation and the sharing of knowledge among all professionals working for or with mentally handicapped people, by offering a unified professional view on the strategies of mental handicap, and by educating the public to accept, understand and respect mentally handicapped people. (APMH Constitution 1977, p.89)

The seeds of advocacy can be seen in this declaration. Indeed, APMH was one of the first professional organisations in the UK to include parents and people with learning disabilities as full members.

Other professional organisations (e.g. British Institute for Learning Disabilities (BILD); British Psychological Society Special Interest Group; National Development Team) may also claim to advocate for people with learning disabilities. However, this tends to be an implicit part of their main role which is the promotion of higher standards of support services and the dissemination of information. In a similar way, educational institutions that provide courses for staff working with people with learning disabilities can claim to have an implicit advocacy role. One higher education institution has sought to make this role more explicit by including people with learning disabilities in the planning, delivering, and evaluating of courses (Earwaker and Gray 2000).

Organisations in the UK with a more explicit advocacy role include Mencap (founded in 1946) and the Campaign for the Mentally Handicapped (CMH, founded in the early 1970s) and now called Values into Action. They can be categorised as a form of 'collective advocacy' (Wertheimer 1998) or 'class advocacy'

(East Nebraska Council for Ordinary Residences (ENCOR) 1981). People First and Advocacy Partners are organisations in the UK that have advocacy as their central purpose: People First promotes self-advocacy and Advocacy Partners supports citizen advocacy. People First was founded in the USA in the 1960s and in the UK in the 1970s, whilst Advocacy Partners developed from groups that sprang up in the 1970s and 1980s. In the UK, 1981 was the year in which five national charities – Mencap, MIND, the Spastics Society, One-to-One and the Leonard Cheshire Foundation – established Advocacy Alliance.

One of the aims of these formal advocacy organisations has been to encourage governments to recognise the critical role that advocacy can play in the development of effective services for people with learning disabilities. There is some evidence to show that governments are now listening:

> Advocacy is central to the new era of care when the planning and delivery of services is designed from the perspective of the service user. (Foreword to *Independent Advocacy: A Guide for Commissioners*: Scottish Executive 2000b)

> Better information, communication and advocacy are central to making any changes and putting the principles into practice. (*The Same as You? A Review of Services for People with Learning Disabilities*: Scottish Executive 2000a, para. 3.1)

> The Government's long-term aim is to have a range of independent advocacy services available in each area so that people with learning disabilities can choose the one which best meets their needs. To achieve this, we will want a partnership with citizen advocacy and self advocacy groups to promote and sustain development of independent local advocacy schemes. (*Valuing People: A New Strategy for Learning Disability for the 21st Century*: Department of Health 2001, para. 4.9)

What is striking here is that notwithstanding this recently accorded recognition, there is surprisingly little written on the subject of advocacy. One of the consequences of this neglect has been that the meaning and purpose of advocacy have not been subjected to sustained critical examination with the result that discussions relating to advocacy tend to occur in a conceptual fog. It is our hope that this book will bring some measure of clarity to what is a confused and confusing field and to raise the level of discussion beyond the kind of superficial aspiration commonly encountered in government publications. If there is a genuine commitment to providing people with learning disabilities with the means to express their views then there has to be a more informed debate about how this can most effectively be achieved. No arrogant claims are being made that this book provides answers to the many questions that currently exist about the nature, value and purpose of advocacy. However, knowing the right questions to ask is an important first step on the path to understanding. This book seeks to ask some of these questions.

The book covers the following topics:

> the principles underpinning different types of advocacy

> the issue of integrity and how this relates to advocacy

> the role of values in the management of advocacy schemes

> the kinds of conflicts that can occur between human service professionals and people with learning disabilities

> legal issues affecting advocacy organisations and the advocate/client relationship

> the experience of self-advocacy by people with learning disabilities

> ways in which advocacy can be made accessible to people with communication difficulties

> advocacy developments in the USA, Australia and New Zealand.

Jan Walmsley (Chapter 2) examines the principles which underpin the two main types of advocacy for people with learning disabilities – citizen and self-advocacy – and invites the reader to consider how far these principles are complementary and compatible. Walmsley argues that some of the criticisms that have been levelled at the principle of normalisation can equally be directed at citizen advocacy, where non-disabled people assume powerful and unassailable positions in the lives of people with learning disabilities. Further, whilst the normalisation principle claims to revalue people with disabilities, it is self-evidently rooted in a hostility to and denial of 'differentness'. This failure to take a holistic view of the person with learning disabilities means that citizen advocacy tends to hold back from intervening in situations where intervention is needed. Walmsley goes on to examine some of the reasons why self-advocacy by people with learning disabilities does not sit easily within the disabled people's movement.

Michael Kendrick (Chapter 3) notes that advocates frequently find themselves in situations where they have to evaluate and even judge the propriety, motives and consequences of the behaviour of others. What advocates need to be aware of is that the standards of integrity that they set for others need to be matched by their own performance. Kendrick identifies a number of dimensions of integrity against which the performance of advocates should be judged.

Tim Clement (Chapter 4) seeks to clarify some of the beliefs and values that exist about advocacy and uses concepts drawn from management and organisational literature to examine these beliefs and values. The point is made that the way in which 'values' are used in citizen advocacy and self-advocacy are rarely subject to close examination and that where definitions are provided they are invariably weak. Clement argues that citizen advocacy and self-advocacy organisations tend to be characterised by ambiguity, where members of organisations have reached agreement about the stated values but have not explored and reached consensus about underlying assumptions.

Colin Goble (Chapter 5) explores the conflicts between human service professionals and people with learning disabilities and the meaning, purpose and practice of advocacy. Attention is drawn to the misguided view which conceives advocacy as a therapeutic rather than a political activity with the result that advocacy is stripped of its radical and emancipatory role. Goble looks at the wider origins and nature of the social construction of professional consciousness and its relationship to issues of service user empowerment and advocacy in health and social care system.

Deborah Baillie and Veronica Strachan (Chapter 6) highlight key legal issues relating to the operation and management of different forms of advocacy organisation. The chapter makes clear the legal responsibilities and duties of advocates and members of management committees and the legal rights of users. Serious difficulties can occur where advocacy organisations do not address such issues. As Kendrick has observed advocacy organisations are quick to identify the deficiencies in other organisations but frequently fail to turn the spotlight on their own shortcomings.

Mike Pochin (Chapter 7) reflects upon some significant issues in the implementation of a citizen advocacy scheme supporting people with learning disabilities. According to Pochin citizen advocacy is not merely one individual speaking up for the needs and wishes of another but a unique bond between two people – the principles governing that bond being independence and loyalty. The two main obstacles to the implementation and growth of citizen advocacy have centred on the lack of funding and the growing diversification in types of advocacy. The argument is advanced that citizen advocacy can be better understood by viewing it as a form of community development rather than an intervention or service. That is to say, the partner is not merely a recipient or 'service user' but also a 'giver' who can contribute to the life of the advocate. A distinction is drawn between long-term and crisis partnerships with a recognition that advocacy goals may often only appear with the passage of time, so that in citizen advocacy it may well be the relationship that determines the goals.

Dorothy Atkinson (Chapter 8) examines recent research in relation to advocacy by, for and with people with learning disabilities. The focus is on self-advocacy research as this raises important issues about the nature of research, and of advocacy, and the relationship between the two. Atkinson makes the point that self-advocacy is about identity and that people in self-advocacy groups are more likely to acknowledge their identity as people with learning disabilities, which can be interpreted as a celebration rather than a denial of differentness. The role and value of participatory research is discussed along with the potential for research to empower the self-advocates.

Members of Carlisle People First explain in Chapter 9 how membership of the organisation has profoundly changed their lives. They describe graphically their sense of anger, frustration and powerlessness when in the past they have been in situations where they have been denied any opportunity to express their hopes, concerns and fears. Through self-advocacy members feel that they have achieved a measure of freedom and influence over the direction of their lives. They indicate how having experienced at first hand the benefits of active involvement in People First, they have gained sufficient confidence to promote the merits of self-advocacy.

Nick Pike (Chapter 10) argues that advocacy for children with learning disabilities and their families is the neglected dimension in the support network for such children and families. He identifies a number of reasons for this neglect: a pervasive 'familist ideology' that places the responsibility for advocacy on the shoulders of parents; the absence of any rational framework for family support; an overabundance of models of service and practice with little in the way of clear roles and framework upon which to build; and, a lack of any obvious theoretical and organisational model for advocacy development. One solution, in Pike's opinion, might be the development of a network of advocates for children with disabilities. This could be achieved by extending either the brief of existing children's rights schemes or the terms of reference of citizen advocacy schemes.

Janet Scott and Janet Larcher (Chapter 11) address the problems in advocacy for someone with a learning disability who has significant limitations in the ability to communicate. In order to be an effective advocate for someone with communication difficulties, it is important for the advocate to know about the different types and degrees of communication difficulty, the effect that these might have on the person and the consequences on that individual's communication partners. At the same time the advocate will need to be aware of, and develop skills in, different techniques used to augment and facilitate non-speech communication and to know how to access more specialist help and advice. The purpose of this chapter is to provide the reader with some understanding of communication disability and how this may influence the advocacy process. Practical suggestions and possible methods for developing a means of communication are discussed.

The final three chapters look at advocacy developments in the USA, Australia and New Zealand. In his observations on the US advocacy scene, Michael Kendrick (Chapter 12) acknowledges that the scale and complexity of that scene make any brief and generalised treatment impossible. A significant feature of developments in the USA has been the ability of the advocacy community to form alliances right across the political and ideological spectrum and to secure funding from a wide diversity of financing sources. As a consequence of the power of advocacy organisations and the proficiency of advocates, the rights and interests of people with disabilities have been recognised and given legal protection. Having identified some of the virtues of the US advocacy scene, Kendrick turns to a number of concerns. Whilst the USA relies more heavily than do other nations on private funds for advocacy, nevertheless US advocacy is deeply dependent on public financing. Kendrick acknowledges that the situation could change and if it were to do so, then it is probable that most formal advocacy would decline. Who then would advocate for people with disabilities? Whilst there has been widespread agreement that people ought to have advocacy, Kendrick notes that less attention has been paid to the adequacy of that advocacy. He questions the uncritical acceptance by advocacy organisations of current priorities in the learning disability field and argues for a more explicit and compelling theory to guide advocates.

Dimity Peter (Chapter 13) indicates that the development of formalised advocacy programmes is a relatively new phenomenon in the Australian sociopolitical context. Unlike the USA, Australia does not have a Bill of Rights for any of its citizens so that there is no right or entitlement to services for people with disabilities. Peter observes that the threat to formal advocacy appears to come from within the advocacy movement, rather than external sources. One weakness is that the learning disability field is divided with competing interests, philosophies and visions of what advocacy is and what needs to be done. This lack of understanding as to the meaning and purpose of advocacy extends not only to the Australian public but also to many services, funders and even people in the advocacy movement itself. A particular problem has been the lack of cohesiveness within the advocacy community. Peter notes that the adoption by government of market ideologies has led advocacy away from clear principles towards concerns with efficiency, outcomes, numbers and turnover, which prompts the question as to who is shaping advocacy in Australia. There is evidence that government interest and support for advocacy in its current forms is diminishing. Notwithstanding the uncertain future, advocacy is still seen as remaining a powerful force in the lives of many Australians with disabilities.

Colleen Brown (Chapter 14) writes from the perspective of a volunteer education advocate for families who have children with special needs in New Zealand. Parents of children with special needs have no right of access to government funded advocacy support service. The view of the government is that the provision of such a service would not be economically feasible. Advocacy services therefore rely on a mix of government funding and voluntary donations. However, advocacy organisations have to tread warily as too strident criticism of government policy can lead to the withdrawal of state funding. Particular attention is drawn to the implementation by the New Zealand government of its policy Special Education 2000, which was designed to introduce a world-class inclusive education system. A key feature of this policy is the notion of 'partnership' between parents and schools. But little consideration has been given to how such a partnership can work, given the hierarchical, autocratic and bureaucratic nature of the education system. The chapter provides first-hand accounts by parents of their experience. Brown concludes that without formal lines of accountability created and fully funded advocacy centres established to safeguard the rights of children with special needs, the Special Education 2000 policy is likely to fail.

Two interrelated themes, which thread their way through these chapters, are operational independence and security of funding. One of the most crucial issues facing an advocacy service is the nature of the funding arrangements for these will influence the extent to which a service can operate independently (Dunning 1995). What is not in doubt is that an advocacy service, which is in receipt of direct funding from a statutory agency, will often find its freedom to represent people constrained or limited.

Where advocacy services are directly funded by statutory services in the UK, there is a growing trend for the adoption of service agreements. There are a number of problems with this kind of arrangement. First, the purchaser–provider model is an inappropriate one given that there is a major difference in the relationship between an organisation that provides a service for an individual client for which the funder pays and an organisation where funds are not linked to individuals but to the provision of an independent service. Second, as soon as an advocacy service is contractually linked with a funder in the provision of its service, it will be directly accountable to that purchaser. That relationship immediately breaches the independent position of the advocacy service. Third, with service agreements there may be pressure to disclose information about the people represented. The perception of the advocacy service as contractually tied to the purchaser is likely to encourage doubts as to the extent to which that service can protect confidentiality. As a result the advocacy service may be seen as an organisational adjunct to the statutory agency which is funding the service. Fourth, service agreements are likely to lead to the bureaucratisation of the service provided (e.g. increased paperwork and form-filling; regular completion of statistical returns). In this connection it is worth noting that one of the reasons for the rise of the citizen advocacy movement was a concern that the statutory agencies had become too bureaucratic and remote from the people they were supposed to be serving (Jackson 1999a).

It is accepted that if public monies are invested in advocacy services that there has to be some mechanism to ensure that the funds are properly and effectively used. There is then a compelling case for funds being channelled through a central government agency or local authority Consumer Protection Department. Where advocacy services are an integral part of national voluntary organisations, there is a risk that the campaigning mission of the voluntary organisation may infiltrate and colour the work of the advocacy service and prejudice its independent and neutral status.

Jackson (1999b) has argued that, like the mayfly, advocacy services funded by statutory agencies may have only a relatively short lifespan:

> *initial phase:* a short period characterised by general enthusiasm for the idea of advocacy
>
> *awareness phase:* when the funders begin to realise the potential threat that advocacy poses
>
> *containment phase:* when efforts are made to rein in the advocacy service as the performance of the funders comes under increasing critical scrutiny
>
> *final phase:* when advocacy services begin to disintegrate as their independence and integrity are progressively undermined by the funders.

One reason for the uneasy relationship between advocacy services and professional workers is because the process of empowering disadvantaged individuals and groups can be interpreted as a challenge to the power, role and status of professional workers (Jackson 1999a; Simons 1993). A further cause of irritation is the fact that it is quite often the advocates and not the professional workers who draw the attention of the people they are representing to their eligibility to different benefits and entitlements.

A further source of friction relates to the role of the advocate. Statutory agencies find difficulty in coping with situations where advocates assume an assertive, proactive and interventionist role. In a study undertaken by Danker-Brown, Sigelman and Bensberg (1979), citizen advocates were found to perform a whole series of defender roles: correcting situations in which their clients were being abused or exploited; educating clients about their legal rights; intervening with an agency to improve services to their client where they were deficient; educating service agencies about the needs of their clients. There are those who strongly contend that the relationship between the advocate and the person represented should be an ongoing one in which the advocate acts as a 'watchdog' to ensure that the person's rights are in no way being infringed, curtailed or denied (Strichart and Gottlieb 1980).

One difficulty, which faces all advocacy services, is reconciling the volunteering principle with the need to have an efficient group of advocates who are able to

> unravel often complex cases quickly
>
> identify and focus on the key issues
>
> present a client's case in an objective manner
>
> create a working partnership with clients based on mutual trust
>
> access a wide range of sources to obtain relevant information and advice.

At the same time advocates need to be aware of the kinds of strategies sometimes employed by statutory agencies and ways of coping constructively with them. As few people coming forward to act as volunteer advocates have all these abilities, there is a need for training. It is at this point that some uneasiness is expressed for it is felt that the objectivity and neutrality of the advocate must necessarily be compromised by exposing volunteers to extensive training. In other words, the advocate changes from being a volunteer to a quasi-professional. However, the alternative of letting loose untrained advocates to deal with sensitive and complex cases provides ammunition for those who question the value of advocacy schemes.

In discussing the importance of operational independence and security of funding, one issue has tended to be overlooked. Given the likelihood of advocacy services being subject to pressures, subtle and blatant, applied by funders, it is essential to have management committees which are prepared to stand up to such pressures and vigorously assert the service's independence. Situations do sometimes arise when in a misguided attempt to placate the funders, management committees cede some measure of a service's independence and in so doing compromise that service's integrity. When that happens it is inevitable that divisions will occur between the advocates and management committee members. No matter how good the team of advocates, if there is a weak, inept and unsupportive management committee, that advocacy service will fail.

If critical issues like operational independence and security of funding are to be properly addressed then there needs to be a coming together of the many disparate advocacy groups into a coalition that has the power and authority, endurance and resolve, leadership and vision, to test the commitment of government. However, such a powerful and united voice may simply prompt the government of the day to respond by choosing the 'silent paths', to which Marcos (2001) alludes, where opposition is disguised behind a façade of rationality. During the 1990s successive governments have confined their commitment to advocacy to the occasional ritualistic obeisance or rhetorical flourish and not to any substantive action leading to the allocation of resources sufficient to create an effective national advocacy network. The key question here is whether any government can afford, politically and financially, to sanction the development of a system that has the potential to expose so openly, relentlessly and mercilessly deficiencies in policy, provision and practice.

References

Americans With Disabilities Act (1990) Washington, DC: Bureau of National Affairs.

Association of Professions for the Mentally Handicapped (1977) *Resources, Responsibilities and Rights*: a collection of papers given at the Association's Fourth Annual Congress, University of York. London: APMH.

Atkinson, D. (1999) *Advocacy: A Review*. Brighton: Pavilion.

Boddington, P. and Podpadec, T. (1991) 'Who are the mentally handicapped?' *Journal of Applied Philosophy 8*, 177–190.

Booth, W. and Booth, T. (1998) *Advocacy for Parents with Learning Difficulties*. Brighton: Pavilion.

Community Care (Direct Payments) Act (1996) London: Department of Health.

Danker-Brown, P., Sigelman, C. and Bensberg, G. (1979) 'Advocate–protégé: pairings and activities in three citizen advocacy programs.' *Mental Retardation 17*, 137–141.

Department of Health (2001) *Valuing People: A New Strategy for Learning Disability for the 21st Century*, Cmd 5086. London: Department of Health.

Disability Discrimination Act (1995) London: Department for Education and Employment.

Downes, C. (2001) 'Direct payments and people with learning disabilities', unpublished BA thesis, King Alfred's College, Winchester.

Dunning, A. (1995) *Citizen Advocacy with Older People: A Code of Good Practice.* London: Centre for Policy on Ageing.

Earwaker, S. and Gray, B. (2000) 'The development of disability studies at one college of higher education in England.' *International Journal of Practical Approaches to Disability 24*, 32–38.

East Nebraska Council for Ordinary Residences (ENCOR) (1981) *Advocacy Training Packet for ENCOR Advisors.* 8/81.

Firth, M. and Firth, H. (1982) *Mentally Handicapped People with Special Needs,* King's Fund Centre Reports 82/45. London: King's Fund Centre.

Further Education Unit (FEU) (1990) *Developing Self-Advocacy Skills with People with Disabilities and Learning Difficulties.* London: FEU.

Gold, M. (1975) 'Vocational training'. In J. Wortis (ed) *Mental Retardation and Developmental Disabilities,* vol. 7. New York: Brunner-Mazel.

Heal, L.W. (1999) 'Are normalization and social role valorization limited by competence?' In R.J. Flynn and R.A. Lemay (eds) *A Quarter-Century of Normalization and Social Role Valorization: Evolution and Impact.* Ottawa: University of Ottawa Press.

Jackson, R. (1999a) 'Learning disability and advocacy: obstacles to client empowerment.' *Journal of Learning Disabilities for Nursing, Health and Social Care 3*, 50–55.

Jackson, R. (1999b) 'Is there a future for citizen advocacy for people with learning disabilities?' *British Journal of Developmental Disabilities 45*, 140–145.

Jessing, B. and Dean, S. (1977) 'Case advocacy: ideology and operation.' In L.D. Baucom and G.J. Bensberg (eds) *Advocacy Systems for Persons with Developmental Disabilities: Context, Components and Resources.* Lubbock, TX: Research and Training Center in Mental Retardation.

Kuhse, H. and Singer, P. (1985) *Should the Baby Live? The Problem of Handicapped Infants.* Oxford: Oxford University Press.

Low, C. (2001) 'Have disability rights gone too far?' Text of speech given at City Insights Lecture, 3 April. Can be found at http://www.city.ac.uk/whatson/low.htm

Mack, T. (2001) 'We'll do it our way.' *Guardian Weekend* 14 April.

McKnight J. (1995) *The Careless Society: Community and its Counterfeits.* New York: Basic Books.

Marcos, I. (2001) 'The word and the silence.' In J. Ponce de Leon (ed) *Our Word is our Weapon: Selected Writings of Subcomandante Insurgente Marcos.* London: Serpent's Tail.

Oliver, M. (1990) *The Politics of Disablement.* London: Macmillan and St Martin's Press.

Oliver, M. (1995) *Understanding Disability: From Theory to Practice.* London: Macmillan.

Schwartz, D. (1992) *Crossing the River: Creating a Conceptual Revolution in Community and Disability.* Cambridge, MA: Brookline Books.

Schwartz, D. (1997) *Who Cares? Rediscovering Community.* Oxford: Westview.

Scottish Executive (2000a) *The Same as You? A Review of Services for People with Learning Disabilities.* Edinburgh: Stationery Office.

Scottish Executive (2000b) *Independent Advocacy: A Guide for Commissioners.* Edinburgh: Scottish Executive Publications.

Simons, K. (1993) *Citizen Advocacy: The Inside View.* Bristol: Norah Fry Research Centre.

Strichart, S. and Gottlieb, J. (1980) 'Advocacy through the eyes of citizens.' In J. Gottlieb (ed) *Educating Mentally Retarded Persons in the Mainstream.* Baltimore, MD: University Park Press.

Wertheimer, A. (1998) *Citizen Advocacy: A Powerful Partnership.* London: Citizen Advocacy Information and Training.

Wolfensberger, W. (1972) *The Principle of Normalization in Human Services.* Toronto: National Institute on Mental Retardation.

Wolfensberger, W. (1983) 'Social role valorization: a proposed new term for the principle of normalization.' *Mental Retardation 21*, 234–239.

Woodward, J.R. (1995) 'What is happening to CILs?' *The Disability Rag and Resource* May/June; a version can also be found at http://www.ragged-edge-mag.com./

World Health Organisation (WHO) (1968) *Organisation of Services for the Mentally Retarded*, Fifteenth Report of the WHO Expert Committee on Mental Health, WHO Technical Reports Series 302. Geneva: WHO.

CHAPTER TWO

Principles and Types of Advocacy

Jan Walmsley

Advocacy is speaking or acting on behalf of oneself or another person or an issue with self-sacrificing vigour and vehemence. (Williams and Schoultz 1979, p.92)

Introduction: who owns advocacy?

This question appeared on the EMPOWER maillist in January 2001. It is an interesting question in the light of the commitment in the UK government's White Paper *Valuing People* both to 'establish a National Citizen Advocacy Network for Learning Disability led by a consortium of leading voluntary organisations' and to 'increase funding for local self-advocacy groups and strengthen the national infrastructure for self-advocacy' (Department of Health 2001, p.47). In committing itself both to citizen advocacy and to self-advocacy the UK government is riding twin horses, but are these horses likely to work in tandem, or are they going to pull in different and contradictory directions?

To attempt to answer these questions, this chapter delves into the principles of the two main types of advocacy in learning disability – citizen advocacy and self-advocacy – and invites the reader to consider how far they are complementary and compatible with one another.

Advocacy and learning disability: an historical review

One way of looking at the history of learning disability is as a history of advocacy, that change and progress has relied heavily on powerful advocates. Peter Mittler actually calls the introductory chapter of his edited book *Changing Policy and*

Practice for People with Learning Disabilities 'Advocates and advocacy' (Mittler and Sinason 1996). His opening paragraph is:

> People with learning disabilities have not lacked advocates who have been prepared to speak out against abuse and for human rights and better services. Courageous individuals have always been ready to make a public protest about inhuman or degrading conditions to which people with learning disabilities have been – and still are being – subjected. (Mittler 1996, p.3)

In the chapter he cites individuals – Stanley Segal, Peggy Jay, Ann Shearer, Richard Crossman, Barbara Castle, Jack Tizard, Herbert Gunzburg, Wolf Wolfensberger – and organisations like Mencap, the National Development Group and National Development Team – as examples of advocates and advocacy. If he were writing today he would no doubt add some names – politician John Hutton and activist/academic Oliver Russell come to mind as people who have worked for a new White Paper and a new vision; while if he were delving further back into the past he would also have mentioned the National Council for Civil Liberties (NCCL, now renamed Liberty) whose campaign in the early 1950s against compulsory detention in mental handicap hospitals spelt the beginning of the end of the draconian Mental Deficiency Act 1913 (Stainton 2000) or indeed the efforts of the liberal Member of Parliament (MP) Josiah Wedgwood to defeat the Mental Deficiency Bill itself in 1912–1913 on the strikingly modern sounding grounds that it contravened civil liberties (Stainton 2000), or further back to Seguin and other great reformers of the past (Kanner 1964).

In some respects, then, the history of learning disability could be cast as the history of advocates speaking for what were then perceived as the interests of people with learning disabilities.

What is striking, though, is that this history until very recently has been the history of non-disabled people acting for people with learning difficulties. As Joanna Ryan put it so elegantly: 'What history they do have is not so much theirs as the history of others acting either on their behalf or against them' (Ryan with Thomas 1987, p.85).

Mittler does mention self-advocacy; however, only 1 of the 17 chapters is about self-advocacy, and that is written not by a self-advocate but by an advocate/supporter, Andrea Whittaker. Prior to the 1970s (the 'official' beginning of self-advocacy in Britain, according to Williams and Schoultz 1979), self-advocacy, as far as written records go, had no history, while the history of advocacy appears to reach as far back as the concept of learning disability itself.

Arguably people with learning disabilities are one of very few groups in society who continue to rely heavily on others to do their advocating for them. As Tara Mack observed:

> People who are the targets of discrimination should be the ones who lead the fight against it – that is the central tenet of just about every pressure group. Except those for people with learning difficulties. (Mack 2001, p.21)

In this, her introduction to a *Guardian* article on self-advocacy, Mack puts her finger on one of the major issues of principle to address with respect to advocacy – who owns it?

To examine this further, the two major types of advocacy in learning disability – citizen advocacy and self-advocacy – are placed within a broader context of two movements where, arguably, they originate. Citizen advocacy was most articulated by normalisation, later social role valorisation (SRV) theorists – self-advocacy has stronger links with the wider disability movement, in particular the social model of disability.

Normalisation, social role valorisation and citizen advocacy

To summarise normalisation here risks relaying information which is so well known to many readers of this book that it is repetitive. However, to understand citizen advocacy it is important to set it in the context of the movement which has given it its most developed set of principles, normalisation.

Normalisation emerged in the early 1960s in Scandinavia as a means to begin to redress the injustices and inequalities which people with learning difficulties experienced. In its Swedish version, it drew heavily on human rights theories:

> The normalization principle means making available to all mentally retarded people patterns of life and conditions of everyday living as close as possible to the regular circumstances and ways of life of society. (Nirje 1980, p.33)

In the slightly later North American formulation of normalisation (renamed social role valorisation c.1983), the emphasis is more on reversing the consequences of social devaluation: 'normalization implies, as much as possible, the use of culturally valued means in order to enable, establish and/or maintain valued social roles for people (Wolfensberger and Tullman 1989, p.131).

Both versions of normalisation themselves represent advocacy – people without disabilities are arguing for improvements in the lives of people with learning difficulties. This is in contrast to the then contemporary movements for civil rights by black people and disabled people (Campbell and Oliver 1996) which were dominated by black and disabled people respectively. Although the ideas which inspired these movements, particularly human rights arguments, were common, it was non-disabled people who articulated and disseminated these ideas in the learning disability context. The original ideas came from academia (Nirje and Wolfensberger), researchers took them up, particularly in the context of deinstitutionalisation, and the policy dictums came from government (for example, the 1979 Jay Report (Jay Committee 1979) and the 1983 All Wales Strategy (Welsh Office 1983) in the UK were heavily influenced by normalisation ideas).

Just as normalisation/SRV was the creation of non-disabled people, so the implementation of it was also to be in the hands of non-disabled allies. The most developed articulation of this was in the concept of the citizen advocate:

> A person who is richly connected to the networks of people and associations that make up community life and is independent of services, is willing, on an unpaid basis, to create a relationship with a person at risk of social exclusion and to understand and respond to and represent that person's interests as if they were their own, thus bringing their partner's gifts and concerns into the circles of ordinary community life. (Butler, Carr and Sullivan 1988, quoted in Williams 1990, p.102)

This quotation bears close examination because it encapsulates a vision which still inspires. Citizen advocates are one of the 'culturally valued' means by which devaluation is redressed. They will be a major vehicle by which people are to be enabled to belong to communities. They are to be unpaid, are to be independent of services, and are to act in such a way as to abnegate self in representing the interests of their 'partner', and they are to put their own networks, ties and connections to community at the disposal of the partner.

Wolf Wolfensberger went so far as to argue that advocacy was a prerequisite for self-advocacy:

> A severely limited person learns self-advocacy best within the demanding shelter, protection, love and friendship of a citizen advocacy relationship, because these processes are especially apt to bring the person towards growth and independence. (quoted in Williams and Schoultz 1979, p.93)

Not only has the concept of citizen advocacy inspired citizen advocacy groups and individuals, but also it has been highly influential in other contexts. Williams and Schoultz link its principles to the roles of self-advocacy supporters:

> Many self-advocacy schemes have been fortunate to find the support of non handicapped individuals who have practiced the principles of advocacy on behalf of handicapped people... The ideal is that a partnership develop between the mentally handicapped people in a self advocacy group and one or a small

number of non handicapped helpers whose conflict of interest is minimal and who are thus free to treat the interests of the group members as if they were their own. (Williams and Schoultz 1979, pp.93–94)

Although this was written in the late 1970s the ideals of self-advocacy support workers acting as if the interests of the group are their own continues to be held dear. One supporter described the role thus: 'the watchword is to listen carefully to what they are saying and act on it, rather than acting on your own decisions, even if you disagree with them. That's the hardest task of all' (quoted in Mack 2001, p.28).

The principles of citizen advocacy have been extended to advice to service providers and parents, through exhortations such as 'Think positive!' (Shearer 1996); Shearer argues that the way people are presented can have a profound effect on the way others perceive them. Thus parents can be advocates through presenting their children, not as a burden but as 'very much part of the family and the community' (Shearer 1996, p.213), whilst service providers are encouraged to act in such a way as to demonstrate that 'we value everyone here equally and expect others to do the same' (Shearer 1996, p.213).

One can also discern the influence of normalisation-based citizen advocacy ideals amongst researchers, particularly those who espouse participatory approaches. Sheena Rolph (2000) approached her task of researching the history of community care by approaching a group of people with learning difficulties to work with her. Their life stories, as told by them to Sheena, are a testimony to their resilience and resistance. She dubbed them 'life historians', a positive role in accordance with SRV principles. However, one is moved to wonder whether her position as advocate-researcher would have been able to encompass stories of criminality, abuse and viciousness equally well. Similarly Booth and Booth (1994) acknowledge explicitly their adherence to the principles of citizen advocacy in their work on parents with learning difficulties: 'our obligations (to the parents) always came before the interests of the research whenever the two appeared to move in different directions' (Booth and Booth 1994, p.24)

Thus they committed themselves to presenting the people they researched in a positive light – this did not permit of interpretations which might present the parents as incompetent or worse.

At one level it seems churlish to argue against positions such as these. People with learning difficulties have had a raw deal, and it is, one might say, only natural justice that people with the power to do so should begin to redress the balance. However, the criticisms levelled at normalisation can equally be levelled at citizen advocacy: that it is a philosophy which accords to non-disabled people an extremely strong, almost unassailable position in the lives of people with learning difficulties (Walmsley 2001); that it is a model for change which has not been adopted by disabled people themselves or any organisations which are accountable to disabled people (Chappell 1997); and that it perpetuates a one-sided view of people with learning difficulties, that of victim and/or innocent, rather than a holistic picture which portrays them warts and all, even acknowledging that at times they may be misguided, and require a more interventionist stance than the citizen advocacy philosophy permits.

If we return to the tenets of normalisation/SRV we can see that the principles on which citizen advocacy are based are inimically hostile to difference: 'one of the central contradictions of normalisation is that while it purports to re-value people with disabilities, it is rooted in a hostility to and a denial of "differentness"' (Szivos 1992, p.126). An acceptance that citizen advocacy is the principal route to redressing devaluation accepts also that impairment is the cause of devaluation, and ignores the sociological tradition of questioning why impairment leads to disadvantage:

> What should concern us is the mystifying fact that so many social scientists…do not regard mental retardation as a social and cultural phenomenon. I say mystifying because nothing in the probabilistic world of social scientific reality is more certain than that mental retardation is a socio-cultural phenomenon through and through. (Dingham 1968, p.76)

We turn now to self-advocacy and explore whether it is indeed compatible with citizen advocacy as part of a twin strategy to 'value people'.

Self-advocacy

In contrast to citizen advocacy, self-advocacy is about people with learning difficulties advocating for their own needs rather than having their needs represented by others. As Kate Eldon, chairperson of People First, Bristol put it: 'It's a way of people with learning difficulties getting a voice and getting their ideas across. It means they can tell people what they want and make decisions for themselves' (quoted in Mack 2001, p.23).

As mentioned earlier, self-advocacy has, officially at least, a very short history, the first self-advocacy group being set up in the UK in the early 1980s. Unlike citizen advocacy, its theoretical origins are unclear, and it is largely to non-disabled allies that the academic author must look for analyses. Hank Bersani (1998) quotes Safilios Rothschild in his chapter 'From social clubs to social movements: landmarks in the development of the self-advocacy movement' (in Ward 1998), in which Rothschild argues for self-advocacy to be seen as a new social movement: 'The time may be ripe for the disabled to generate a social movement patterned after the at least partially successful examples of the Black Movement and the Women's Movement'.

The characteristics of self-advocacy that Bersani (1998) cites (largely from a North American context) as evidence that self-advocacy is a 'new social movement' include developing a sense of history, a set of principles, a commitment to justice and solidarity, organisation and attention to language. Whilst all these factors do apply to the self-advocacy movement, its provenance as such is compromised by the fact that it is a non-disabled person (arguably an advocate!) who is making these arguments. It would be inconceivable for a similar account of the black people's movement to be written by a white person – or of the women's movement to be written by a man.

Positioning self-advocacy as a new social movement aligns it specifically with movements like the disabled people's movement. I have argued elsewhere (Walmsley 2001) that the linguistic shift from 'mental handicap' to 'learning disability' which took place during the late 1980s and 1990s tends to underline the alignment of people with learning difficulties with disability broadly (not a foregone conclusion – in legislative terms people with learning difficulties have often been grouped with people with mental health problems as in the Mental Health Act 1959). Positioning self-advocacy as a part of the disabled people's movement can be helpful in that it places its philosophy within the social model of disability. The social model of disability does offer an alternative explanation of the social exclusion experienced by people with learning difficulties. The much-quoted Union of the Physically Impaired Against Segregation (UPIAS) definitions are a useful starting point:

> Impairment – lacking part or all of a limb, or having a defective limb, organism or mechanism of the body.

> Disability – the disadvantage or restriction of activity caused by a contemporary social organisation which takes no account of people who have physical impairments and thus excludes them from mainstream social activities! (UPIAS 1976, quoted in Oliver 1990, p.11)

Thus in contrast to normalisation/SRV which tacitly accepts that devaluation is a consequence of impairment which should therefore be redressed by using culturally valued means (like citizen advocacy), the social model firmly places the responsibility for disadvantage at the door of society, not the individual's deficits. Moreover, one consequence of the social model has been to celebrate difference, through disability arts, through reclaiming terms such as 'cripple' and using them with pride (Mairs 1986). Thus rather than denying, minimising or hiding difference, as is the principle on which normalisation/SRV is based, the adoption of the social model opens the way for a defiant reassertion of pride in the disabled body or mind.

However, self-advocacy sits in many ways uneasily within the disabled people's movement. The uncertain place self-advocacy occupies can be illustrated by three points. The first is the use of language. The slogan 'Label Jars not People' adopted by UK-based People First groups owes as much to normalisation/SRV, drawing as it does on deviancy theory, as it does to celebration of difference, a characteristic of most new social movements – Gay Pride, Disability Pride, and so on. The contrast with Mairs's use of 'cripple' is underlined by Cooper's reaction to the labels she had been given earlier in her life: 'some of them, like the names they called you in them days, hurt a bit' (Atkinson and Cooper 2000, p.18). At present, it is hard to imagine people with learning difficulties embracing words like 'defective' and 'moron'. The preference that self-advocates show for the term 'learning difficulties', implying the potential to learn (Goodley 2001), rather than the permanency of oppression encapsulated in the term 'disabled people', is symptomatic of a wish to minimise rather than rejoice in difference.

The second related point is that although nominally embraced by the broader disability movement, self-advocacy groups have a very tenuous place in that movement (Chappell 1997) and the emphasis on bodily impairments in the writings of disabled activists effectively marginalise the interests of people with learning difficulties. We can see in the UPIAS definitions the tendency identified by Chappell (1997) to privilege physical impairment in the social model. Simone Aspis argues that this is not mere oversight, but deliberate:

> People with 'learning difficulties' face discrimination in the disabled people's movement. People without learning difficulties use the medical model when dealing with us. We are always asked to talk about advocacy and our impairments as though our barriers aren't disabling in the same way as disabled people without 'learning difficulties'. (Aspis 1997, quoted in Campbell and Oliver 1996, p.97)

A third point is associated with self-advocates' ability to represent and theorise their own position. Much of the literature on self-advocacy is 'grey literature'. The material that finds its way into more widely available forms of print is largely written by, or with, non-disabled academics. Connections with the social model have been made, not by self-advocates themselves, but by academics, like myself (Walmsley 2001) and Chappell, Goodley and Lawthorn (2001) arguing on behalf of people with learning difficulties, very much in the tradition of advocacy.

The relative isolation of self-advocacy in the context of the broader disability movement has left it to some extent at the mercy of others who, argues Simone Aspis, misuse it. Of all UK self-advocates, Aspis is the one who has most clearly articulated its vulnerability. She identifies a tendency for self-advocacy to be annexed by service providers as a tool to find out what people want from services. Thus, a potentially radical movement becomes confined in a context where services, not citizenship or liberation, are the focus of attention:

> As more and more service providers offer self-advocacy within their services or provide service agreements to independent self-advocacy groups the greater the control these people have over what people with learning difficulties should speak up about. As a result, self-advocates will be forced into only speaking up about choices of services which are provided by the local or health authority. (Aspis 1997, p.652)

The danger that this tendency represents is well illustrated in the 2001 White Paper *Valuing People* where self-advocacy, alongside citizen advocacy, is seen as part of the UK government's long-term aim to 'have a range of independent advocacy services available in each area so that people with learning difficulties can choose the one which best meets their needs' (Department of Health 2001, para. 4.9). Whilst laudable in many ways, the possibility that self-advocacy becomes one of a range of advocacy services from which consumers might choose appears to undermine its potential as a radical force for change, and reduce it to the type of tool which Aspis (1997) deplores. It would be difficult to conceive of any contemporary western government having the temerity to attempt to annexe black people's, disabled people's or women's groups in a similar way.

In summary, then, it is less easy to place self-advocacy neatly into a box associated with new social movements such as the disability movement. Connections there are, but often in the minds of academics more than in the practice of individual self-advocacy groups. Whether there is a permanent gulf between self-advocacy and the radical movements of other socially excluded groups, or whether this is merely a state of the art at the present time it is hard to say. Certainly there are issues around the ability of self-advocates to speak out about their situation in the way that Oliver (1990), Morris (1993) and Barnes (1996) have succeeded in capturing the intellectual territory on behalf of disabled people. However, to place self-advocacy alongside citizen advocacy as one of a range of types of advocacy from which people are free to choose does risk its being tamed into a process which is 'managed and controlled by the same people who have the power to oppress those who have been labelled as having "learning difficulties"' (Aspis 1997, p.653).

Advocacy and difference

One area which advocacy of any type has to address is the question of difference. In their basic forms both citizen advocacy and self-advocacy are based on the assumption that learning disability is *the* major difference that needs to be addressed. Thus 'pure' citizen advocacy requires a 'citizen' regardless of race, gender, age or any other social characteristic who is willing to put his or her skills, networks and prowess at the disposal of a devalued person; while the tenets of self-advocacy are that 'speaking up' is an individual or group process in which the solidarity engendered by having a learning difficulty is enough to ensure commonality of interest.

Within self-advocacy, difference based on characteristics such as gender, class, degree or nature of impairment have largely been ignored. Questions about the ability or indeed willingness of individual self-advocates, often themselves with mild impairments, to represent the interests of more severely disabled people, or people from a different racial or cultural background have been raised, again by Jackie Downer, who argues that white men with relatively mild learning difficulties dominate the movement ('in every group I go to men are shouting the loudest') and that women only or black people only groups need to be set up to counteract this tendency. As Downer puts it: 'At some stage everybody needs their separate groups' (Walmsley and Downer 1997, p.18). Downer is challenged by the assumptions of individualism in self-advocacy which is particularly unfortunate for people with more severe impairments:

> I'm so used to saying 'my needs' tough luck about the others. They're somewhere else. I think it can work but it takes time. And we people with learning difficulties, we've got no time. (Walmsley and Downer 1997, p.44)

It is particularly in this area of severe impairments that there is arguably a place for citizen advocacy – certainly this is the view expressed in *Valuing People* where it is stated that: 'Citizen advocates make a vital contribution to enabling the voices of people with more complex disabilities to be heard' (Department of Health 2001, para. 4.6).

Whether this position is viewed as sustainable depends upon the belief that people can sublimate their own views and perspectives to the extent that they are able to overcome differences in social background, culture and characteristics. In their powerful edited volume of writings on normalisation, Hilary Brown and Helen Smith (1992) pulled together a number of critiques of normalisation which questioned the whole concept of normal. What is normal for a white middle-class male is not 'normal' for a black person, a woman, and so on.

As citizen advocacy is based on the premises of normalisation/SRV, questions must be raised about the potential of citizen advocacy to cater for difference. Certainly black people have been suspicious of the ability of white people to advocate for them. Jackie Downer, a black self-advocate, takes issue with the view that a white researcher is a suitable person to seek out and represent the perspectives and experiences of black families with members with learning difficulties, arguing that black families have so much experience of being marginalised or ignored they will be suspicious of such an overture (personal communication).

However, the risks of fragmentation are great if it is accepted that only black women, for example, can adequately represent the views of people like them. The level at which this operates can be reduced to absurd levels if and when all shades of difference are treated with this degree of respect, and the potential for representing the views of people with learning difficulties as an oppressed group is correspondingly diminished. This has been a subject of vigorous, sometimes acrimonious debate in disability circles with 'first wave' scholars arguing against splitting the movement along the lines of identity politics, while feminists and black people argue for a more pluralistic approach (Vernon 1996). Such debates have yet to reach citizen or self-advocacy; however, there is a need to problematise the relationship advocacy has with difference, and from personal observation I can suggest that male supporters and female self-advocates can set up problematic, though unarticulated, power relationships.

Conclusion

In this chapter I have examined two major types of advocacy, citizen advocacy and self-advocacy, and argued that they are based on strikingly different principles. The chapter opened with the question 'Who owns advocacy?' and it is to this question that I return. In an ideal world, advocacy would be unambiguously owned by self-advocates themselves, with the potential to call on others as allies, indeed as advocates, as and when necessary. The reality in learning disability is rather different. Advocacy on behalf of people with learning difficulties preceded self-advocacy by several centuries. There is a long tradition, to which I and other contributors to this book belong, of non-disabled people taking up the pen to address injustice and to speak for people who lack the confidence and means to speak for themselves. This tradition is slow to give way to self-advocacy. Some commentators, like Wolfensberger and Williams and Schoultz (quoted above), see self-advocacy as complementary to other forms of advocacy, coexisting harmoniously, one a precursor to the other, or shading imperceptibly from one to another.

In this scenario, the supporter is a type of advocate, willing to assist people in developing, articulating and asserting their views, and, in the tradition established by citizen advocacy, denying themselves a voice or opinion. In practice, I have suggested, this type of happy coexistence is the vision of the White Paper *Valuing People*, where self-advocacy is but one of several types of advocacy to be used as deemed appropriate by consumers.

The dangers of relying on advocacy by powerful others can be illustrated if one revisits the past. Earlier in the chapter I suggested that one perspective on the history of learning disability is that it is the story of advocates pressing for change. From the standpoint of the present, it becomes relatively easy to single out the goodies and the baddies, to distinguish advocates from enemies. However, there have been equally powerful voices arguing for the interests of people with learning difficulties to be, for example, kept in institutional care (Rescare) – one person's advocate can look like another person's enemy.

An alternative view, one best articulated by Simone Aspis (1997), is that to allow self-advocacy to become just one of several equally valid forms of advocacy is to reduce its potential as a radical force for change, and to make it just another part of the service provider's toolkit. Comparing self-advocacy with other social movements, such as the disabled people's movement, suggests that self-advocacy has a long way to travel before it can shake off the reliance on those very people who wield more power. Whether, with this particular group, which is essentially heterogeneous and includes a minority for whom self-advocacy is hard to visualise, true ownership of advocacy can ever be achieved is a moot point. At our present state of knowledge and skill, I would say that it cannot. However, I should love to be proved wrong.

References

Aspis, S. (1997) 'Self-advocacy for people with learning difficulties: does it have a future?' *Disability and Society 12*, 647–654.

Atkinson, D. and Cooper, M. (2000) 'Parallel stories.' In L. Brigham, D. Atkinson, M. Jackson, S. Rolph and J. Walmsley (eds) *Crossing Boundaries: Change and Continuity in the History of Learning Disabilities*. Kidderminster: British Institute of Learning Difficulties (BILD).

Barnes, C. (1996) 'Disability and the myth of the independent researchers.' *Disability and Society Vol.11* (4), 107–110.

Bersani, H. Jr (1998) 'From social clubs to social movement: landmarks in the development of the international self-advocacy movement.' In L. Ward (ed) *Innovations in Advocacy and Empowerment*. Chorley: Lisieux Hall.

Booth, T. and Booth, W. (1994) *Parenting under Pressure*. Buckingham: Open University Press.

Brown, H. and Smith, H. (eds) (1992) *Normalisation: A Reader for the Nineties.* London: Routledge.

Butler, K., Carr, S. and Sullivan, F. (1988) *Citizen Advocacy: A Powerful Partnership.* London: National Citizen Advocacy.

Campbell, J. and Oliver, M. (1996) *Disability Politics: Understanding our Past, Changing our Future.* Leeds: Disability Press.

Chappell, A. (1997) 'From normalization to where?' In L. Barton and M. Oliver (eds) *Disability Studies: Past, Present and Future.* Leeds: Disability Press.

Chappell, A., Goodley, D. and Lawthorn, R. (2001) 'Making connections: the relevance of the social model of disability for people with learning difficulties.' *British Journal of Learning Disabilities 29,* 45–50.

Department of Health (2001) *Valuing People: A New Strategy for Learning Disability for the 21ˢᵗ Century,* Cmnd 5086. London: Department of Health.

Dingham, H.F. (1968) 'A plea for social research in mental retardation.' *American Journal of Mental Deficiency 73,* 2–4.

Goodley, D. (2001) 'Learning difficulties, the social model of disability and impairment: challenging epistemologies.' *Disability and Society 16,* 207–231.

Jay Committee (1979) *Report of the Committee of Enquiry into Mental Handicap Nursing Care.* Cmnd 7468. London: HMSO.

Kanner, T. (1964) *History of the Care and Study of the Mentally Retarded.* Springfield, IL: C.C. Thomas.

Mack, T. (2001) 'We'll do it our way'. *Guardian Weekend* 14 April.

Mairs, N. (1986) 'On being a cripple.' In *Plaintext: Essays 9–20.* Tucson, AZ: University of Arizona Press.

Mental Health Act (1959) London: HMSO.

Mittler, P. (1996) 'Advocates and advocacy.' In P. Mittler and V. Sinason (eds) *Changing Policy and Practice for People with Learning Disabilities.* London: Cassell.

Mittler, P. and Sinason, V. (eds) (1996) *Changing Policy and Practice for People with Learning Disabilities.* London: Cassell.

Morris, J. (1993) *Independent Lives: Community Care and Disabled People.* London: MacMillan.

Nirje, B. (1980) 'The normalization principle.' In R.J. Flynn and K.E. Nitsch (eds) *Normalization, Integration and Community Services.* Baltimore, MD: University Park Press.

Oliver, M. (1990) *The Politics of Disability.* London: Macmillan.

Rolph, S. (2000) *Community Care for People with Learning Difficulties in East Anglia: A History of Two Hostels.* Unpublished PhD thesis, Milton Keynes: Open University.

Ryan, J. with Thomas, F. (1987) *The Politics of Mental Handicap.* London: Free Association Books.

Shearer, A. (1996) 'Think positive: advice on presenting people with a mental handicap.' In P. Mittler and V. Sinason (eds) *Changing Policy and Practice for People with Learning Disabilities.* London: Cassell.

Stainton, T. (2000) 'Equal citizens? The discourse of liberty and rights in the history of learning disability.' In L. Brigham, D. Atkinson, M. Jackson, S. Rolph and J. Walmsley (eds) *Crossing Boundaries: Change and Continuity in the History of Learning Disability.* Kidderminster: BILD.

Szivos, S. (1992) 'The limits to integration?' In H. Brown and H. Smith (eds) *Normalization: A Reader for the Nineties.* London: Routledge.

UPIAS (1976) *Fundamental Principles of Disability.* London: Union of the Physically Impaired Against Segregation.

Vernon, A. (1996) 'Fighting two battles: unity is better than enmity.' *Disability and Society 11*, 285–291.

Walmsley, J. (2001) 'Normalisation, emancipatory research and inclusive research in learning disability.' *Disability and Society 16*, 187–206.

Walmsley, J. and Downer, J. (1997) 'Shouting the loudest: self-advocacy, power and diversity.' In P. Ramcharan, G. Roberts, G. Grant and J. Borland (eds) *Empowerment in Everyday Life: Learning Disability.* London: Jessica Kingsley.

Ward, L. (1998) (ed) *Innovations in Advocacy and Empowerment for People with Intellectual Disabilities.* Chorley: Lisieux Hall.

Welsh Office (1983) *All-Wales Strategy for the Development of Services for Mentally Handicapped People.* Cardiff: HMSO.

Williams, P. (1990) *Networks, Workbook 2 of Learning Disability: Changing Perspectives* (K262). Milton Keynes: The Open University.

Williams, P. and Schoultz, B. (1979) *We Can Speak for Ourselves.* London: Souvenir.

Wolfensberger, W. and Tullman, S. (1989) 'A brief outline of the principle of normalization.' In A. Brechin and J. Walmsley (eds) *Making Connections.* Sevenoaks: Hodder and Stoughton.

CHAPTER THREE

Integrity and Advocacy

Michael Kendrick

Introduction

The rise of advocacy, as an institutionalised feature of contemporary formal human services, is a relatively recent development. Not surprisingly, with the emergence of a novel area or phase of human activity, there comes a period in which much is left ambiguous. It seems that the issue of integrity as it relates to advocacy falls into this category. In such instances, one may be tempted into thinking that novelty provides some measure of insulation from the vast prior experience of human beings with sustaining the integrity of themselves and their all too human institutions. This would be illusory, as all human activities are bound by questions of moral and ethical scrupulousness, and advocacy in this contemporary form, should not be exempted from comparable scrutiny.

The question of integrity is actually highly pertinent to advocacy. In advocacy, like all other undertakings that people take on, integrity relates to how virtuous people are when they are involved in whatever they are doing. This refers to advocacy done both by individuals and collectively by groups or organisations. Although it may need to be made clear what advocacy 'done well' looks like, one's faithfulness to such an ideal could eventually be evaluated. Integrity would then be bound up in whether a person or group performed as expected given such ideals. Something is usually considered to lack integrity when it is revealed as being contradictory, incoherent and undependable. All people are prone to such failings of conduct and, as a consequence, there has long been admiration for people who behave consistently in an honourable way. People who break shared codes of honourable conduct are, not unexpectedly, thought to be lacking in integrity.

Another meaning or nuance of integrity relates less immediately to matters of a personal or organisational character. Here, the focus is on the unity between expected norms of conduct and actual actions. In this sense, it means that advocacy has stayed within its boundaries of being advocacy, and has not become in practice something that might be thought of, for simplicity sake, as being 'non-advocacy'. In other words, advocacy is what it claims to be. Were advocates or advocacy organisations undertaking activities that were essentially 'unauthorised', by a generally understood sense of what was a proper purview for advocacy, then that party might be transgressing against the integrity of a particular model of advocacy. The key here is not the legitimacy of the substitute activities, so much as it is their misrepresentation as being coherently within the agreed upon boundaries of a specific type of advocacy. Thus this particular failure of integrity is in the falseness of the characterisation of the activities. Such actions in the case of persons, who are unaware of the fact that they have strayed into other roles or activities, need to be evaluated somewhat differently from instances where the failure to act with integrity is more conscious than oblivious.

Advocacy 'done well' constitutes a kind of promise to many parties that a set of functions is to be carried out, or various human interests are to be protected, in good faith. Practitioners ask the public to see them as being what they claim to be, undertaking their work within the context of an implied public trust. It is certainly true that such a trust or promise may be very amorphous, but it commonly requires of advocates that they stand as defenders and allies of the group that is being advocated for. For an uninvolved 'public', this creates a sense that their concerns for the vulnerable group are being pursued faithfully and with due diligence. They are then free to believe that the responsible pursuit of the matter has been reliably entrusted to the advocacy group who has created these expectations.

As described here, the achievement of integrity is not a light matter at all, as its realisation brings many burdens for the aspirant. This is concordant with any estimable human achievement, in that it exacts a price or cost upon those who would seek to rise to its standard. This is the more ancient meaning of 'quality' that refers to recognition of the enduring presence of tested and proven excellence that (fundamentally more embodied within given persons than institutions) has led to and resulted in distinctive success. The recognition of the inherent difficulties involved in maintaining one's integrity explains why we laud those who without interruption uphold standards of integrity particularly in challenging times.

It is quite a routine matter for advocates to be privy to many of the shortcomings of persons involved in roles of authority and responsibility. Not uncommonly, these lapses need to be pointed out and challenged, as they harm the interests of the people the advocate may be speaking for or with. Advocates may find themselves having to evaluate and even judge the propriety, motives and consequences of the behaviour of others. Frequently, this may have to be done in relatively public ways, and may even result in penalties of one kind or another for the offending party. In this way, advocates develop a kind of precision of attack on, and intolerance of, lacklustre integrity. Consequently, in a reciprocal way, advocates may be unwittingly helping to erect the very same standards of coherent conduct against which they can be evaluated, however unconscious they may be of this fact. A compelling standard of integrity requires that the scrutiny of advocates be just as unrelenting as the advocate's is of others. This is only fair.

What follows here are a selection of substantive dimensions of integrity that advocates might find useful to examine. In each instance, a proposition and justification are made for its inclusion as a possible aspect of desirable integrity. To the more broadly read observer, it will become immediately clear that these recommendations are hardly novel, as they have arisen in countless instances in the past in relation to integrity. This is not unexpected. While formalised human service advocacy may be novel, the question of human integrity is decidedly not. This observation does not confer on these propositions any greater inherent legitimacy.

Advocates need to have exacting principles about how human beings 'should be' treated

It is central to the role of advocates that they champion the well-being and interests of people. However this may be construed in particular instances, the well-being of people is impossible to defend or buttress unless one has first made clear what it is about people that constitutes good or appropriate treatment of them. By implication, this leads to greater clarity about what is unacceptable or damaging to treatment of people. In essence, it is important to have a sense of how people *ought* to be treated. The basis for such a set of judgements has to rest upon various principles or beliefs about what, at its origin, endows people with such qualities or entitlements. This could be their Creator, the Cosmos, Nature, the law of the land, natural law, a constitution or whatever. Nevertheless, the practical result is a set of principles about how people should be treated and thus the means by which poor treatment can be recognised and challenged.

An advocate who fails to have and uphold such principles, may be at risk of being unable properly to advocate for people, since they can neither recognise nor justify appropriate treatment. After all, they have no standards for doing this. They would be impotent and paralysed to act, since the grounds for their advocacy action remain to be established. In the instance of a person who was being genuinely badly treated, they would fail to act. They would therefore lack integrity as an advocate, since they had not done what a responsible advocate should have done. Such an instance is a helpful starting point to begin to illuminate the important role that such guiding principles, about how people should be treated, play in regards to the quality of advocacy and its outcomes.

It is not all that easy to be clear about such principles and how they might apply. Nevertheless, it is good to remember that there exists some measure of agreement about what are the rights of people across many diverse groups and times, so the advocate does not need to start from within a vacuum. What is 'right' or 'wrong' is not quite so obscure as much of the hair-splitting that attends such questions suggests. Even so, an advocate cannot expect to be able to claim to have integrity if he persistently fails to have and uphold some enduring principles about how people should be treated. After all, advocates claim to be there to benefit people, and this requires that the basis of such benefit be explicated so that it can be evaluated.

Advocates should be willing to 'bear witness' to the dark side of our nature, our communities and our social institutions

It is commonly the case with disadvantaged, marginal and even outcast people that they face an uphill struggle simply to get their mistreatment recognised by legitimate authorities. Their complaints and testimony are often not taken seriously, or are distorted in such a way that their credibility is questioned or reduced. Frequently, few will believe them with quite the same ease, as those who enjoy social approval and institutional legitimacy. This bias towards favouring established authorities, institutions and even central cultural mythologies, is rarely seen for what it is. It masquerades as an unacknowledged preference for preserving faith in the cherished values and illusions of a society about itself (i.e. that it is fair, humane, democratic, rational, and exalted). Nonetheless, all people and communities do have a dark side that is difficult to see fully.

Scapegoating, and other vilifications of people, serve to shield those who are more truly responsible for the character of our world from having to take responsibility for their conduct. People who are powerless and unable to exert much pressure on the social order can well find themselves as practical and psychic pawns in the hands of others. This hidden bias towards favouring the established, the familiar and the socially established, typically contributes to the mistreatment of people who are none of these things by rendering them to have less value and importance. Their social devaluation becomes the backdrop against which harm done to them is harder to recognise for what it is. It is so easily thought of as somehow more 'natural' that what such persons deserve by way of fair treatment need not be taken into account, at least in comparison to people who are more socially favoured.

Socially devalued people are therefore at proportionately greater risk of harm of all kinds, and the ultimate culprit may well be the social order itself. The poor of any nation are too readily made into human sacrifices in order to preserve the advantages built into the social order. Advocates may therefore face the unattractive task of having to be the bearer of painful news about the true nature of what is going on. In simply advocating for people to be better treated, the advocate must recognize that they are engaged in a rebalancing of social forces in which the morality, credibility and integrity of our communities may sometimes be put to the test. If the advocate is unable to bear this responsibility, because of their own unacknowledged stake in upholding such social, psychological, moral or even economic mythologies, then they may well be unprepared for their duties.

It is not that all advocacy has this dimension. Rather it is that advocates cannot advocate effectively if they are encumbered by the belief that all social appearances are what they seem or claim to be. They must be willing to look beneath the respectable rationales that are proffered in defence of the status quo, to the possibility that something is more amiss than meets the eye. This is not a preference for cynicism or even scepticism, it is simply a willingness arising from a duty to those being advocated for, to go where the facts lead, even if that damages the authority of our social institutions by unmasking their inevitable contradictions. It does require of advocates that they have the integrity to be able to discern that their principal loyalty as an advocate is to advocate well. In fact, if they are too solicitous of the needs of our social institutions, they might well compromise their obligation. Naturally, such an advocate can face the wrath of those who are 'found out' either directly or symbolically. Such is one of the many hard tests of integrity.

Advocates should clearly be acting upon and accountable for the best interests of those they claim to speak on behalf of

There is no way of knowing if advocates have shown loyalty and fidelity to the people they are to assist, if there is not erected a standard that is sufficiently rigorous as to determine whether the advocates have done their job. This 'job' is normally expressed as being the defence of the person's best interests or overall well-being. This often, but not always, includes the defence of the expressed wishes of the people to be advocated for. To do this, the advocate must acknowledge that such interests exist, that they can be damaged or advanced by advocacy, and that these ought to be independently appraised if necessary. To be fair, 'best interests' are always difficult to keep clear, but this does not mean that they are not real and have real effects on the well-being of people.

The integrity of the advocate rests on whether they feel bound to act in regard to the best interests of people. Even in instances where the people themselves choose to act in ways that promise to harm their own interests, it is still the duty of the advocate to advise against such choices. Such advice is not inherently coercive, as the individual being advocated for remains able to act freely, and expressed disagreement with the views of this individual hardly rises to the level of a compulsion. For the advocate, the task is to seek to identify and uphold these interests, and to take responsibility for not doing so if it is within their power to do so. It does not oblige them uncritically to accede to the expressed wishes of the party being advocated for, but it does oblige the advocate to seek to clarify 'best interests' with them.

Such a standard ultimately invites people, other than the advocate, to evaluate the advocate's performance, by the measure to which those being advocated for had their interests properly defended and advanced. It is a measure of the integrity and accountability of the advocate that such a transparent evaluation be undertaken. Such an evaluation may never be requested or required but leaves the conduct of the advocate open to probing scrutiny. Thus the more practical meaning of this standard is that it provides the advocate with a personal or collective obligation against which their judgements and practice must be assessed.

Advocates or advocacy groups must free themselves from conflicts of interest that would impair their ability to advocate faithfully

It is almost inevitable that advocacy groups or individual advocates will find themselves in situations where the interests of other parties than those being advocated for come into conflict with those being advocated for. This may arise from 'structural' relationships as when advocacy groups accept controlling funding from the same system they must challenge or when the advocate has personal relationships and loyalties to parties that are involved in the situation where the people being advocated for have their dispute. These sorts of conflicts of interest arise with great frequency and it is quite possible that these will set the stage for decisions and conduct by the advocate that dilutes or harms the kind of principled advocacy the people deserve.

The ideal in this case is that the advocate be independent of any compromising interest that renders the advocate incapable of putting the needs and interests of the party being advocated for first. Normally, this is accompanied by a sense that not only should there not be a conflict of interest but also there should be the appearance of probity. The fact that there may be reasonable doubt as to whether an advocate is compromised should be sufficient justification for an advocate with integrity to withdraw from the advocacy role.

Advocates should reasonably persevere

It would seem obvious that very little will be accomplished where the starting point for advocacy is some manner of short-term dabbling in the challenging of injustices. So many things that oppress people cannot be quickly resolved in a matter of hours or even months. Not uncommonly many of the enduring evils that advocates must confront are far more persistent than such 'light' remedies would alleviate. Thus advocacy must be taken up within an ethical framework that properly acknowledges the often long-term nature of 'best interests' and the forces that work against these.

This recognition does not in any way inhibit whatever necessary actions might be taken in the short run, providing the limits of these are properly articulated. What it does do, is raise the question of whether the advocate shows appropriate and proportionate responsibility in regard both to what is taken on and how this is viewed or presented. The long term may be remote, but it does exist, and it is all too easy to sacrifice it unwittingly in the near term. In a similar sense, the way forward over the long term might well be jeopardised by injudicious short-term actions and thinking. Perhaps a classic instance of this is seen in the indifference of many advocates to what follows for people when they leave institutions and move into the community. While getting people out of such places may well be ultimately advantageous, it does not make sense if the person enters avoidable and perilous community conditions. As many have pointed out, the person 'dies with their rights on'. In this sense, the 'best interests' problem over the long term is better construed as assuring good community supports rather than, more narrowly, simply being liberated from residential institutions.

Such a remedy is clearly more difficult and long term in nature than simply getting people freed from oppressive institutions. For this reason, the more responsible and ethical advocate is likely to be the one that both recognises this long-term issue and does what is possible about it. Naturally, advocates cannot settle such matters single-handedly, but they can take all feasible steps to persevere where this is possible. There is clearly a matter of proportionality in such a responsibility thus making the discernment of proper advocacy conduct a very challenging question. Nevertheless, the question of what constitutes integrity remains latent in a host of situations where any number of short-term interventions could impair long-term interests. Additionally, the alternative to 'dabbling' is not undertaking unsustainable long-term commitments but rather a wise and judicious sense of the limits and enduring consequences of today's actions.

Advocacy is not about winning at all costs with no regard for truth and fairness

It is easy enough, in the abstract, to see the distinction between ends and means. However, in the heat and passion of dispute and conflict, the temptation to seek pathways that favour one's case, even if they are a violation of truth and fairness, is understandable. We live in a world that seems quite proficient at bending the rules, shading the truth, employing deception, 'spinning' appearances, and casting dubious facts as being moral and justified when they can be used to advance one's interests. Hence, the classic challenge to integrity of trying to size up whether the means selected to advocate is as moral as the cause being championed.

It may be easy to strengthen one's case by exaggerating the failings of those in opposition, and by employing clever rhetoric and language. However skilful one is at such things, there still remains a duty for an advocate to know and uphold truth and fairness, otherwise any tactic or stratagem is justified if the end result benefits the aggrieved party. Thus, more principled advocates ought to try to win but do so in an honourable way. Their methods should not mirror the sleazy ruthlessness of the 'hired gun' version of some lawyers but rather should emulate the genuine skilfulness of talented advocates who achieve their victories without a consequent price being paid to truth and fairness. As partisan as advocacy ought to be, partisanship should not be confused with unscrupulousness.

Advocates should not celebrate conflict and division but should hold out for whatever reconciliation and restitution is feasible

It may seem to some people that the sign of a good advocate is a willingness to embrace conflict and to risk division in the pursuit of justice. It may even be heard that the advocate must be doing something right since everyone speaks poorly of them and that encounters with them are dreaded by people in authority. It may even be the case that some advocates pride themselves on their ability to seed division and conflict. All of these things do not necessarily indicate the actual merit of an advocate, as they merely describe the presence of conflict. It remains to be seen if the actual conflict in question was necessary in the first instance and ultimately fruitful in advancing the party's interests. One has to look past conflict and division in order to appraise them. This requires some kind of higher order principles with which one can evaluate conflict and one's integrity in relation to it.

Perhaps a key principle of this kind is that conflict should not be seen as an end in itself, but at best as a poor substitute for resolving matters straightforwardly and in a peaceable measured way. In this sense, the ideal to emulate is to reconcile the differing parties, and overcome, to whatever degree possible, the division between them in accord with the demands of justice and appropriate restitution. In other words that the desirable state for human beings is not conflict but rather some form of 'at oneness' if this is possible to achieve. Even if there are conflicts, it is better that these are dealt with with this aim in mind. Consequently, conflict may be a necessary evil, and even one in which one enjoys prowess, but it is a much less desirable state than to craft solutions that lead to greater unity between people rather than division. In such a view, unnecessary conflict and division may signal ineptness or even an underlying attitudinal problem in an advocate as shown in the advocate's inability to envision and pursue solutions that lessen rather than exacerbate conflict.

This is not an argument for the demonising of conflict, as it is inconceivable that it can be escaped entirely. Merely taking up an issue that polarises people may lead to conflict. In this sense, the forthright pursuit of valid conflicts may be precisely the kind of healing that is necessary. However, an advocate, acting with integrity must question whether any conflict or division is essential to reconciliation. This cannot be answered in terms of conflict itself but must involve some manner of calculation of whether the interests of the party being advocated for are indeed best addressed by pursuing a particular conflict, in a particular way and at a particular time. Thus, again, the merit of things lies not in the conflict itself but rather in what lies 'beyond' it.

Advocates should search for visions of authentic improvement

It is unlikely that simply crafting remedies that conform to today's status quo can ever satisfactorily address the best interests of people. It is probable that at least some matters can be advanced only if we create a genuinely better world. To a staggering degree much of human suffering may have to be tolerated because we don't know how to do better, or even have a sense of what 'better' might be. It is not enough simply to solve matters by reference to what the world currently provides, it is essential that people look past today's possibly inadequate options towards what might some day become a better option. To remain passive and to continue operating solely within the realm of the immediately practical may ultimately be a disservice to what people actually need.

What may lie between an unsatisfactory present and a more beneficial future is the presence of a vision that permits proactive forward movement. It is not defensible simply to await passively the arrival of a better future. The advocate must consider the question of whether there is a place for imagining and ultimately pursuing 'better'. Oddly enough, the way forward may be best facilitated not by conforming to today's reality but by forcing oneself to become 'sensibly unrealistic', in being willing to look over the horizon at what should be created and is essential to people's well-being. Advocacy without this commitment is an inverse way to settle for the world as it is. This stance lacks integrity if the advocate is sincere about pursuing people's best interests.

At the same time, it would be very unwise to assume that any or all advocates can and should fashion themselves as visionaries, since this is clearly utopian and wildly impractical. It is not, however, so outlandish to assume that advocates cannot show sufficient integrity in their role that they cannot recognise that vision is needed, even if they lack the particular aptitudes to develop the vision. Hence, this element of integrity has been deliberately cast as a duty to search for needed vision rather than be the source of it. Visions worth the time can be expected to be elusive so the fidelity of the searching matters more than whether the search is always fruitful. Advocacy cannot be a triumph over all shortcomings in the human condition but it can be one of many catalysts to make life's prospects better rather than worse.

Advocates should know and acknowledge the difference between their own voice and that of those who they claim to represent

It is a perennial concern with any arrangement where people claim to speak for themselves or others that they can lose their way. This may come about because of an inability to distinguish one's own voice from that of others which may occur in the heat of the moment. The reality is far more sobering, of course, since good intentions and confused self-interest are often at the root of any number of ethical lapses made by people who are deeply convinced that they are the 'good guys'. The amount of moral righteousness one feels does not always equate to actual virtue, even if it feels like it does.

The implications of this dilemma are far ranging but progress can be made if advocates are willing to see themselves as possibly being a potential danger. This danger can be reduced if advocates are able to see the ethical dangers of substituting their own voice for that of others, as well as being alert to the ways which this can occur. Of course, this is a prescription for a kind of ethical scrupulousness. Not surprisingly, it is relatively easy to see how such a quality can assist with the integrity of advocacy. In fact, it is baffling to try to imagine what integrity might be if it were not grounded in ethical scrupulousness.

In practice, the matter is complicated by the fact that there may not be a clear and self-evidently crisply defined 'voice' for any party. Thus there needs to be a relentless searching for and verification of the authenticity of what is actually people's 'true voice'. Thus, the faithfulness and fidelity of the search may be more significant than may initially be apparent. In fact, one might well wonder about those advocates who are uncritically certain that their voice and that of others never get confused. This seems inconsistent with human nature and may well reveal moral conceit and complacency. Such features have a long history of promoting ethical lapses rather than preventing them. In a similar way, self-questioning and a willingness to doubt one's automatically assumed virtue can be construed as a sign of progress.

Vigilance

The evils that humans can commit are continuously innovative whether at the level of persons or at the level of social institutions. It is a truism that harmful things continuously get portrayed as beneficial, and good things often get treated as if they are the problem. Advocates are continuously thrown into a world in which these claims must be sorted out and the truth of things evaluated. One never knows where harm will come from or what form it will take. Nevertheless, one can find oneself much better prepared if one has anticipated the enduring, disguised and infinitely nuanced way in which various evils take root.

This is not an argument for some sort of paranoia or preoccupation with perversity. Rather, it is a statement about the duty of an advocate to defend people and their interests and this is not well served when the advocate is too ready to take things at face value, or finds it convenient to assume that all things are well simply because an immediate tragedy or travesty is not 'in one's face'. Advocacy works best when it sees itself as a safeguard up and against that which harms people. To not remain alert to, and anticipatory of, emergent menace, is hardly the best way to guard against anything. The advocate who is not looking to see what is coming will indeed be quite unprepared when it arrives. Thus it is not too much to claim that the standard of due vigilance is a sign of the integrity of the advocate.

Conclusion

As has been indicated earlier, what has been offered here, as possible dimensions of integrity for advocates, are not new elements, as each has a long history in the search for viable ethics for integrity. Nor is it necessary to agree with them simply because they are offered. Nevertheless, it would be wise not to dismiss these kinds of concerns simply because they are unconvincing at the moment. The meditation on these sorts of issues and concerns will, in all likelihood, be fruitful even if other conclusions are ultimately drawn. It is hard to imagine integrity of any calibre that comes about without personal self-examination and reflection. Such is the nature of integrity.

Note

This chapter is an edited version of a keynote presentation originally offered at the Scottish Advocacy 2000 Conference, Edinburgh, Scotland on 23 February 2001.

CHAPTER FOUR

Exploring the Role Of Values in the Management Of Advocacy Schemes

Tim Clement

Values have to be cherished... insensitive trampling on cherished values quickly results in demotivation and lengthy argument. (Hudson 1995, p.37, original emphasis)

How can it be that supporters of different types of advocacy end up arguing with one another? Surely we all want the same thing? Perhaps we do, but the means of achieving the same ends is characterised by clashes of beliefs about advocacy. And as we know, people are prepared to defend their beliefs with great passion. In this chapter I look at some of the beliefs that exist about advocacy, and use concepts that exist in the popular management and organisational literature to engage with them. In doing so I share some of my own beliefs about types of advocacy and hope to open up an area that is worthy of systematic future research.

Introduction

I still have the notes that I wrote in March 1985 from a one-day seminar in Cardiff on Citizen Advocacy. I had been told that as a service worker I could not justly represent the interests of people with learning difficulties. In the early stages of my career, and passionate about my role in helping to resettle people from an institution into community-based services, I found this somewhat upsetting and mildly incomprehensible.

If you were the coordinator of a citizen advocacy organisation, I would imagine that it would likewise be distressing to be told that you are running little more than an expensive befriending scheme. Or if a citizen advocate, you may feel uneasy to hear that your voice is drowning out your partner's attempts to speak up for him or herself. It may be possible that you are a person with learning difficulties who has a position on a self-advocacy committee in a day centre, in which case you may be offended to hear that your efforts are not 'real' self-advocacy.

Such views are reported in the literature about types of advocacy (see Brandon, Brandon and Brandon 1995; Dowson 1991; Tyne 1994) and reflect *beliefs* about professionalised services, the role of citizen advocacy and where self-advocacy should take place. They may, of course, not be beliefs that are shared by yourself.

'Advocacy' has come to mean so many different things, and is used in so many ways that it is difficult to write and talk coherently about it. Since the late 1960s and early 1970s the tagging of advocacy onto other words to create new terms has mushroomed, adding to the general confusion over meaning. Anyone trying to disentangle the meaning of advocacy can soon become lost in a terminological forest.

What are my beliefs about types of advocacy? What are yours? If I volunteered as a citizen advocate in an organisation where you were the coordinator, would we share the same beliefs about citizen advocacy? Would a People First organisation in Scotland have the same beliefs about self-advocacy as an organisation in North America? Is it possible to explore, write and talk sensibly in relation to the beliefs that exist about advocacy?

What goes on in a citizen or self-advocacy organisation can be examined at different levels of analysis. Dipboye, Smith and Howell (1994) distinguish between micro- and macro-levels of organisational analysis. Looking at how a coordinator gives support to citizen advocates or how members of a steering group in a self-advocacy organisation work together are micro-level issues, whilst examining how a self-advocacy organisation is structured and how it fits into the larger welfare system would be a macro-level analysis.

The citizen and self-advocacy literature has a number of accounts about how to run organisations that promote these types of advocacy. There are the distilled experiences of coordinators and advisers (for example, Forrest 1986; Novak 1973; O'Brien 1984; People First (Scotland) undated; Sang 1984; Thomas 1973; Worrell 1988), guidance from organisations that have an interest in promoting citizen and self-advocacy (Butler, Carr and Sullivan 1988; Crawley *et al.* 1988; Dowson and Whittaker 1993; Wertheimer 1998; Zauha and

Wolfensberger 1973) and the experiences of people with learning difficulties (Schaaf and Bersani 1996; Whittell *et al.* 1998).

However, it is not possible to reconstruct what these authors really mean in their accounts of advocacy. Any interpretations are inevitably projections of my own beliefs and reactions to their accounts (Schein 1997). For example, what reactions do I have to two recent manifestations of advocacy, Bateman's (2000) formalisation of 'Professional Advocacy' and the proposals to establish the 'Patient Advocacy and Liaison Service' (PALS) in the National Health Service (NHS) Plan (Department of Health 2001)?

In the early 1970s Wolfensberger (1973) pointed out that there were a number of programmes in existence that resembled or were claimed to be the equivalent of the fledgling concept of citizen advocacy. The words that he wrote then seem equally true today, especially in relation to the two types of advocacy mentioned above.

> Any professional who believes that human service needs should be met only on the professional and/or agency level, or under professional or agency direction, is – I have no other word for it – crazy. (Wolfensberger 1973, p.30)

Over time I have come to believe that it is impossible for people that are employed by professionalised human service organisations to consistently represent the interests of service-users and in doing so I now share Wolfensberger's belief.

The case for citizen advocacy emerged from a critique of the services that existed at the time. Although there have been some major changes in the delivery of services, the original list of shortcomings has some resonance some 30 years later. Wolfensberger (1973) suggested that services were impersonal, bureaucratic and poorly administered. They were staffed by people with an inherent conflict of interest, operating in an environment where the options available to service users were limited and services were rationed. The existing safeguards that were in place to protect service users did not work.

Zauha and Wolfensberger (1973) went as far to suggest that any modifications of the ideas on which citizen advocacy were based would merely reduce the concept to the one in existence that had already failed. I believe that professional advocacy is no more than committed service workers going about the job they are paid to do, with all the difficulties that follow. I also believe that the claim put forward by the Department of Health (2001) that patient advocates in the PALS scheme are independent is seriously flawed (Hall 2000).

However, using 'advocacy' as an umbrella term can be a starting point for looking at similarities and differences between types of advocacy. For example it could be suggested that proponents of self-advocacy and professional advocacy are on the same side. Whether you are representing your own interests or somebody is doing that for you, a common aim is to make positive changes in people's lives.

Nonetheless, there are also real differences between types of advocacy, and as Tyne (1994) suggests, we need to be clear about and respect these differences. Any reading of the advocacy literature shows that this is not a simple task, because there is interplay between these types of advocacy that causes much of the confusion (Brandon *et al.* 1995). As Atkinson (1999) points out, the confusion is not just about the specific details but fundamental disagreements about who advocacy is for and who 'owns' it.

What is required is a way in, a means of exploring types of advocacy so that any points of similarity can be clarified and the differences exposed. My own particular interest is in organisations and as most efforts at promoting advocacy take place in an organisational context, I am interested in what insights might be gained by looking at advocacy through the application of some of the ideas that exist about 'beliefs' in the organisational literature.

Belief in 'the cause'

What seems to be given great prominence in the aforementioned accounts of citizen and self-advocacy is the notion that people are drawn to work or volunteer in citizen and self-advocacy organisations because they believe in their causes and are committed to the values espoused by these organisations.

Handy (1988) puts forward a caricature of people who join voluntary organisations. He suggests that such people are not motivated by money. If they were, they would be in the business world, with its emphasis on management, organisation and bureaucracy. People join voluntary organisations because they want to be there. Although this is a parody, an emphasis on values and a rejection or marginalisation of the organisational and management literature is also evident in much of the cited writing on citizen and self-advocacy. For example, Wertheimer (1998, p.62) reminds people who are recruiting paid staff in a citizen advocacy context that 'skills can be developed and knowledge can be acquired'. In doing so she is guiding people to put an onus on beliefs and attitudes, such as, 'a commitment to and an enthusiasm about citizen advocacy' (Wertheimer 1998, p.62). By recruiting volunteers made of the right stuff, organisations seek to minimise the impact of beliefs that are alien to their own.

Additionally, Dowson and Whittaker (1993) report that during the workshops that gave rise to their book on the role of the adviser, that participants questioned the need for organisational structure. It appears that the participants were concerned that it 'would encourage (self-advocacy) groups to imitate the power games and hierarchies of the rest of society' (Dowson and Whittaker 1993, p.38).

However, Handy (1988) suggests that voluntary organisations reject ideas about management and organisations at their peril. Surely people in citizen advocacy and self-advocacy organisations recognise that it is better to be organised, than it is to muddle along guided only by the cause? Amongst other things this literature can tell us how to motivate people; give us an understanding of the workings of groups; advise us how to structure an organisation effectively and develop a culture that instils the organisation's goals in all its members.

Similarly it is useful to know something about voluntary organisations in particular. For although citizen advocacy and self-advocacy organisations have coordinators and advisers in key paid positions respectively, they rely on people who give their time and energy voluntarily. Using the insights from the literature specifically about voluntary organisations may tell us how these organisations work and may help people in these settings to avoid repeating common mistakes (Wolfensberger 1984).

Space does not allow me to address all of these or other interesting issues in this short chapter, but I hope that raising such concerns will at least alert you to the possibilities of making links with a rich seam of knowledge. In the remainder of this chapter I wish to focus my attention on the subject of beliefs and values, since they feature so prominently in my reading of the literature.

The importance of values

It is not too contentious to state that values are very important in health and social welfare organisations. Indeed, Emerson, Hastings and McGill (1994, p.209) write: 'It nowadays appears to be accepted as something of a truism that such a "value base" underpins the very existence of welfare services and exerts a pervasive and powerful influence upon their everyday practice'. Pahl (1994) goes slightly further by suggesting that: 'at the heart of social work [are] certain values either unique [to the profession] or more influential than in other occupations' (Pahl 1994, p.192, citing the Barclay Report 1982).

Hudson (1995), writing about not-for-profit organisations, would categorise citizen and self-advocacy organisations as 'values-led organisations'. In truth, however, values play an important role in all organisations, but it would appear that Handy's (1988) assertion that people are attracted to the voluntary sector because they are committed to certain values is not far fetched. But what are 'values' and what are the specific ones that people are attracted to?

It should be apparent that some of the ideas that I have referred to above are based on certain beliefs. Citizen advocacy is needed because services have a number of shortcomings. Citizen advocacy has certain features that must not be tampered with. 'Real' self-advocacy takes place in an independent organisation. Only citizen advocates with the right values should be recruited.

Unfortunately the term 'values' is used liberally in the literature, and not only is it rarely defined, but it is also used interchangeably with other concepts, like beliefs, principles, morals and ethics (Marsh 1994). For example, Zauha and Wolfensberger (1973) refer to the 'essential features of citizen advocacy'; Butler *et al.* (1988) the 'principles' and Wertheimer (1998) the 'basic principles'. With regard to self-advocacy, People First (Scotland) discuss 'values and principles' and in 1996 the International League of Societies for Persons with Mental Handicap (ILSMH) published *The Beliefs, Values, and Principles of Self-Advocacy.*

Is it possible to get to the basic beliefs about types of advocacy and in doing so distinguish the concepts from one another? Analysing what people have written about citizen and self-advocacy may show whether this is a useful way to proceed, always keeping in mind my earlier remark that this may say more about my own beliefs. Indeed how you react to what I have written will tell you something about your own beliefs.

What are values and whose values are we talking about?

The way that 'values' are used in citizen and self-advocacy organisations has not been subject to serious scrutiny. Stackman, Pinder and Connor (2000) suggest that what we know about values and the roles they play in relation to people's behaviour has been compromised by the poor definition of the values construct, both by researchers and by practitioners.

Neither does the citizen and self-advocacy literature make much distinction about whose beliefs or values we are referring to. Very rarely does an author state explicitly, as I have tried to do, 'these are my beliefs about self-advocacy'. For example, whose beliefs are those in the ILSMH's (1996) document *The Beliefs, Values, and Principles of Self-Advocacy?* Are they merely those of the people with learning difficulties and their supporters who wrote them? Or do they belong to all the members of the ILSMH organisation? Since the ILSMH is not an organisation run by people with learning difficulties are they shared by People First organisations, which might claim to be a more authentic voice of self-advocacy?

In attempting to understand values in organisational culture research, the most frequently used work is that of Rokeach (Ashkanasy, Wilderom and Peterson 2000). Rokeach (1968) believed that the first step towards understanding would come from initially distinguishing between concepts such as beliefs, value systems, values, and attitudes, and then using them in distinctively different ways.

We all hold certain 'beliefs'. We accept that a fact, statement or thing is true. A commonly held belief about people with learning difficulties is that bad things happen to them. For example, People First (Scotland) (undated, p.2) write: 'We start from the position that the lives of most people with learning difficulties are difficult'. Some typical experiences of people with learning difficulties are listed as ridicule, segregation, abuse and being dehumanised.

These beliefs are organised into a 'total belief system', all of a person's beliefs about the self, the physical and social worlds. Rokeach (1968) distinguished between five different types of belief, varying in intensity, verifiability and inconsequentiality. For Rokeach a value is

> a type of belief, centrally located in one's total belief system, about how one ought or ought not to behave, or about some end-state of existence worth or not worth attaining. Values are thus abstract ideals, positive or negative, not tied to any specific attitude, object or situation, representing a person's beliefs about modes of conduct and ideal terminal goals. (Rokeach 1968, p.124)

Not surprisingly, a definition such as this alerts us to the fact that we are dealing with a complex concept. Although Rokeach was writing about individual beliefs and values, the values construct is applied to higher levels of abstraction. In the sections that follow I will move between micro- and macro-levels, from the individual to the more abstract concepts of the organisation and society. It is worth making the point here, that organisations do not really have values. We attribute values to organisations metaphorically (Stackman *et al.* 2000). People in organisations have values, and these may be shared by people in the organisations and reflected in formal documents such as the ILSMH's.

The ILSMH (1996) document *The Beliefs, Values and Principles of Self-Advocacy* (see Box 4.1) is one of the few that provide any definitions. Beliefs and values are 'things of the heart which you believe in', whilst principles are 'guidelines that we follow in making decisions' (ILSMH 1996, p.9).

Box 4.1 The Beliefs, Values, and Principles of Self-Advocacy (ILSMH 1996)	
Beliefs and values	*Principles*
Being a person first	Empowerment
Being able to make our own decisions	Equal opportunity
Believing in my value as a person	Learning and living together
Having other people believe in you as a person	Non-labelling

The ILSMH's definition and distinction between 'values' and 'principles' is weak and over-complicated, and thus exemplifies the claim by Stackman *et al.* (2000) that what we know about values is compromised by poor definitions in practice. Not only should an adviser in a self-advocacy organisation believe that people with learning difficulties can make their own decisions, but also the adviser's behaviour should be guided by that value. Whatever the principle of 'empowerment' actually means, it could just as easily appear as a value, as all values guide behaviour.

'Empowerment' fits more neatly into Rokeach's (1968) definition of a value, as a positive abstract ideal that can be applied to different situations. It refers to both how people should behave, in an 'empowering' manner, and an end-state of existence, 'empowerment'. The point here is not to be pedantic, but to suggest that common understanding will result only from thorough use of terms and the claims we make about them.

Vision and mission

In order to clarify the values of an organisation and its purpose, it has become fashionable to produce 'vision' and 'mission' statements. Macdonald (1998, p.174) writes that: 'the concept of a set of guiding values as being at the heart of, and essential to, the long-term successful organisation now appears to be proven and accepted by the leading proponents of management thought'.

Hudson (1995) suggests that the 'vision' and 'mission' concepts have a special place in organisations whose aims are more social than economic. His use of 'vision' relates to a desirable future situation that an organisation is unlikely to achieve on its own. There is clear parallel between Hudson's 'desirable future situation' and Rokeach's 'end-state of existence worth attaining'.

Thus, self-advocacy organisations may have a vision of playing a part in the creation of a better society. Worrell (1988) claims that:

> Self-advocacy is also part of a large movement in our society that challenges the way society works...self-advocacy can play a vital historic role to promote (positive cultural) values and challenge some of the fundamental ways society functions...the day that labelled people are truly empowered will be the day when the world will be transformed. (Worrell 1988, p.7)

The ILSMH also has a picture of a better world for people with learning difficulties: 'the vision of the ILSMH is that, some day, people with a mental handicap will be appreciated and respected for what they are and get the possibility to live like other people on their own terms' (ILSMH 1996, back cover).

The future looks bright, if a bit fuzzy. The desirable future is characterised by contestable and undefined terms like 'empowerment', 'respect' and 'appreciation'. Handy (1988) cautions about setting such lofty goals and asserts that they are one of the reasons why voluntary organisations are full of careworn individuals. He suggests that these organisations should set less ambitious goals as 'to bring peace to the world is the sort of task that only gods should take on' (Handy 1988, p.6).

An organisation's 'mission' is more concerned with its common beliefs, the reason why it exists and gives a clearer sense of how to achieve the vision (Hudson 1995).

Again there is a link with Rokeach's (1968) definition of a value, for in order to achieve a vision, one has to behave in a certain way. Hudson (1995) suggests that the idea of 'mission' has two essential components, and he makes an explicit link with the concept of values:

> The first element of mission is the **common values** held by people in the organization... Second, the mission is the organization's raison d'être. It explains why the organization exists and who benefits from it. From this perspective the mission is the intellectual rationale for the organization... Mission is therefore concerned with both **hearts and minds**: the beliefs that come from the heart and the rationale that comes from the mind. (Hudson 1995, pp.94–95, original emphasis)

Of course not everyone follows a textbook when describing their mission. In a section entitled 'Values and principles – what do we believe?' People First (Scotland) (undated) state:

> We believe that having an intellectual disability is not a shameful thing. It is not something to be avoided or side-stepped. By accepting people, regardless of their differences, and accepting and valuing the differences that people have, we can create a society where genuine inclusion is more likely... In the People First movement, we value people because they are people. We try to advance ideas of mutual support and inter-dependence. We try to support the values of acceptance, tolerance and inclusion. (People First (Scotland) undated, p.4)

To quote from the ILSMH again: 'The overall purpose of the ILSMH is to fight for the human rights of persons with a mental handicap and their families' (ILSMH 1996, back cover). Between them, these two organisations use the two elements of Hudson's idea of 'mission'. People First (Scotland) identify a number of values and the ILSMH state that it should be people with learning difficulties and their families that should benefit from their existence. It is easy to see why employees and volunteers would buy into organisations that found themselves on such ideas. In appealing to hearts and minds, organisations encourage people to align themselves with ideals that fit in with what they themselves believe in (Marsh 1994).

However, many health and social care organisations have been criticised for writing noble 'mission' and 'vision' statements but continuing to provide the same low quality services. Value statements can be nothing more than empty words, printed in glossy brochures that no longer have the power to motivate and inspire (Burton 1998). The statement put forward by People First (Scotland) that they accept people regardless of their differences, and value the differences that people have, is reflected in the slogan – 'Celebrate the Difference'. I believe that the idea that all people are accepted unconditionally regardless of their differences does not stand any serious challenge.

Part of the rationale for developing these statements is to make sure that the values of an organisation are understood by everyone in that organisation. Values were one of the eight attributes identified by Peters and Waterman (1982) in their research that characterised excellent companies. One role of the organisation's leadership is to communicate the values and purpose clearly (Macdonald 1998). The idea is that organisations can create strong unified cultures by stating and strengthening the values of the organisation through policies, language and behavioural standards that over time are adopted by all employees. This management approach became labelled as 'values engineering' (Martin and Frost 1996).

Organisational typologies

Although Clegg and Hardy (1996) make the point that different theoretical approaches to organisational studies have removed any certainty about what an organisation is, for the purpose of this chapter we might agree that citizen advocacy and self-advocacy organisations exist predominantly for the promotion of these respective activities.

One way of trying to understand organisations has been to classify them into different types. A reason for doing this is that it is claimed that different structures impact on an organisation's 'culture' (Handy 1993), a term that I will return to later.

The advent of disabled people forming their own organisations saw the distinction between 'organisations of disabled people' and 'organisations for disabled people' (Oliver 1996). The distinction makes a clear statement about issues of power and control in these organisations and Oliver (1996) suggests that 'organisations of disabled people' are at the heart of the empowerment of disabled people.

By using this classification of organisations it becomes clearer, in relation to people with learning difficulties, that an organisation recruiting citizen advocates is fundamentally different in character from a self-advocacy organisation. To caricature these organisations, one is an organisation for disabled people where non-disabled people represent the interests of people with learning difficulties, and the other is an organisation of disabled people where people with learning difficulties organise collectively to represent themselves.

Alternatively Rhoades (1986) described four types of self-advocacy organisation, the autonomous, divisional, service system and coalition models. Dowson (1991) was severely critical of people and organisations that sought to smother the potential of self-advocacy. He argued that this is easily done by people without learning difficulties keeping control, or by organisations incorporating self-advocacy into their agenda-setting and decision-making processes. With such an understanding, the autonomous model is put forward as the preferred model. Indeed Dowson and Whittaker (1993) co-designate the autonomous model as the ideal model for self-advocacy.

We can see that certain beliefs are behind the conception of these typologies and the promotion of the autonomous model. People with learning difficulties are more likely to become empowered in their own self-advocacy organisation. As many activities initiated by services in the name of self-advocacy remain under the control of services (Dowson and Whittaker 1993), 'real' self-advocacy can take place only in the context of an independent self-advocacy organisation. An unintentional side-effect of this belief is that the efforts of people with learning difficulties in other settings are made to seem less legitimate, and even less worthy.

Typologies allow organisations to be classified according to prescribed dominant features, but as Goodley's (2000) exploration of self-advocacy in different types of organisation showed, typologies do not so clearly exist in reality. Goodley (2000) found that in his research that the organisations transcended the types identified by Rhoades (1986).

Empowerment

In her review Atkinson (1999) suggests that advocacy is about empowerment, autonomy, citizenship and inclusion. Since the literature that I have quoted suggests that empowerment lies at the heart of organisations of disabled people, will reflect a transformed world and is a principle that guides decision-making in relation to self-advocacy, let us have a look at it as a value in relation to two types of advocacy, citizen and self-advocacy. Can empowerment really lie at the heart of both types of advocacy?

The term 'empowerment' was not common currency when the citizen advocacy concept was first being formulated, but it has crept into later writings. The original conception of citizen advocacy is rooted in 'protective services' – 'those services and activities which are undertaken by an individual or agency on behalf of other individuals who are not fully able to act for themselves' (Helsel 1973, p.132). Thus for Wolfensberger (1973) there were some people who needed to be protected from neglect, abandonment, abuse, exploitation or other forms of mistreatment. (This belief is similar to that outlined earlier by People First (Scotland), a self-advocacy organisation, that bad things happen to people with learning difficulties.)

The original use of the term 'protégé' to refer to the disabled person in the citizen advocacy relationship reflects this protective stance, for protégé is used in this instance as someone who is under the care and protection of another. As I suggested earlier there has been a reaction against this conceptualisation of citizen advocacy because it is said to reinforce the powerlessness of disabled people, where non-disabled people take responsibility for those who are vulnerable or excluded (Tyne 1994) and in doing so create a new pattern of dependency (Brandon *et al.* 1995).

So in more recent writings we find that protégé has been transformed into partner (Butler *et al.* 1988; Wertheimer 1998) although an objective of citizen advocacy is still to: 'protect those who may need protection' (Wertheimer 1998, p.7).

We also find that empowerment, a term associated with organisations of disabled people, has been adopted by some citizen advocacy organisations (Tyne 1994). Butler *et al.* (1988, p.1) write: 'Citizen advocacy's objective is to empower those who have been kept powerless and/or excluded'.

In a similar tone Jackson (1999, p.52) states: 'Citizen Advocacy, with its mission to empower disadvantaged individuals and groups, presents a challenge to the power, role and status of professionals'. It is my belief that if citizen advocacy is about one person representing the interests of another person then it makes no sense to talk of the protégé being 'empowered'. It is citizen advocates, drawing on their sources of power, who are trying to influence another person to change their behaviour or modify their attitude towards the protégé.

If it is a professional who is being addressed by the citizen advocate then I agree that his or her power, role and status are being challenged. But you can be sure that the professional is drawing upon his or her sources of power in return. The person who holds the balance of power will win.

It may be the case as Wolfensberger (1973, p.11) recognised that: 'in contrast to the agency which has many voices and much power, [a person with learning difficulties'] voice and power, for instance, are zero unless someone else speaks for him'.

However, if you substitute self-advocacy in either of the quotations from Butler *et al.* (1988) or Jackson (1999), then it makes sense to suggest that a person with learning difficulties could become empowered. However, an empowered state is not always the guaranteed outcome for people with learning difficulties. It may be the case that the balance of power lies with the professional and the agency he or she works for, and that in not getting the result he or she wanted, the person with learning difficulties feels even more helpless than before.

The idea that the empowerment of people with learning difficulties is a central value to both citizen and self-advocacy seems unlikely to me. Empowerment is another of those terms that is poorly defined and liberally used, typically without any reference to concepts of or understanding of power. My own view is that citizen advocacy organisations have reacted to the challenge of self-advocacy and assimilated the currency of empowerment into their own values, and in doing so have muddied the notion of what citizen advocacy actually is.

Brody (1993, p.34) suggests that: 'every organization would benefit from a periodic examination of its values to determine which need clarifying or modifying'. It appears that Citizen Advocacy Information and Training (CAIT) have made an effort to do this. The statement quoted above by Butler *et al.* (1998) that citizen advocacy's objective is to empower those who have been kept powerless is missing from the second edition of their handbook (Wertheimer 1998). Instead, Wertheimer (1998, p.7) writes: 'citizen advocacy's objectives are to include those who have been excluded and protect those who may need exclusion'.

We can see that how values operate in practice is extremely complex. An individual holds many values, organised into a value system. Rokeach (1968) suggested that values are hierarchical structures, with substructures, and that they are further rank-ordered along a continuum of importance. He believed that: ' a person's value system [represents] a learned organization of rules for making choices and for resolving conflicts – between two or more modes of behaviour or between two or more end-states of existence' (Rokeach 1968, p.161). Thus, neither the belief that there are some people with learning difficulties that need others to speak up for them, nor the belief that people with learning difficulties should speak for themselves are right or wrong. Both can exist at the same time, in the same person and within the same organisation. Although an individual may have a 'rule' for deciding when to speak up for someone and when to let people do so for themselves, the same may not be true for an organisation.

Organisations generally do not take the time to arrange their values in a hierarchical arrangement, and neither do they go beyond attempting to specify a small number of core values. It is additionally quite likely that members of an organisation do not share the organisation's core values or have misperceived them.

It is easy to misconstruct a concept of citizen advocacy that is overly paternalistic or maternalistic. For although Wolfensberger (1973, p.22) wrote: 'the [citizen] advocacy concept calls for the vigorous protection of the interests of impaired persons', one needs to add in Wolfensberger's words of caution:

> Protective services of the past have a tendency to function on an 'all-or-nothing' basis. Within the proposed [citizen] advocacy schema, recognition of the continuity of human needs and a commitment to the maintenance of human dignity imply an avoidance of 'protective overkill', and adoption of a strategy of 'minimal [citizen] advocacy'. (Wolfensberger 1973, p.28)

Thus citizen advocacy and citizen advocates should hold the values of 'protection' and 'avoidance of protective overkill' in their value system and if Rokeach (1968) is right, there should be rules for making choices and for resolving conflicts between the two values.

So in practice a citizen advocate probably should not represent a protégé when that person can speak for him or herself. However, Wertheimer (1998, p.8) writes that there may be occasions when a 'citizen advocate will have to act without their partner's permission or even against their wishes'. It is almost impossible to believe that such a statement could be made in the context of self-advocacy, and illustrates why someone might argue that citizen advocacy could swamp the voice of disabled people.

Rokeach (1968) thought that beliefs are organised into systems that have properties which can be measured and described. We can see from the above discussion that mapping these beliefs would be hard for one person, let alone for aggregations of people in citizen and self-advocacy organisations. For although we think that values determine people's attitudes, that they have a role in decision-making and the way people behave, Stackman *et al.* (2000, p.38) write: 'it remains a mystery how values cause preferences to be formed, and it is even more mysterious how values cause individuals to act upon their preference'.

However, the above discussion suggests that we need to analyse values in a way that moves beyond practitioner guidance statements and superficial vision and mission statements.

Organisational culture

Values are central to another concept that has received a lot of attention in the management literature, that of organisational culture, often poorly defined and about which there is little agreement (see Ashkanasy *et al.* 2000 for example). One model of organisational culture that has received much attention is Schein's (1990, 1997).

Schein (1997) defines the culture of a group as:

> a pattern of shared basic assumptions that the group learned as it solved its problems of external adaptation and internal integration, that has worked well enough to be considered valid and, therefore, to be taught to new members as the correct way to perceive, think, and feel in relation to those problems. (Schein 1997, p.12)

Although on first reading the definition appears complicated, the 'culture' concept has a number of strengths. Schneider (2000) suggests that it is a relatively complete specification of the deep psychological attributes (values, meanings, beliefs) that can be used to characterise culture. What, for example has a citizen advocacy organisation learned about being a citizen advocate that it wishes to pass on to a new volunteer?

It is also useful for tracking the development of a culture over time. An organisation may start with certain beliefs about citizen advocacy, but these can alter as the organisation struggles with problems thrown up inside and outside of the organisation. A change in the external environment, for example, challenges to the concept of citizen advocacy from advocates of the social model of disability (Oliver 1996) will cause tension inside a citizen advocacy organisation.

Schein's model of culture distinguishes between three levels of cultural phenomena, observable artefacts, values and basic underlying assumptions. If you were to go to visit a self-advocacy organisation you would get a feeling about the organisation. How are the offices arranged? How do people dress? How do people speak to each other? You would be able to examine written and pictorial documents, perhaps minutes from meetings or statements about self-advocacy. Schein (1990, 1997) calls these artefacts things we can observe, 'feel' and react to. However, artefacts are hard to make sense of. We may interpret them incorrectly if we do not know how they relate to the underlying assumptions that people have in the organisation (Schein 1990, 1997).

Values determine beliefs about what is important and how things should be in an organisation. One can study a citizen advocacy organisation's values through its formal documents or by talking to organisational members about how people feel and think, and ask them about why things happen the way they do.

If you were to ask an adviser or a coordinator about the values of the self-advocacy or citizen advocacy organisations where they work, they would probably be able to articulate them, although they probably go about their job without continually referring to them. Thus, the literature that I have referred to may be nothing more than artefacts or they may merely be 'espoused values', public pronouncements that reflect what people will say but not what they actually do (Schein 1997).

Lying deeper in the heart of an organisation are unconscious basic assumptions about the organisation and the people who inhabit the organisation. With this model of culture it is typically the unconscious underlying assumptions that determine how, for instance, people behave, feel and think about self-advocacy.

It is quite possible for citizen and self-advocacy organisations to be characterised by ambiguity, if members of an organisation have reached agreement about the stated values, but not explored and reached consensus about the underlying assumptions. The ILSMH's (1996) values (Box 4.1) may not therefore be underpinned by agreed assumptions. The opposite is also true, in that people may agree about the underlying assumptions, but there may be conflicting values that cause people to behave in contradictory ways.

I think that this is a helpful way of examining some of the contradictions that exist within the citizen and self-advocacy literature, and explaining some of the deep-seated conflicts that exist between some organisations where these activities take place.

Box 4.2 outlines two sets of the espoused values of citizen advocacy, the five essential features identified by Zauha and Wolfensberger (1973) and the basic principles suggested by Wertheimer (1998). Zauha and Wolfensberger (1973) believed that it was essential to maintain their five features of citizen advocacy in order to distinguish it from other protective services. Getting to the fundamental assumptions about what these authors believe about citizen advocacy is not possible from merely reading their literature. I can only make inferences about the fundamental assumptions in this instance, at the risk of being accused of claiming to know the beliefs of others when I do not. Fundamental assumptions are hard to articulate and require a certain approach to research properly.

Box 4.2 Important beliefs about citizen advocacy

Zauha and Wolfensberger (1973) **Essential features to safeguard**	Wertheimer (1998) **Basic founding principles**
Independent location and funding for a citizen advocacy organisation	Independent location, funding and administration for a Citizen Advocacy Office
A paid coordinator or director	A coordinator whose primary focus is identifying partners, recruiting advocates, preparing for the citizen advocacy role, matching partners and advocates, follow-up and support for citizen advocates
Emphasis on long-term relationships between citizen advocates and protégés	A long-term relationship
Mechanisms for providing instrumental and expressive citizen advocacy and formal and informal roles	
Unpaid citizen advocates who are totally in no way compromised in representing their protégés' interests	Citizen advocate independence from the citizen advocacy organisation, agencies and family Loyalty to partners No payment or other compensation

	One-to-one relationship
	Diversity (in terms of citizen advocates and partners in relation to sex, age, ethnicity, and so on)
	Active seeking-out of people that need a citizen advocate
	Management committee with local people committed to the fundamental principles of citizen advocacy
	Use of positive imagery and interactions

These authors agree that one of the essential features of citizen advocacy is an independent location and funding for an office. As Zauha and Wolfensberger (1973, p.181) write, this is 'to make it as free as possible from outside dictation and interest conflict'. Independence in time, organisation and finance are similarly listed as advantages of the autonomous self-advocacy model (Dowson and Whittaker 1993). However, in order to survive both citizen advocacy and self-advocacy organisations have accepted money from NHS trusts and social service departments (Jackson 1999; Wertheimer 1998), in effect a 'deal with the devil'.

Insecure funding of citizen advocacy is undoubtedly problematic for the day-to-day running of an organisation. The coordinator and the management committee may find it difficult to forward plan, or an atmosphere of despondency can grow amongst the volunteers as insecurity grows about the future of the organisation (Sim and MacKay 1997). Time may be wasted filling in endless unsuccessful grant applications.

In violating this 'essential feature' citizen advocates may be reticent in vigorously advocating for their protégé (Wertheimer 1998) or the funders may impose bureaucratic tasks at odds with the main purpose of a citizen advocacy organisation as a means of controlling the organisation (Jackson 1999). The culture of citizen advocacy organisations may therefore change over time, and the nature of citizen advocacy itself may change over time as organisations wrestle with their financial security.

In securing short-term funding it is possible that greater harm may be done to the organisation itself by creating conflict with its values or underlying assumptions. Or citizen advocacy may mutate into an ineffective form no different from other agencies trying to protect the interests of people with learning difficulties.

Schein (1997) argues that culture starts with leaders who impose their own values and assumptions on a group. Over time, if others socially validate these views, they will become shared assumptions. Thus the concept of citizen advocacy incorporates the assumptions of early leaders like Zauha and Wolfensberger (1973), Sang (1984) and O'Brien (1984), but over time the concept comes to embrace the shared learning of the many people involved in citizen advocacy, not just the original leaders.

Trying to provide leadership from outside an organisation through publications like CAIT's *Handbook on Setting Up and Running Citizen Advocacy Schemes* (Wertheimer 1998) is hard. The advice given by external 'leaders' may not work because their solutions, based on their values, may not work reliably in practice (Schein 1997). In this way a value held by CAIT gets challenged directly, or is not adopted at all because it is at odds with people's own experiences and the conclusions that people draw from their own experience are extremely resistant to change.

Jackson's (1999) article is an excellent example of this dynamic in practice. As a result of his experience of running a citizen advocacy organisation, his experiences caused him to question what he believed to be the underlying principles of citizen advocacy. Amongst other proposals, Jackson (1999) suggests that volunteers, another of Zauha and Wolfensberger's (1973) essential features, must be abandoned and replaced by full-time and paid citizen advocates. Is such a proposal a sensible shift in a changing world or taking citizen advocacy in the wrong direction?

In this context what Schein's (1997) concept of culture usefully does is to emphasise the importance of how individual people perceive, think and feel about advocacy. It explains why there are likely to be variations between people with learning difficulties about the meaning of self-advocacy within the same organisation, let alone between organisations. It provides a vehicle for explaining not only the seemingly irrational conflict that exists between proponents of citizen and self-advocacy, but also why there is common understanding.

Alan Tyne (1994, p.254) wrote in relation to the different movements that are concerned with improving the situation of disabled people that 'over time we may hope that our sense of what we have in common will seem greater than what divides us'. To establish a common language about advocacy, to distinguish between concepts and use them in distinctive ways requires a longer project and deeper analysis than I have provided in this chapter. My hope is that clarifying beliefs about advocacy will go some way towards establishing common ground, and I believe that the ideas I have outlined in this chapter are one useful way to proceed.

References

Ashkanasy, N.M., Wilderom, C.P.M. and Peterson, M.F. (2000) 'Introduction.' In N.M. Ashkanasy, C.P.M. Wilderom and M.F. Peterson (eds) *Handbook of Organizational Culture and Climate*. London: Sage.

Atkinson, D. (1999) *Advocacy: A Review*. Brighton: Pavilion with Joseph Rowntree Foundation.

Barclay, P.M. (1982) *Social Workers: Their Roles and Tasks*. (The Barclay Report) London: Bedford Square.

Bateman, N. (2000) *Advocacy Skills for Health and Social Care Professionals*. London: Jessica Kingsley.

Brandon, D., Brandon, A. and Brandon, T. (1995) *Advocacy: Power to People with Disabilities*. Birmingham: Venture.

Brody, R. (1993) *Effectively Managing Human Service Organisations*. London: Sage.

Burton, J. (1998) *Managing Residential Care*. London: Routledge.

Butler, K., Carr, S. and Sullivan, F. (1988) *Citizen Advocacy: A Powerful Partnership*. London: National Citizen Advocacy.

Clegg, S.R. and Hardy, C. (1996) 'Organizations, organization and organizing.' In S.R. Clegg, C. Hardy and W.R. Nord (eds) *Handbook of Organizational Studies*. London: Sage.

Crawley, B., Mills, J., Wertheimer, A., Whittaker, A., Williams, P. and Billis, J. (1988) *Learning about Self-Advocacy (Booklets 1–5)*. London: Campaign for People with Mental Handicaps (CMH).

Department of Health (2001) *The NHS Plan*. Http://www.doh.gov.uk/nhsplan/npch10.htm. Accessed 3 January 2001.

Dipboye, R.L., Smith, C.S. and Howell, W.C. (1994) *Understanding Industrial and Organizational Psychology: An Integrated Approach*. Fort Worth, TX: Harcourt Brace.

Dowson, S. (1991) *Keeping it Safe: Self-Advocacy by People with Learning Difficulties and the Professional Response*. London: Values into Action.

Dowson, S. and Whittaker, A. (1993) *On One Side: The Role of the Adviser in Supporting People with Learning Difficulties in Self-Advocacy Groups*. London: Values into Action and King's Fund Centre.

Emerson, E., Hastings, R. and McGill, P. (1994) 'Values, attitudes and service ideology.' In E. Emerson, P. McGill and J. Mansell (eds) *Severe Learning Disabilities and Challenging Behaviour: Designing High Quality Services*. London: Chapman and Hall.

Forrest, A. (1986) *Citizen Advocacy: Including the Excluded*. Sheffield: Sheffield Advocacy Project.

Goodley, D. (2000) *Self-advocacy in the Lives of People with Learning Difficulties*. Buckingham: Open University Press.

Hall, C. (2000) 'MP in fight to save patients' watchdog.' *The Times* 28 December.

Handy, C. (1988) *Understanding Voluntary Organizations*. Harmondsworth: Penguin.

Handy, C. (1993) *Understanding Organizations*, 4th edn. Harmondsworth: Penguin.

Helsel, E. (1973) 'History and present status of protective services.' In W. Wolfensberger and H. Zauha (eds) *Citizen Advocacy and Protective Services for the Impaired and Handicapped*. Toronto: National Institute on Mental Retardation.

Hudson, M. (1995) *Managing without Profit: The Art of Managing Third-sector Organizations*. Harmondsworth: Penguin.

International League of Societies for Persons with Mental Handicap (ILSMH) (1996) *The Beliefs, Values, and Principles of Self-Advocacy.* Cambridge, MA: Brookline Books.

Jackson, R. (1999) 'Learning disability and advocacy: obstacles to client empowerment.' *Journal of Learning Disabilities for Nursing, Health and Social Care 3*, 1, 50–55.

Macdonald, J. (1998) *Calling a Halt to Mindless Change: A Plea for Commonsense Management.* New York: Amacom.

Marsh, N. (1994) *The All Star Company: People, Performance and Profit.* Toronto: Inclusion Press.

Martin, J. and Frost, P. (1996) 'The organizational culture war games: a struggle for intellectual dominance.' In S.R. Clegg, C. Hardy and W.R. Nord (eds) *Handbook of Organizational Studies.* London: Sage.

Novak, L. (1973) 'Operation of the citizen advocate program in Lincoln Nebraska.' In W. Wolfensberger and H. Zauha (eds) *Citizen Advocacy and Protective Services for the Impaired and Handicapped.* Toronto: National Institute on Mental Retardation.

O'Brien, J. (1984) 'Building creative tension: the development of a citizen advocacy programme for people with mental handicaps.' In B. Sang and J. O'Brien, *Advocacy: The UK and American Experiences.* London: King Edward's Hospital Fund.

Oliver, M. (1996) *Understanding Disability: From Theory to Practice.* London: Macmillan.

Pahl, J. (1994) '"Like the job – but hate the organisation": social workers and managers in social services.' In R. Page and J. Baldock (eds) *Social Policy Review no. 6.* Canterbury: Social Policy Association.

People First (Scotland) (undated) *On a Short Leash: A Handbook for Advisers to People First Groups.* Edinburgh: People First (Scotland).

Peters, T.J. and Waterman, R.H. Jr (1982) *In Search of Excellence: Lessons from America's Best-Run Companies.* New York: HarperCollins.

Rhoades, C. (1986) 'Different organizational models for self-help advocacy groups that serve people with developmental disabilities.' *Journal of Rehabilitation* October/November/December, 43–47.

Rokeach, M. (1968) *Beliefs, Attitudes and Values: A Theory of Organization and Change.* San Francisco, CA: Jossey-Bass.

Sang, B. (1984) 'Citizen advocacy in the United Kingdom: a first attempt.' In B. Sang and J. O'Brien, *Advocacy: The UK and American Experiences.* London: King Edward's Hospital Fund.

Schaaf, V. and Bersani, H. Jr (1996) 'People First of Oregon: an organizational history and personal perspective.' In G. Dybwad and H. Bersani Jr (eds) *New Voices: Self-Advocacy by People with Disabilities.* Cambridge, MA: Brookline Books.

Schein, E.H. (1990) 'Organizational culture.' *American Psychologist 45*, 2, 109–119.

Schein, E.H. (1997) *Organizational Culture and Leadership*, 2nd edn. San Francisco, CA: Jossey-Bass.

Schneider, B. (2000) 'The psychological life of organizations.' In N.M. Ashkanasy, C.P.M. Wilderom and M.F. Peterson (eds) *Handbook of Organizational Culture and Climate.* London: Sage.

Sim, A.J. and MacKay, R. (1997) 'Advocacy in the UK.' *Practice 9*, 2, 5–12.

Stackman, W.R., Pinder, C.C. and Connor, P.E. (2000) 'Redirecting research on values in the workplace.' In N.M. Ashkanasy, C.P.M. Wilderom and M.F. Peterson (eds) *Handbook of Organizational Culture and Climate.* London: Sage.

Thomas, G. (1973) 'The initiation of Nebraska's first two advocacy services.' In W. Wolfensberger and H. Zauha (eds) *Citizen Advocacy and Protective Services for the Impaired and Handicapped.* Toronto: National Institute on Mental Retardation.

Tyne, A. (1994) 'Taking responsibility and giving power.' *Disability and Society 9*, 2, 249–252.

Wertheimer, A. (1998) *Citizen Advocacy: A Powerful Partnership – A Handbook on Setting Up and Running Citizen Advocacy Schemes*, 2nd edn. London: Citizen Advocacy Information and Training (CAIT).

Whittell, B., Ramcharan, P. and members of People First Cardiff and the Vale (1998) 'Self-advocacy: speaking up for ourselves and each other.' In L. Ward (ed) *Innovations in Advocacy and Empowerment for People with Intellectual Disabilities.* Whittle-le-Woods: Lisieux Hall.

Wolfensberger, W. (1973) 'Citizen advocacy for the handicapped, impaired and disadvantaged: an overview.' In W. Wolfensberger and H. Zauha (eds) *Citizen Advocacy and Protective Services for the Impaired and Handicapped.* Toronto: National Institute on Mental Retardation.

Wolfensberger, W. (1984) *Voluntary Associations on Behalf or Societally Devalued and/or Handicapped People.* Downsview, ONT: National Institute on Mental Retardation.

Worrell, B. (1988) *Advice for Advisors.* Downsview, ONT: National People First Project.

Zauha, H. and Wolfensberger, W. (1973) 'Funding, governance and safeguards of citizen advocacy services.' In W. Wolfensberger and H. Zauha (eds) *Citizen Advocacy and Protective Services for the Impaired and Handicapped.* Toronto: National Institute on Mental Retardation.

CHAPTER FIVE

Professional Consciousness and Conflict in Advocacy

Colin Goble

Introduction

This chapter is about conflicts between human service professionals and people with learning difficulties and their allies about the meaning, purpose and practice of advocacy. I begin by briefly outlining some key points of conflict as identified by Gathercole (cited in Brandon, Brandon and Brandon 1995). These points of conflict can be seen as, at the very least, inhibiting forces on professionals in terms of their capacity to act as advocates. Nonetheless, some human service professionals have taken advocacy to be a key and, some have claimed, 'defining' aspect of their role. This claim is discussed with particular reference to nursing, a profession in which it has indeed been made. I shall then argue, with reference to work by Seedhouse (2000), that this is, at best, a misguided view which misconceives advocacy as a therapeutic rather than a political activity, and, at worst, a potentially dangerous delusion arising from a distorted professional worldview, which is capable of disarming advocacy of its more radical, emancipatory role. Underlying such a worldview, I go on to argue, is the 'construction' of professional consciousness, and its expression in authoritative scientific and managerial discourses; products of modernist and rationalist philosophical frameworks which still largely underpin western social thought. The conception of people with learning difficulties arising from these discourses serves to 'other' them, and construct them in turn as human service clients, or 'cases' rather than as citizens with their own life stories and experiences. Particular reference is made here to the critique of professionalised services in human service systems by McKnight (1992). The ultimately disempowered situation to which this gives rise is then illustrated by reference to 'Angela,' a woman with whom I formerly worked, whose life situation is, I would argue, tragic testimony to the capacity of professionalised consciousness and discourse to pathologise the behaviour of people with learning difficulties. Such behaviour, if seen as communicative rather than psychopathological, would lead to very different forms of response of a sociopolitical, rather than biomedical nature. First, let me begin however, by making an important distinction between types of advocacy.

It is important from the start, I believe, to distinguish between what I term advocacy with a small 'a', and advocacy with a capital 'A'. By advocacy with a small 'a' I mean advocacy which is conducted within the limits and constraints of service systems. This, I would contend, is a perfectly legitimate, even essential, aspect of the role of service professionals. More important for people with learning difficulties as an oppressed, if loose social grouping however, is advocacy with a capital 'A'. This is social and political, rather than systemic in nature, inextricably linked to the struggle of people with learning difficulties and their allies for empowerment and self-determination. As such it confronts and challenges services and professionals in ways that are often fundamental in terms of their place and role in people's lives. This is an advocacy role which, I will argue, can be taken on only by people with learning difficulties themselves, or their independent allies, not service professionals, embedded as they are within the very systems and agencies which are often at the root of the problem.

Points of conflict

Brandon *et al.* (1995) provide us with a useful review of debates around these issues. For instance, they cite five categories of conflict between professional and advocacy roles. These are, first, 'organisational', where the capacity for advocacy is inhibited or compromised by the survival interests of the service agency. This might be powerful enough even to inhibit reportage of outright abuse, neglect and exploitation. One response here, it might be argued, is 'whistle-blowing' as a distinct, 'heroic' (to use Brandon's term) form of advocacy. Professional status, and appeal to professional codes of conduct may actually be assets in this kind of situation. However, the inhibiting power of organisations and professions on even this kind of 'emergency advocacy' should not be underestimated. This leads us into the second point of conflict, that of 'professional' interest. Here the key factor is defence of the good name and role of the profession itself over the needs and interests of the client group they supposedly exist to serve. An example of this might be the way medicine, nursing and other health professions persist in conflating the categories of illness and disability, promoting pervasive, and often invasive, interventions in the lives of people who are not actually ill. It is worth noting, however, that professionals can also act as powerful advocates for change in service structures and practices. The widespread promotion and adoption of 'normalisation' principles and ideals in the 1980s is an example. Professionals can all too easily retain the 'we know best' position however, including taking over advocacy groups and movements and shaping them to their needs, rather than to the purposes of people with learning difficulties. Third, and closely linked to the above, are 'managerial' interests. The distinctiveness of this category in the UK has emerged more strongly with the managerialisation of human services in recent decades. Issues of financial constraint and control are perhaps the most obvious point of conflict here. Fourth, there are 'personal' interests, where conflict is essentially over the competing interests and values of service workers and service users. An example of this from my own experience is the imposition by members of staff with strong religious beliefs of negative judgemental views on peoples' sexual behaviour and orientation. Finally, there are 'competing' interests of other individual clients or groups of service users. Like 'managerial' interests, this category has become more significant perhaps in recent decades as more severe rationing of resources has become the norm. On a day-to-day basis however, and again from my own experience, people with learning difficulties often spend their days having to compete with three or four others for the time and attention of a single staff member – a situation which makes constructive, individualised or even enjoyable activity, virtually impossible.

Overall then, it can be strongly contended that the capacity of professionals and service workers to advocate for people with learning difficulties is severely restricted, and some would say fatally compromised by the fact that they are salaried by agencies which are often the major sources of oppression.

The professions themselves can, and do challenge this view, contending that advocacy is an important part of their role in people's lives. Brandon *et al.* (1995) give us the example of Graham (1992), who argues from a nursing perspective that 'nurses are in the best place to carry out the advocacy role. Nurses have knowledge of the system, alternative treatments, and other disciplines, while still being able to relate to patients on their own terms' (Graham 1992, p.30). Underlying such an assertion is, of course, the assumption that it is knowledge of the system, alternative treatments and other disciplines that people need. Whilst this may indeed be true to an extent, it is also, perhaps typically, a view which fails to look beyond services.

The meaning of advocacy

Perhaps one problem here is a lack of clarity about what advocacy actually is? Nursing is an interesting example to explore in this respect because some nurse theorists have laid special claim to advocacy as a key, or even, a defining role of nursing. Seedhouse (2000) makes this point in his challenge to nurse theorists such as Gadow (1980) over the very nature, purpose and meaning they attribute to advocacy. He argues that there is clear confusion in the writings of these theorists about what advocacy actually is and what activities it embraces.

In his discussion Seedhouse distinguishes between what he calls the 'normal' sense of advocacy, where an advocate sides with a person to argue for their interests, and notions of advocacy from nurse theorists which appear to embrace offering information, helping the patient/client find meaning in their experience, helping the person clarify their needs and intentions, and doing things for someone that they are unable to do for themselves; all legitimate activities for nurses surely, but is this advocacy? Seedhouse (2000), correctly in my view, questions whether the meaning of advocacy has not been stretched too far here. In latching on to advocacy as the 'big idea' of nursing these theorists have expounded a model which appears to embrace a broad range of caring, counselling and helping activities, all of which may be laudable, but none of which actually constitutes advocacy in Seedhouse's 'normal' sense. Quite apart from the fact that, as Seedhouse also points out, there is nothing about advocacy which makes it specifically an activity of 'nursing' as such, there is also the more serious problem that such broad definitions risk disarming and sanitising advocacy of its more radical role of challenging systems, and power within systems. Nurses may well be able to function as advocates within health and social care systems (advocacy with a small 'a'), but these are actually very narrow and service orientated contexts within which to work. Also, Marks (1999) reminds us that not all professions have the same degree of power and influence, and, in many contexts nurses are often in subordinate roles. Thus, even where they may seek to pursue an emancipatory ideal, their capacity to advocate may actually be severely limited. People with learning difficulties are very often in need of advocacy that looks and seeks to act beyond such confines and discourses (advocacy with a capital 'A'). A major constraining factor here, I would argue, is professional consciousness itself, which we will now begin to focus on more specifically.

The social construction of professional consciousness

Underpinning the kind of misconceptions about what advocacy is referred to above, are, I would argue, two fundamental issues. First, a failure to recognise that advocacy is not a therapeutic, but a political activity, in which the advocate needs to challenge power structures. As we have already seen, this is questionable ground for professionals whose roles and identities are embedded in those very structures. Second, but inextricably linked to this first point, professional consciousness itself is often shaped by and embedded within powerful discourses by which professions construct those identities and roles. These discourses, and the philosophical and methodological conventions they derive from, have a strong political dimension in that they are also the means by which professions legitimise themselves within broader sociopolitical spheres. To step outside of them is often to risk bringing this legitimacy into question. I would like now to try and explore something of the wider origins and nature of this 'social construction of professional consciousness' and its relationship to issues of service user empowerment and advocacy in health and social care systems. I will make extensive reference here to the critical analysis of 'welfare capitalist' service systems in the USA by John McKnight (1992). This analysis I believe to be particularly useful given that this is the path that the UK welfare state has sought to emulate since the NHS and Community Care Act 1990, often with service user empowerment (or at least involvement) as a stated goal.

The broad political context

The current social era has been dubbed, in one famous critique of professional systems, as 'the age of professions' (Illich 1992). Illich predicted that social analysts of the future will identify this current era as

> the time when politics withered, when voters, guided by professions, entrusted to technocrats the power to legislate needs, renounced the authority to decide who needs what and suffered monopolistic oligarchies to determine the means by which these needs shall be met. (Illich 1992, p.12)

Illich further predicted that such a system would ultimately decline into a benign totalitarianism. The spectre of the welfare states degenerating in such a manner was, ironically, one subsequently used by the so-called 'New Right' in the USA and the UK to argue for the dismantling of the institutions and systems of 'welfarism' in order to combat the alleged 'culture of dependency' it had created. The New Right naturally blamed socialism as the 'evil' behind this process. However, it can be contested that this view fails to recognise that the creation of large-scale dependency is, and always has been a central process in capitalism. Welfare states in western Europe, North America and the westernised world have never actually existed outside the context of capitalism, and were, arguably, very much a capitalist creation during a particular phase in its historical development. The restructuring of welfare provision in the closing decades of the twentieth century can be viewed as part of subsequent trends of later capitalist restructuring, reflecting globalisation and declining national economic integrity. It can also be seen to reflect the shift away from primary production and manufacturing based economic life which has been identified as an important element in the expansion of human services (Wolfensberger 1991).

The creation of services and the professions which 'inhabit' them then, is, it can be argued, very much a product of capitalism, and of the modernist, rationalist philosophical perspectives influencing it. From philanthropy, through eugenics, to psychiatry, behavioural psychology, and on to the burgeoning genetic medicine, it is important to be mindful of this when we examine the construction of professional identities, and service systems relating to people with learning difficulties (Goodley 2000).

McKnight (1992) identified the importance of the growth of human services to the economies of modern societies where an increasingly large proportion of gross national product (GNP) is related to, and reliant on their provision; so much so in his view that he describes them as 'serviced societies'. He also notes the underlying anti-democratic trend of the growth of what he describes as 'an ideology that converts citizens to clients, communities to deficient individuals and politics to a self-serving debate by professionals over which service system should have a larger share of the Gross National Product' (McKnight 1992, p.90). The underlying agenda of services in this context is not the creation of a new, more competent and libertarian society of empowered individuals and communities, but a society of citizens converted to clients, not just reliant upon, but actually subservient to, more or less consciously articulated professional identities.

McKnight's analysis is not confined to the macro socio-economic level however. He also looks in depth at the micro-level of human service professionals interacting with their client groups. Central in this analysis is the importance he attaches to the linguistic, or discursive symbols on which such interaction is constructed. The term 'care' is itself a particularly potent example. 'Care', McKnight (1992) asserts, is symbolic of the 'expression of love', and he points out that such symbolism frequently underlies the individual and collective expression of values given by human service professionals for choosing to do the work they do. In just such an instance of this kind of usage of that term, Seedhouse (2000) points out that 'care', like advocacy, is another 'big idea' to which nursing has attached itself as a defining concept. For McKnight however, the use of such symbolism serves to mask the underlying political interests of services and professions. As he puts it: 'the politico-economic issues of services are hidden behind the mask of love', however '[beyond] that mask is simply the servicer, his systems, techniques and technologies – a business in need of markets, an economy seeking new growth potential, professionals in need of an income' (McKnight 1992, p.73). McKnight is at pains here to point out that this 'mask' is not a false face however, and that he is not implying hypocrisy or conspiracy. What he is highlighting rather, is the pervading power of the ideology at work here that makes it virtually impossible to distinguish between the mask and the face. As he says: 'the modern servicer believes in his care and love, perhaps more than the serviced. The mask is the face' (McKnight 1992, p.73).

Likewise, the symbolism of the term 'need', McKnight argues, should be closely examined if we are to distinguish between the mask and the face. If 'love' and 'care' are human needs, then services which purport to provide them will consequently be characterised as meeting the needs of the people to whom they are delivered. A similar point is made by Wolfensberger (1991):

> this kind of society needs unproductive types of employment in order to circulate wealth, and one of these types of employment happens to be human services. Thus, the very service system that is supported to be curative, therapeutic and habitational actually services the unconscious societal function of increasing, or at least maintaining a certain needed – and in our case large – percentage of the population in a state of dependency. (Wolfensberger 1991, pp.10–11)

Such a society, suggests Wolfensberger, actually manufactures devalued people in 'need' of professional care. 'Need' then, becomes more and more defined by professionals requiring raw materials and markets in which to earn their living.

Disabling effects of professional consciousness

McKnight goes on to identify what he calls the 'disabling effects' which arise from professional assumptions applied to people designated as having 'needs' requiring the intervention of human services.

First, 'needs' become synonymous with deficiencies. As McKnight (1992, p.78) puts it: 'professional practice consistently defines a need as an unfortunate absence or emptiness in another'. There is an important 'individualist' emphasis in such a definition which strongly correlates with dominant political ideologies in western, capitalistic societies. These can be identified as underlying the consciousness of those making the definition, and its location of the 'problem' in an unfortunate individual rather than in a societal response to difference in physical, behavioural or cognitive functioning. Oliver (1995) characterises this as the 'individualised' conception of disability, and argues that it is a cornerstone of medical hegemony in services for disabled people. Rooted in a biomedical conception of disability, this characterisation easily becomes transmuted into social scientific characterisation as well.

The result of locating the problem in the individual rather than the sociocultural context in which they find themselves is that human services then provide 'remedies' which are isolated from the wider social context, both physically and conceptually, even when professionals themselves may recognise that their clients' problems are 'social' in origin. In another article McKnight (1989) describes the way that human services frequently surround the person, isolating them from communities, even when they may appear to be situated in them, a phenomenon noted too in the UK version of community care (Sinson 1993).

McKnight also identifies 'specialisation' as a further disabling effect arising from professional assumptions of clients' needs. This leads to the client being 'broken down' into 'a set of managed parts' each with its own corresponding service mechanic (McKnight 1989, p.81). Likewise clients are 'pieced out in time', with needs specified according to age related, developmental criteria. Thus compartmentalisation is added to individualisation and takes us a stage further still down the road of disempowerment. As McKnight (1989, p.82) puts it: 'while individualising need may disable by removing people from the social context, this compartmentalisation of the person removes even the potential for individual action. People are, instead, a set of pieces in need, both in time and space'.

From such assumptions arise the perfect rationale for professionalised responses. First, 'if you are the problem' then 'I am the answer'. This response characterises the person as the recipient of specialised, professionalised help, isolated from peers, family and wider community, all potentially strong sources of empowerment and advocacy for the valued and connected individual. Thus, all apart from professionals are effectively deemed to be not competent to respond to the persons needs, and the professional is, in turn, deemed as indispensable. And by so doing, professionals have made their own presence the very mark of a caring society. As Brandon (1990) puts it: 'the development of a healthy medical, social work, nursing, or teaching profession is presented as if it were entirely concomitant with the growth of a healthy society' (Brandon 1990, pp.27–28). This is at the very heart of what Illich (1995) has called 'social iatrogenesis', where services maintain dependence rather than fostering self-help and community competence, and 'structural iatrogenesis', where people's competence to deal with their own problems is undermined by professionalised services. Here is the undermining of personal and community competence which McKnight argues is so anti-democratic.

A further manifestation of this is, McKnight suggests, the necessity to ensure that the 'remedy defines the need'. By this he means that the creation of more elegant and sophisticated tools and techniques of treatment and therapy creates the imperative to use them. This is surely no truer than when applied to the medical profession with its love affair with high-tech machinery and pharmacy. It is also true of those twin pillars of 'head medicine' in western society, clinical psychology and psychiatry. The (over)use of psychoactive medication is the obvious example in relation to people with learning difficulties.

Science and professional discourse

Underlying this use of techniques and technologies is, of course, the notion of the application of 'science' and 'scientific know how', arguably the most socially and politically potent discourse of all. Nunkoosing (2000) has illustrated how science provides the ideal model for the 'expertise' of the professional. Components of this expertise and associated discourses include classification of phenomena, the categorisation of affected individuals, the diagnosis of their problems, and the knowledgeable, rational and skilled wielding of therapeutic responses. Here, the hegemony of the professional is completed, as is also the reduction of the role of the individual in understanding and articulating their own needs. The power of the scientifically informed, expert professional is now virtually total. This power 'allows the professional to use his shiny new remedy, it also defines the citizen as people who cannot understand whether they have a problem – much less what should be done about it' (McKnight 1992, p.85). The client thus ceases to exist as a potentially competent citizen altogether, and areas of their lives that formerly might have fallen within the sociopolitical sphere are reduced to technical problems with technological fixes.

This leads us to a further 'disabling effect' – arguably the most disabling of all. That is, the 'encoding' of the problem into a language and discourse comprehensible only to the professional expert and the expert community to which they belong. McKnight (1992, p.86) argues that this 'mystifies both problem and solution so that citizen evaluation becomes impossible'. Any possibility of a dialogue is also effectively destroyed, or at least reduced in importance to a level, which does not threaten the continued dominance and authority of the professional expert. The very words used by the person to describe their own situation are nullified. Frieri (1972) has described this kind of process as nothing short of a direct act of oppression. Such a degree of control and manipulation of language does more than merely mystify. It ultimately removes from people the very ability to imagine that things could be any different from how they are. Disability provides us with a good illustration of this. Rioux (1997) points out, that the dominant image of disability in western societies is one shaped by medicine. Disability is portrayed in medical discourse as pathological in nature, synonymous with disease, and to be responded to as such. Although weakened to some extent in recent years, this approach still dominates, not only medicine, but also the various therapies and 'allied' professions, including nursing and social work, and stretches even beyond, to areas like the teaching and legal professions. One result of this is, what Marks (1999, p.54) has called 'epistemic invalidation', where medical discourse is so privileged as to invalidate alternative explanations or accounts, especially personal and subjective accounts which are deemed unscientific. It is only relatively recently that 'social model' theorists have challenged such a conception of disability.

For people with learning difficulties there are even greater barriers of 'invalidation' to be faced however. For people with physical or sensory impairments, barriers can be overcome more easily because they are more likely to be deemed competent to both judge and articulate their needs and experience. For people with intellectual impairments, however, such competence is always open to question. Simpson (1999) places competence at the centre of her analysis of developments in learning disability services in the UK since the advent of community care. In tracing shifting discourses relating to people with learning difficulties over the past two centuries she argues that, despite changes, a continuity is also discernible. As she puts it:

> [that] continuity is provided in the way in which competence and liberty are connected to one another, the underlying theme being that people with learning difficulties must demonstrate their competence prior to being granted autonomy. This is the direct inversion of the principle of social intervention which holds for the rest of us. (Simpson 1999, p.154)

Community care may have helped instigate a reduction in the emphasis on medical pathology, in which competence is judged by behavioural criteria, but new 'managerial' and 'market' criteria such as 'consumer choice' and 'cost efficiency' have replaced, and in some cases been added to them.

Part of the New Right project in reforming health and welfare systems in the UK in the 1980s and 1990s was an attempt to take on and roll back entrenched professional elites and their power. It has since become apparent that they seriously underestimated the power and prestige of the medical profession in particular; a power rooted in the combined scientific and moral authority of its discursive practices, reinforced widely in popular culture and media. In fact, New Right influenced government policy merely created and elevated a new managerial professional power elite in health and social care systems. This has created whole new discursive conventions and structures, including the appropriation of the language and channels of 'complaint', often undertaken in the name of consumer and service user empowerment. McKnight (1992, p.88) has described the consumer movement as the 'handmaiden of the service society'. He argues that the basic assumption of the consumer movement is that they are 'enabled' by their power as consumers. He goes on to point out, however, that the consumer movement implicitly accepts the service ideology which channels people into understanding satisfaction only in terms of becoming service clients rather than citizens with problems to be solved. In fact people with learning difficulties have often effectively become the commodities rather than consumers in this system, being bartered, sold and appropriated by service systems for whom they become valuable assets to be accumulated and retained at all costs (Collins 1994).

So where does all this leave people with learning difficulties? To illustrate this I would like at this point to introduce 'Angela'. 'Angela' is based on a woman with learning difficulties with whom I worked for a number of years.

Angela

Angela lives in pain. At 45 years of age she has spent most of her life living in NHS residential care, first in a mental subnormality hospital for 20 years, then in a 25-bedded hostel on the edge of a large suburban housing estate; in, but not of, the community. Angela has a mild learning difficulty. She reads and writes, is articulate and physically able, if bordering on the obese. Her pain is psychological, and its sources are multiple. There is the troubled relationship with her family – a dead father she has never been allowed to mourn properly; a mother whose visits are awaited with agonising anticipation for three months or more, and who is gone within the hour; a sister whose phone calls come out of the blue, raising Angela to the heights of ecstasy with the 'Hello, how are you love?' then plunging her to the depths of despair with the final 'click, brrrr'. There is also an unrequited, deeply frustrated sexuality, shattered self-esteem, abysmal self-image, and a deep and clearly articulated desire to live elsewhere, with other people, to have more money, more choice, more control. And then there is the anger. Seething rages that leave furniture, possessions, nerves and her own and everyone else's quality of life in tatters. Rages that bring the further diagnosis of 'severe challenging behaviour', which in turn brings the behavioural programmes, the cobbled together counselling, the psychotropic drugs…and the bitter remorse. If Angela wasn't sick when the NHS took her in, she is now. She is depressed – deeply and chronically. And like most people who are depressed, she is right to be. Though her understanding and experience may be limited, she knows the situation she is in, and that it is unlikely to change for the better.

Although the sources of Angela's pain are complex, her main problem is, I believe, quite simple to identify. The fundamental problem, as is often the case with people with 'challenging behaviour', is one of communication. But for Angela it is not a case of any communicative impairment that is the problem. Rather it is the communicative conventions and limitations of the professionalised culture and systems that embrace her. These are the disabling barriers that prevent Angela growing, healing, living. Angela is trapped in a world where key professionals communicate about, but not with her.

Attempts by myself (in the role of a learning disability nurse) and others to advocate for Angela using an outline of her life situation and history such as that given above, met with repeated dismissal as 'overly subjective'. This concurs with research findings by Gillman, Swain and Heyman (1997) who found that people with learning difficulties frequently have their life stories reduced to 'case histories' which suit the purpose of professions and service systems rather than the individuals concerned. We found ourselves overruled constantly by combined psychiatric and managerial discourses, which conceived of Angela primarily as a potentially costly 'psychotic case' in which drugged incarceration was the most cost effective response, at least in the short-term time-frames into which a management corralled into yearly budget balancing were forced. Responses which might have included alternative, more immediately costly, though possibly more long-term cost-effective interventions, such as bereavement counselling, family therapy to rebuild her relationship with her mother, sex education and supported individual living and employment, went either unsupported, or were cobbled together by an already overstretched support team with limited time and expertise. Needless to say, most of these interventions ended in failures which made further attempts to set up something new more difficult still. For Angela, each failed intervention merely seemed to reinforce her sense of hopelessness. And so Angela continues to live 'cared' for by sophisticated medical and managerial human service systems responding to her 'needs'. The mask of love continues to smile outward, reassuring managers, psychiatrists and wider society that the unfortunate Angela, and many others like her, are cared for, while lamenting that the hell in which they spend their lives is of their own making.

The fundamental root of conflict

It was conversations with Angela which inspired me to undertake research which involved interviewing other people in similar situations to see how they perceived the staff who worked with them and the services of which they were 'users' (Goble 1999). The results of that study were disturbing, if not wholly unexpected. The accounts of the people interviewed strongly suggested that, notwithstanding some individual differences, they live in a world where, although they are almost completely reliant on staff for their physical and emotional well-being, they have little or no knowledge of who these people actually are, the rationale behind, or the structures governing, their roles in their lives. And this is not because of any inability to understand these things on the part of interviewees. They have just never been told. Consequently they have no means of negotiating what staff roles should be, or even that negotiation is possible. They appear to live subject to the vagaries of mysterious, powerful others, who they call by their first names, even refer to as friends, but who they actually seem to hardly know at all as people, let alone as agents of, what one informant aptly described as 'the secret service' (Goble 1999, p.456). McKnight (1992) describes this situation in terms instantly recognisable as that in which my study participants could be said to exist:

> If I cannot understand the question or the answer – the need or the remedy – I exist at the sufferance of expert systems. My world is not a place where I do or act with others. Rather, it is a mysterious place, a strange land beyond my comprehension or control. It is understood only by professionals who know *how* it works, *what* I need and *how* my need is met. I am the object rather than the actor. My very being is as client rather than citizen. My life and our society are technical problems rather than political systems. (McKnight 1992, pp. 86–87, original emphasis)

It is difficult to conceive of a more disempowered situation in which to exist than this, apart perhaps from situations of war or slavery.

Here, for me, is the fundamental root of the conflict between professional consciousness, identity and roles, and the very purpose and meaning of advocacy. And it is important to grasp the fundamental nature of this conflict, I would contend, in order to prevent advocacy being sanitised of its personally and collectively empowering potential for people with learning difficulties.

Simons (1998, p.265) asks the question that I feel is most important here: 'What really matters to people with learning difficulties?' The answer to that question is both mundane and profound. Mundane because, as Simons (1998) and others (e.g. Aspis 1999) have shown, it is essentially what most people in our society want – money, education, work, choice, a decent place to live, and so on; profound because the response to that question has traditionally come, not from the people affected at all, but from their professional 'carers' and experts, and has usually appeared in the shape of a list of services. Aspis illustrates this by referring to the Open University learning pack *Learning Disability: Working as Equal People* (1996, cited in Aspis 1999). As she puts it: '[in] the Open University pack (1996, p.24) one of the questions asked was "What makes it possible for people [with learning difficulties] to live in the community?"' Then in apparent answer to the question it suggests:

> Did you think of group homes, foster families, hostels, supported living, training centres, supported employment, families, schools and benefits? – which are all indicators of dependency. This is emphasised by what is missing from the list: community opportunities such as work, education, inclusive politics and leisure, and living in your own home with or without support (thus indicating that there is a choice). (Aspis 1999, p.180)

A similar phenomenon can be seen when looking at the British Institute of Learning Disabilities (BILD) Life Experiences Checklist (Ager 1998). This is a tool for helping to measure the quality of life of people with learning difficulties living in the community. It measures across five 'domains': home, relationships, leisure, freedom and opportunities. What is interesting however, as with the Open University example, is what is missing. Areas which either don't get a look in at all, or only peripherally so, include work and sex. What is particularly interesting here is that the 'domains' identified are, it is claimed (invoking the philosophy of normalisation) those constituting a valued lifestyle according to 'ordinary citizens', and the tool comes complete with a supporting 'normative' data set for comparison. I would argue that they actually represent a typically impoverished, professional conception of the quality of life of people with learning difficulties. Most disturbing of all here is the fact that the Open University and BILD are two of the more 'radical' organisations working in health and social care related education and research.

Simons (1998) rightly makes the point that services can play an important part in supporting people with learning difficulties to live valued, and valuable lives. But he reminds us that

> ultimately all these organisational issues are really a means to an end. Services exist to support people with learning difficulties. Yet all too often organisational concerns have come to dominate. The kinds of services on offer, and the way they are delivered, owe less to the needs and wishes of people with learning difficulties and more to the needs of the organisations that provide them. (Simons 1998, p.266)

The reason this aim gets lost, I would argue, is because people with learning difficulties are still largely viewed using a 'professional gaze' (to adapt a phrase from Foucault 1973), which 'others' them (to use Nunkoosing's term: 2000, p.59), more or less unconsciously, to the convenience of powerful and authoritative groups in society – and it matters not whether medical or managerial. This 'othering' is achieved most powerfully through the creation, and perpetuation of authoritative, scientifically and politically legitimised discourses which remove from people the right and ability to name and speak their own lives and realities.

Even where professions, such as nursing, with a better track record of working in solidarity with their clients are concerned, there is a real danger that, if the influence of these discourses is not acknowledged, the meaning and purpose of advocacy will unconsciously be usurped, and that even the self-advocacy movement may find itself redefined and reshaped to suit professional, rather than people with learning difficulties, interests. Aspis (1997) warns of the dangers here, in her critique of some forms of self-advocacy training where service providers retain control. 'This leads people with learning difficulties only being able to see what they want in terms of services and only receiving the benefits of change depending on the manager or staff on duty in a particular service' (Aspis 1997, pp.652–653). This is what can happen when professionals latch on to advocacy and make it their own.

Conclusion

Angela, and thousands of others like her, do not need an advocacy which cannot see beyond the group home garden gate, or which helps them reach some kind of esoteric, existential acceptance of their situation. They, I would contend, need an advocacy which is a based on a complete reconception of disability as a socially created, rather than a biomedical phenomenon, and services, as those systems of support due to any citizen in need of help to achieve and maintain integration in mainstream social life.

References

Ager, A. (1998) *The Life Experiences Checklist.* Kidderminster: British Institute of Learning Disabilities.

Aspis, S. (1997) 'Self-advocacy for people with learning difficulties: does it have a future?' *Disability and Society 12*, 4, 647–654.

Aspis, S. (1999) 'What they don't tell disabled people with learning difficulties.' In M. Corker and S. French (eds) *Disability Discourse.* Buckingham: Open University Press.

Brandon, D. (1990) *Zen in the Art of Helping.* London: Arkana.

Brandon, D., Brandon, A. and Brandon, T. (1995) *Advocacy: Power to People with Disabilities.* Birmingham: Ventura.

Collins, J. (1994) *When the Eagles Fly: A Report on the Resettlement of People with Learning Difficulties from Long-Stay Institutions.* London: Values into Action.

Foucault, M. (1973) *The Birth of the Clinic: An Archaeology of Medical Perception.* New York: Pantheon.

Frieri, P. (1972) *Pedagogy of the Oppressed.* Harmondsworth: Penguin.

Gadow, S. (1980) 'Existential advocacy: philosophical foundation of nursing.' In S. Spicker and S. Gadow (eds) *Nursing: Images and Ideals.* New York: Springer.

Gillman, M., Swain, J. and Heyman, R. (1997) '"Life" history or "case" history: the objectification of people with learning difficulties through the tyranny of professional discourse.' *Disability and Society 12*, 5, 675–693.

Goble, C. (1999) '"Like the Secret Service isn't it?" People with learning difficulties perceptions of staff and services: mystification and disempowerment.' *Disability and Society 14*, 4, 449–461.

Goodley, D. (2000) *Self-Advocacy in the Lives of People with Learning Difficulties.* Buckingham: Open University Press.

Graham, A. (1992) 'Advocacy: what the future holds.' *British Journal of Nursing 1*, 3, 148–150.

Illich, I. (1992) 'Disabling professions.' In I. Illich, I. Zola, J. McKnight, J. Caplan and H. Shaiken, *Disabling Professions.* London: Marion Boyars.

Illich, I. (1995) *Limits to Medicine: Medical Nemesis – the Expropriation of Health.* Harmondsworth: Pelican.

McKnight, J. (1989) 'Do no harm: policy options to meet human needs.' *Social Policy* (summer) *20*, 1, 5–14.

McKnight, J. (1992) 'Professionalised service and disabling help.' In I. Illich, I. Zola, J. McKnight, J. Caplan and H. Shaiken, *Disabling Professions.* London: Marion Boyars.

Marks, D. (1999) *Disability: Controversial Debates and Psychosocial Perspectives.* London: Routledge.

Nunkoosing, K. (2000) 'Constructing learning disability: consequences for men and women with learning disabilities.' *Journal of Learning Disabilities 14*, 1, 49–62.

Oliver, M. (1995) *Understanding Disability: From Theory to Practice.* London: Macmillan.

Open University (in association with People First and Mencap) (1996) 'Learning disability: working as equal people. Workbook 3.' In *Equal People: Working Together for Change.* Milton Keynes: The Open University.

Rioux, M. (1997) 'When myths masquerade as science: disability research from an equal rights perspective.' In L. Barton and M. Oliver (eds) *Disability Studies: Past, Present and Future.* Leeds: Disability Press.

Seedhouse, D. (2000) *Practical Nursing Ethics: The Universal Ethical Code.* Chichester: John Wiley.

Simons, K. (1998) 'What really matters? Helping people with learning difficulties to shape services.' In L. Ward (ed) *Innovations in Advocacy and Empowerment for People with Intellectual Disabilities.* Chorley: Lisieux Hall.

Simpson, M. (1999) 'Bodies, brains, behaviour: the return of the three stooges in learning disability.' In M. Corker and S. French (eds) *Disability Discourse.* Buckingham: Open University Press.

Sinson, J. (1993) *Group Homes and Community Integration of Developmentally Disabled People: Microinstitutionalisation.* London: Jessica Kingsley.

Wolfensberger, W. (1991) 'Reflections on a lifetime in human services and mental retardation.' *Mental Retardation 29,* 1, 1–15.

CHAPTER SIX

The Legal Context
Of the Advocacy Service

Deborah Baillie and Veronica M. Strachan

Introduction

In this chapter the key legal issues surrounding independent advocacy will be examined. Independent advocacy is not about giving advice, even legal advice, and is therefore quite distinct from citizen advocacy or the legal representation of clients in legal or quasi-legal proceedings. Essentially there are two legal aspects surrounding independent advocacy, namely those relating to the legal responsibilities of the service providers and those that relate directly to the advocate–client relationship.

Legal issues affecting advocacy organisations

Introduction

Just as there are a variety of types of advocacy used, there are a variety of business structures that advocacy services may take. The service could be provided by a voluntary organisation with a management committee, or a company with a board of directors. Where the advocacy service is being provided by professionals, as part of their professional duty, such as nurses, this form of advocacy is not independent from the service provider, and is therefore outside the scope of this chapter. The format of the organisation is key in determining the legal rights and duties of those involved with the organisation, especially when it comes to determining the rights and liabilities of members of management committee or directors.

Types of organisation

As many services are provided in the voluntary sector, it is often the case that the service formed is focused on the needs that it will be addressing rather than the legal implications for those involved in establishing the service. Indeed for many organisations, constitutions are often prepared as part of the process of obtaining government funding. It is only once organisations have been established and begin to develop or expand that the legal structure of the organisation is considered. Sometimes it will be in the organisation's interest to change the format of the organisation for the purposes of bank borrowing.

Legal effect of an unincorporated organisation

Many organisations in the voluntary sector take the form of an unincorporated association. In many ways this is the entry-level type of organisation, involving little formality. This type of organisation will normally have a constitution and a management committee, but it does not have to have anything in writing. For many voluntary sector organisations, a constitution will probably have been developed for the purpose of obtaining grant funding. The constitution is really a contract, a legal agreement, between management and the individual members of the organisation.

The key point with an unincorporated body is that in law it is not a distinct legal entity from those persons in charge of it. This means that the organisation cannot own property for itself – it either holds the property on behalf of its members or on behalf of the public. However, although management committee members may enter agreements on behalf of the organisation, if debts are incurred or damages result, then the persons ultimately responsible for meeting the debts of the organisation are the individual members of the organisation not the management committee (if they are not also members). Individual members of the management committee are liable however, if they have acted outside the duties and powers given to them in the constitution. It is therefore very important that both new and existing members of the management committee are aware of their potential liability. It is likely that the larger the organisation becomes, the more contracts of employment and other obligations that it acquires, the greater the need for the members to obtain protection. This protection is through the organisation acquiring limited liability status.

It is interesting to note that in Scotland an unincorporated organisation can be sued in its own name, that is not the names of the individual members, in the Sheriff Court. However if the organisation were to be sued in the Court of

Session, the action would be in the names of the members. This would obviously have consequences for members, not least in respect of their financial affairs, such as their personal credit rating.

Legal effect of an incorporated association: limited company

An advocacy service could be run as a limited company, a more complex, legal form of organisation. This form of organisation is more common in medium to large-scale organisations. Whilst like the unincorporated body the limited company will have a 'constitution', referred to as its memorandum and articles, the key difference in law is that the members and directors of the limited company are not liable for all debts of the company – their liability is limited. This limited liability is achieved either by the members guaranteeing to pay the debts of the organisation up to a specified amount, or by the members having invested in shares.

However, even within a limited company, those appointed as directors can still find themselves legally liable either to third parties or the company. Such liability could arise if the director purports to enter into a contract but does not disclose that they are acting for the company, or where the directors have exceeded their authority, as specified in the company documents. The directors of an incorporated body have certain duties that cannot be ignored. Directors are personally liable in a number of respects. They are personally liable for data protection issues, health and safety matters, and they may find themselves liable for the debts of the service, if the service was found to have been wrongfully trading. Wrongful trading occurs where the directors have continued to trade when they knew or ought to have known that there was no prospect of the service avoiding insolvent liquidation, and the directors failed to take all necessary steps to reduce the loss to the creditors of the service.

Accountability/independence of the advocacy service

Having established that the nature of the organisation of the advocacy service may determine the potential liability of the management committee or directors, it is important also to consider to whom the advocacy service is legally accountable. Whilst many advocates strive for independence there are a number of issues that can affect that position, and the service providers need to know to whom they are accountable.

The difficulty for some advocacy services, especially where the service offers a specific form of advocacy against one provider, is that they may not, in practice, be entirely distinct from the service provider. Indeed it is not uncommon for some kinds of advocacy services to be located in service providers' premises, using facilities paid for by the service provider. Clearly in such circumstances the service needs to balance the advantage of convenient, free premises with the likelihood that clients may not then see the advocacy services as being completely independent.

Financial dependence/accountability

Where the advocacy service is funded in part by, or receives assistance from, another organisation, local authority or health boards, it is important to be aware of any issues in the financial arrangement that may compromise the independence of the service. The independence of a service could be compromised if the service provider was to have a say in how the advocacy service should operate. It may however be appropriate to have a member of the funding organisation on the management committee or steering group provided they have no voting rights. Legally, unless otherwise provided in the service agreement (which is a contract between the advocacy service and the finance provider), a finance provider will be entitled only to require the advocacy service to have to account to the finance provider as to how the money provided was spent. They do not have a general right to participate in the management of the advocacy service or to access files or other materials of the advocacy service; however, it is not uncommon for this right to be specifically required in terms of the service agreement. Indeed, it is recommended that any attempt by the finance provider to acquire management rights should be avoided. In the event that the finance provider has acquired management rights, these should be made clear to the users of the advocacy service.

It is encouraging to note that the Scottish Executive's (2000a) *Independent Advocacy: A Guide for Commissioners* recommends: 'Do acknowledge that an advocate's primary loyalty must be to the person or group they are advocating for, not a commissioner or provider of services'. Such advice is to ensure independence and avoid conflict of interests. However, where the advocacy service relies on the service provider as their main source of funding, it is possible that outsiders may not perceive the service as being truly independent. This is especially so when the advocates are employees of the advocacy service, and know that the funding of their job is dependent on future funding.

Conflict of interest

In the event that for whatever reason, an advocacy service is of the opinion that its independence in a particular matter is compromised, then they are in a conflict of interests position. Whilst there is nothing in law to prevent the advocacy service from continuing to provide its services, it would be good practice to advise the client of the potential conflict, and to offer to refer them to an alternative source of advocacy should they so wish. Many clients will however consent to the advocacy service continuing to operate in the conflict situation.

The accountability to the client is addressed below; nonetheless it is essential to stress that ultimately when a service is offered, the organisation is liable to the client if the organisation fails to perform to a reasonable standard of care. Failure to perform to the standard of care required is negligence, for which, potentially, the service could be sued for damages.

Contracting for work issues

Whilst some advocacy services are established to focus on a specific form of advocacy, often linked to a particular hospital or other organisation, many other advocacy services provide advocacy to a broad spectrum of clients. Originally it was thought that contracting was not appropriate for advocacy organisations and funders such as social work departments. In the Scottish Council for Voluntary Organisations, *Voluntary Sector Code of Practice for Community Care Contracting* (1991) it was argued that grant aid not contracting services should remain available for the voluntary sector, including advocacy.

However, as the number of different bodies in the voluntary sector expand, it is not uncommon for voluntary agencies to enter into contracts with each other. Advocacy services may therefore consider entering into contracts with other organisations to provide an advocacy service on their behalf. Obviously, the advocacy organisation should ensure that they are legally able to contract for work. This means that the type of work being contracted for is to fulfil the stated purposes of the advocacy service and also that there is nothing in either their constitution or other contracts (such as loans or other finance agreements) that prohibit such activity. Organisations that have charitable status should be very careful about agreeing to undertake paid work for fundraising where the work itself is not related to the purpose of the organisation.

In law, the basic position is that once an offer has been accepted a contract has been formed. Therefore, the key legal issue in entering a contract is to ensure that the contractual agreement covers all relevant matters. Such matters may include the duration of the service required, how and when payment is to be made, to whom the advocate is to report. All of these matters, as well as to how any disputes should be resolved, must be decided in advance. Especially where the advocacy service and the commissioning organisation are likely to want to do business again in the future, it is prudent to require disputes to be resolved by non-court means. There are several methods available for resolving disputes without resorting to the court, such as arbitration or alternative dispute resolution (ADR), such as mediation.

Where as a result of an additional contract, the advocacy service has to employ an additional advocate it is important for the advocacy service to consider the long-term implications. If after a few years the contract is not renewed, will the advocate be made redundant? If so will they be legally entitled to any payment, because if they are this will have to be paid from the advocacy service – and ultimately the members could be personally liable for the debts if there are no funds to meet this obligation.

Taxation issues arising from contracts

If the organisation is a charity for the purpose of revenue law, then any profit will not be assessed for income tax purposes provided that:

> the trade is exercised in the course of carrying out a primary purpose of the charity, or

> the work in connection with the trade is mainly carried out by beneficiaries of the charity (Income and Corporation Taxes Act 1988).

Provided the organisation generally meets the above, it will not be liable to tax.

Agreements or contracts with clients

It should be normal practice to enter into an agreement with a new client as to the advocacy service to be provided. This agreement will include a statement regarding confidentiality. Even although these agreements may actually be signed by the advocate, provided the advocate has been given the authority to sign such agreements by the management committee, the advocate is acting as an agent for the advocacy service, and the agreement is therefore legally binding on the advocacy service. Having entered into a contract, the advocacy service is legally obliged to perform the service agreed. Moreover, it should be noted that the advocate could also be liable to the client under the laws of negligence if they fail to provide a reasonable standard of care in their dealings with the client. What is reasonable will be judged against what would have been expected from a reasonably competent advocate.

Responsibilities to employees and volunteers

During the 1990s the rights of employees have been extended, often as a result of European legal requirements, and indeed some legislation applies not only to employees but also to all workers. Whether a volunteer could qualify under the heading of worker is really dependent on the nature of the work undertaken. Certainly the issue becomes more important where the volunteer is carrying on work, such as in a fundraising shop, and is receiving some regular payment (other than reimbursement of actual expenses such as travel). When considering employing an advocate, the organisation should note that they have common law and statutory duties, which entitle the employee to rest breaks, to time off for sickness, to maternity benefits, to redundancy benefits and which offer the employee protection in terms of health and safety.

Health and safety duties

There is a general duty of all occupiers of premises to take reasonable care for the safety of all lawful visitors on those premises (Occupier's Liability Acts 1957 (England), 1960 (Scotland)). This duty rests with the person in overall daily control of the premises, not the owner of the premises. Therefore this duty will cover all clients and volunteers. Failure to take reasonable care is negligent, and may result in the service being sued for damages. As a matter of practice, when anyone is injured on the premises, this should be recorded.

Conclusion

When agreeing to get involved in setting up or running an advocacy service it is easy to focus on the client needs that are to be addressed. It is often less easy to appreciate the legal implications of participating in such an organisation. However, it is best that members and directors confront their legal responsibilities sooner, rather than later, once something has gone wrong. Likewise, it is important that employees and volunteers of the service are made aware of their legal responsibilities. These will be addressed in the next section of this chapter.

Legal issues affecting the advocate–client relationship

Introduction

According to Advocacy 2000 (2000) 'advocacy is about standing up for and sticking with a person or group and taking their side. It is about standing alongside people who are in danger of being pushed to the margins of society and it is a process of working towards natural justice'. Some people either have no one to help them to speak out or feel that their relatives or carers do not always represent their best interests. These people may benefit from an independent advocate who has no conflict of interest and no fear of speaking out for the client.

The rights of the client

At present, no person has a general legal right to an independent advocate, although the Millan Committee has recommended in Scotland that the law should be changed to give such a right in relation to mental health issues. However, the Patient's Charter in Scotland did state as far back as 1991 that all users of health services have a right to advocacy. The Disabled Persons (Services, Consultation and Representation) Act 1986 did make provision for disabled people to appoint representatives, but this part of the Act has never been brought into force.

Where a client is able to access an independent advocacy service, the client has a right to an advocacy service that is independent of any service funder. Issues relating to potential conflicts of interest should be addressed by the organisation in its service agreements with funders and advocates should make it clear to professionals, such as health or social workers that advocacy is not about mediation or negotiation.

The client also has a right to be empowered to speak up for himself or herself and the right to be treated impartially by the advocacy service. Finally, the client has a right to access information held about him or her by the advocacy service and the right to confidentiality. Good practice suggests that clients should be given a statement of the principles which underpin the work of the advocacy organisation.

The Data Protection Act 1998

There are two aspects of data protection which need to be addressed. The first is whether the organisation is required to notify the Data Protection Commissioner of its processing of data (formerly called registration). The Act exempts 'not for profit' advocacy organisations from notification as long as the following criteria are met:

> the organisation processes data only in relation to persons receiving advocacy

> the data processed are necessary for the purpose of offering an advocacy service

> disclosure of data is made to third parties only when necessary for the provision of the advocacy service

> data are kept only for as long as necessary for the purposes of providing the advocacy service.

This information is the position as stated in February 2001. However, the Office of the Data Protection Commissioner is continuing to issue guidance on the implementation of the Act and organisations should therefore check their own position.

The second aspect to be addressed is that of the data protection principles. Even where an organisation is exempt from notification, it is still required to comply with these principles. The principles are as follows.

1. Personal data shall be obtained and processed fairly and lawfully

In order to comply, the organisation must either obtain the consent of the data subject or, if he or she cannot consent, the processing must be necessary to protect the vital interests of the data subject. Compliance is particularly important where 'sensitive personal data' are being processed, such as in relation to health, racial or ethnic origin, sexuality or criminal offences. Where clients have the capacity to do so, it would be prudent to ask clients to sign a consent form in relation to storage of information. If a client has a person legally appointed to act for them, that appointee could sign a consent form.

2. Data may be held only for the purpose of the provision of the advocacy service

3. Data must be adequate, relevant and not excessive for that purpose

As regards this principle and the first principle, particular care should be taken when storing information in a client's file which relates to third parties. For example, a person may disclose information about another family member. Consideration should always be given as to whether it is necessary to store that information in the client's file for the purposes of offering an advocacy service to that client. Advocates may also be given information about a client's potentially dangerous behaviour if it is felt necessary for the health and safety of the advocate. Where information is being recorded and it may not be obvious why it is relevant, the advocate should note the purpose in the client's file.

4. Data must be accurate and up to date and must be amended if inaccurate

5. Data must not be kept for longer than necessary

There is no clear guidance on how long information should be kept, but many organisations consider seven years to be appropriate; however, it would be prudent for organisations to check whether everything in the file needs to be kept for the same period.

6. Personal data must be processed in accordance with the rights of data subjects

These rights include the right to know whether data about him or her are being processed, the right to receive a copy of that data in intelligible form and the right to know the source. In addition, the data subject has the right to prevent processing which is likely to cause him or her damage or distress.

7. Data must be secure and there must be no unauthorised access, alteration, disclosure to third parties or accidental loss

This raises issues about the security of computerised records and manual files, particularly where advocates take files home with them. It is suggested that where advocates (paid or volunteer) have to keep files outside the office, they should be provided with a secure, lockable container in which to store the files. It is a criminal offence to disclose information unlawfully and the maximum penalty is currently £5000. Directors may also have personal liability for unlawful disclosure.

8. Transfer of data outside the European Economic Area is restricted

Since October 2001 these principles have applied to manual files and computerised files.

As the Data Protection Act 1998 allows a data subject to have access to his or her file, it may be easier for everyone if the organisation has a policy of open access to his or her file by a client.

A question which may arise relates to who owns the client's file. If the organisation allows open access to the file, it would seem appropriate to recognise that the file belongs to the client. In the case of a client file held by a solicitor, it is recognised that the client is entitled to ask for the file, with the exception of file notes made by the solicitor for his or her own benefit or protection. It is quite clear that client files do not belong to the funder or funders of the advocacy organisation and if the organisation is to be wound up, clients should be given the option of having their files returned to them or having them passed to another organisation.

Confidentiality

In general terms, an individual has the right to confidentiality when consulting a professional person in a professional capacity and may claim damages in the civil courts for breach of confidentiality. An advocacy organisation should have a written policy on confidentiality and should insert a condition into the contract of employment about the requirement to keep information confidential. Volunteers, directors and members of management committees should also be required to sign an agreement relating to confidentiality. The policy should make it clear to clients that information will be kept confidential within the organisation, unless the client agrees to disclosure, but should allow for confidentiality to be breached in exceptional circumstances where the client discloses information which suggests that either the client or a third party may be at risk of significant harm. This is particularly important if the organisation is providing a service to children. It would always be good practice for an advocate to discuss the need to breach confidentiality with the organisation's manager or coordinator and all attempts should be made to encourage the client to agree to confidentiality being breached.

The Human Rights Act 1998 may also have to be taken into consideration in relation to confidentiality. Article Eight of the European Convention on Human Rights gives an individual a right to respect for his or her private life and this right would include a right to confidentiality. Since advocacy organisations may be 'public authorities' within the meaning of the Act, they would need to take care in making a decision to breach confidentiality and should consider whether it is necessary to breach confidentiality when balancing the risk against the right to respect for private life. In other words, the need to breach confidentiality must be proportionate to the perceived risk.

Some advocacy organisations state in their policy on confidentiality that advocates will not even acknowledge a client outside the advocacy setting, unless the client acknowledges the advocate first. Some organisations ask clients to sign a document stating that they have read and understood the organisation's policy on confidentiality. In the light of the Data Protection Act 1998, it would be prudent to have a form which covers confidentiality and processing of information. Advocacy organisations should also have forms for clients to authorise access by the advocate to medical and social work files.

Confidentiality and data protection are linked issues. Organisations should ensure that in addition to procedures for the security of client files, they have procedures for security of items such as diaries, address books and computer discs which may otherwise be left on workers' desks when the office is not occupied.

The duties of the advocate

To some extent, the advocate's duties mirror the rights of the client. The advocate must be independent, empowering and impartial and must recognise when there may be a conflict of interest, either in relation to the client or the particular nature of the client's problem. In particular, an advocate should not act for a client and a relative of the client at the same time. An advocate must not act on behalf of the client, unless he or she has instructions from the client and an advocate must not offer his or her views and must cease acting for the client, if required to do so. An advocate must normally keep information about a client confidential and must not give legal advice to a client about the best course of action for that client. The advocate is there to inform and support, but must recognise when a client needs professional advice and make it clear to the client that they cannot offer advice of any kind, including legal advice. However, since many clients now seek help from an advocate in relation to issues such as refusal to provide services or charging policies, the advocate should have a working knowledge of the key areas of law which may affect the particular client group, particularly as they may be faced with professionals who are far from clear about the legal basis for decisions which have been made about the client. Advocates need to be aware that some clients may find it very difficult to form their own opinions as they may have become institutionalised and used to having decisions made for them.

Sometimes, it may not be possible for an advocate to obtain instructions from a client because the client lacks legal capacity to give such instructions. In these circumstances, advocates sometimes find themselves assuming more of a safeguarding role. This can lead to difficulties when challenged by other professionals or family members. Many parents of adults with a learning disability believe that they may legally make decisions about their son or daughter. The law does not permit an adult to act legally for another adult, unless officially appointed to do so. Some professionals may also question the legality of the intervention by an advocate, but the advocate may in fact have a mandate to operate by virtue of a service agreement between the authority responsible for the adult, e.g. local authority or health, and the advocacy service. When working with clients who lack full legal capacity, advocates should attempt to establish whether the person is able to express a view or preference or whether that person previously expressed views or preferences. This would be in keeping with the spirit of principles set down in the Adults with Incapacity (Scotland) Act 2000.

In relation to children as clients of an advocacy organisation, legally a child under 16 can instruct an advocate, if they have a general understanding of what they require the advocate to do for them. The advocacy organisation would not require parental consent and nor would it be able to inform parents that it was providing the service to the child.

Advocates should not accept gifts from clients and nor should they make promises or commitments which they cannot fulfil. In addition, it is important that the advocate–client relationship remains professional at all times and that it does not transform itself into that of befriender–client, otherwise, the independence of the advocate could be compromised.

Complaints

Advocacy organisations need to have a clear procedure for dealing with client complaints. The procedure must be fair and as impartial as is possible in what may be quite a small organisation. It is good practice to give a client a copy of the complaints procedure at the start of the advocate–client relationship.

Negligence

Negligence is the failure of a person to act with a reasonable level of care or to fail to do something that they should have done, as the result of which a person suffers loss or injury. A person who suffers loss or injury as a direct result of the negligence of another person may raise a civil court action to seek compensation (damages) for the loss or injury caused. An award of damages will be made against the employer, rather than the individual employee.

The duty of care owed by an advocate to a client will be that of the ordinary, competent, independent advocate. It is therefore imperative that advocacy organisations give adequate training to both paid and unpaid advocates. If it is alleged that an advocate has breached the duty of care, a court will examine the circumstances surrounding the event in question. It is therefore very important that adequate records are kept by the organisation, in order to show how and why particular decisions were made and that the decisions were in accordance with the written policies of the organisation. The question for the court will be whether the advocate acted reasonably in the circumstances. As already mentioned, advocates should be particularly careful in relation to confidentiality, giving commitments over which they have no control and giving advice to clients.

Advocates should also take great care when writing letters on behalf of clients. The letter should make it clear that it is written on behalf of the client and it should only contain factual information. If any opinions are expressed in the letter, it should be clear that they are the opinions of the client, unless the advocate is acting in a safeguarding role. Ideally the letter should be signed by the client and the advocate, with the advocate designating themselves 'independent advocate on behalf of...[client]'.

Conclusion

When providing an advocacy service, it would be easy to focus on the helping part of the relationship and to ignore legal responsibilities. This chapter has highlighted the importance of law to advocacy organisations and it is hoped that directors, members, employees and volunteers will confront their legal responsibilities and that the organisation will benefit as a result.

Further information

Data Protection Commissioner, Wycliffe House, Water Lane, Wilmslow, Cheshire SK9 5AF. www.open.gov.uk/dpr/dprhome.htm.

References

Adults with Incapacity (Scotland) Act (2000) London: HMSO.
Advocacy 2000 (2000) Key Ideas on Independent Advocacy. Edinburgh: Advocacy 2000.
Data Protection Act (1998) London: HMSO.
Disabled Persons (Services, Consultation and Representation) Act (1986) London: HMSO.
Human Rights Act (1998) London: HMSO.
Income and Corporation Taxes Act (1998) London: HMSO.

Occupier's Liability Act (1957 (England and Wales), 1960 Scotland).

Scottish Council for Voluntary Organisations (1991) *Voluntary Sector Code of Practice for Community Care Contracting.*

Scottish Executive (2000) *Independent Advocacy: A Guide for Commissioners.* www.scotland.gov.uk/library3/health/iagc-00.asp

Further reading

Barker, C., Elliot, R.C. and Moody, S.R. (1996) *Charity Law in Scotland.* Edinburgh: W. Green.

Scottish Executive (2000) *Report on the Review of The Mental Health (Scotland) Act 1984.* www.scotland.gov.uk/millan

Scottish Office (1998) *Advocacy: A Guide to Good Practice.* Edinburgh: Scottish Office.

CHAPTER SEVEN

Thoughts From a UK Citizen Advocacy Scheme

Mike Pochin

Ideas

The term 'citizen advocacy' seems so familiar and well accepted that any attempt to analyse it would appear unnecessary. Is it not, like the five accomplishments enumerated by John O'Brien (1987), seen as part of the very fabric of good practice in support of those who have learning difficulties?

Beneath this superficial consensus, however, the picture is less certain. What exactly is citizen advocacy? How has it been developed in the UK? What constitutes good practice in citizen advocacy? Put these questions to a cross-section of even well-informed individuals, and their answers are likely to be tentative or ambiguous. The analogy with the five accomplishments can perhaps be taken a little further; though both the accomplishments and citizen advocacy are seen as significant aspirations, it is not always clear how they inform or change what happens in practice.

This chapter does not attempt to provide a definitive account of citizen advocacy, nor does it attempt to assess its overall impact within the UK. Rather, it seeks to identify some core citizen advocacy values and to reflect on some significant issues in the implementation of citizen advocacy as experienced in one citizen advocacy scheme supporting people who have a learning difficulty.

Although the term citizen advocacy is sometimes used to describe any situation in which one person speaks up for another, it properly refers to a distinctive form of advocacy developed in North America in the 1960s and 1970s. The idea for citizen advocacy came from Wolf Wolfensberger, and its principles were set out in the manual *Citizen Advocacy Program Evaluation* (CAPE) written by Wolfensberger and John O'Brien (O'Brien and Wolfensberger 1979). O'Brien's (1987) later work, *Learning from Citizen Advocacy Programs*, is the source of perhaps the best known definition of citizen advocacy:

> A valued citizen who is unpaid and independent of human services creates a relationship with a person who is at risk of social exclusion and chooses one or several of many ways to understand, respond to, and represent that person's interests as if they were the advocate's own, thus bringing their partner's gifts and concerns into the circles of ordinary community life. (O'Brien 1987, p.3)

At the heart of this model is the idea, not merely of one individual speaking up for the needs and wishes of another, but also of a unique bond between the two people. The principles which govern this bond are independence and loyalty.

The principle of independence governs the implementation of citizen advocacy in a number of ways:

> *The independence of advocates.* Advocates can speak up freely about shortcomings in services only if they are independent of those services. Similarly people who have learning difficulties can trust only advocates who are not controlled or influenced by service organisations.

> *Independence of partnerships.* It is a distinctive feature of citizen advocacy that advocates are not managed nor directed by the advocacy scheme. Instead, the advocates and their 'partners' (the individuals they support) are encouraged to own the partnership. In this way, the partnership can develop as a human relationship, rather than as a service intervention.

> *Independent identification of those needing advocacy.* Citizen advocacy schemes are encouraged to be proactive in finding those who want and need advocacy; simply to accept referrals from social workers or other professionals may lead to a failure to help those who are excluded from care service provision.

> *Independent scheme management.* Just as advocates should not work for the services received by their partners, so citizen advocacy schemes should be structurally independent of health and social services, in order to avoid conflicts of interest.

> *Independent sources of funding.* In order for citizen advocates, and citizen advocacy schemes, to be able to act with maximum

independence, CAPE also recommends that funding for schemes should as far as possible come from sources independent of health and social services. This requirement has proved difficult for many citizen advocacy schemes in the UK.

If the principle of independence distinguishes the role of advocacy from that of service provision, and enables advocacy partnerships to act in ways that are not prescribed by service providers, the principle of loyalty seeks to define the internal force which drives those partnerships: the principle of loyalty is implemented in the following ways:

> *Citizen advocates do not act for financial reward.* In citizen advocacy, it is essential that advocates act, and are seen to act, solely out of commitment to their partner. Paying advocates not only would impair this motive, but also would imply that people with learning difficulties must live outside the bonds of freely given help that characterise community life at its best. In other words, it would further exclude and devalue them.

> *Citizen advocates are not experts.* Advocates are sometimes described as neutral or impartial. This carries the implication that they can adjudicate the best interests of, say, someone who has profound learning difficulties. Such a view is mistaken; citizen advocates speak up for the wishes and interests of their partner as they have come to understand them during the course of the partnership. They speak up from a place within that person's life, and not as an independent arbitrator.

> *Loyalty means that many partnerships will be long term.* In times of difficulty, most of us would prefer to have a trusted friend, rather than a well-meaning stranger, at our side. Similarly, advocates will often be able to speak up with conviction for someone who has a learning difficulty only if they have spent time getting to know them, and have established a bond of trust with them. In the course of developing this bond, advocates may also offer their partner friendship and access to wider opportunities.

> *Advocate loyalty demonstrates the possibility of a more inclusive society.* Whilst people who have learning disabilities are not formally segregated in the way that they were under the hospital system, there are nonetheless still many whose only interactions from one day to the next are with paid care workers and other service users. In

established advocacy partnerships, it is not uncommon for the advocate to refer to the partner as being 'like one of the family'. The freely given and informal nature of the partnership asserts the partner's value even before any formal advocacy has taken place. Citizen advocacy is not merely a mechanism for commenting on the suitability or effectiveness of community care services; it is also a living reminder of the limits to what even the best services can achieve. Inclusion is as much an issue for society as it is for care services.

This brief review of the core citizen advocacy principles of independence and loyalty has presented citizen advocacy as a credible and positive force in the lives of people who have learning difficulties. However, in its development in the UK, it has not been immune to challenge. These challenges have been of both a theoretical and a practical nature. On the theoretical side, both self-advocates and the wider disability movement have sometimes been suspicious of a form of advocacy which seems to assume that people with learning difficulties need the intervention of able-bodied advocates if their needs and wishes are to be taken seriously (see Atkinson 1999, p.25). Is this not simply reinforcing the devalued status of the partners and perpetuating images of their dependency? The debate cannot be resolved here but it can perhaps be clarified by suggesting that citizen advocacy and the disability movement have differing, if closely related, goals. The disability movement places equality at the centre of its demands, an attitude well summarised in the demand for 'Rights not Charity'. The citizen advocacy movement, whilst it certainly endorses the demand for equality, focuses more especially on the process of inclusion. From this standpoint, as we have seen, an advocacy partnership is not a form of paternalism, but a practical demonstration of inclusiveness. In an ideal world, equality and inclusion would perhaps mean the same thing; in an imperfect world, they may sometimes appear to be in tension.

Practical obstacles to the implementation and growth of citizen advocacy have centred on two main issues: lack of funding and the diversification in types of advocacy. Voluntary organisations have traditionally struggled to attract adequate and secure funding within the UK. For some organisations, this problem was alleviated with the implementation of Care in the Community in 1993; by agreeing service contracts with their local health or social services departments, they were assured income in return for providing a given service. Some citizen advocacy schemes have taken this route, but it poses major difficulties. First, not all local authorities have recognised a responsibility to purchase advocacy, so provision has been patchy. Second, most citizen advocacy schemes would not describe themselves as services, so agreeing contract terms has been problematic. Third, and most importantly, it is very difficult for schemes to challenge a service provider who is also their funder; there is potentially a large conflict of interest. The absence of clear and appropriate mechanisms for citizen advocacy funding has undoubtedly hindered its development.

At the same time, citizen advocacy has also been hampered by uncertainties surrounding its identity. In the early 1980s, citizen advocacy was probably the only form of advocacy in the UK. Over the years, other forms of advocacy have sprung up: peer advocacy, self-advocacy and casework advocacy, to name but three. Some of these sprang from a conscious wish to do something different from citizen advocacy, but others grew from a desire to implement some of the CAPE principles, whilst rejecting others as unrealistic or inappropriate in a UK context. Thus it is not now easy to say, for example, where citizen advocacy ends and volunteer advocacy (using volunteers as casework or 'issues-based' advocates) begins. The citizen advocacy movement still has work to do in order to define a relationship with other forms of advocacy which allows it to be both distinctive and yet tolerant of these other approaches.

Experiences

For all these challenges, citizen advocacy endures and flourishes in the UK. Dozens of schemes identify with, and seek to implement, all or most of the principles laid down in CAPE. In their day-to-day existence, these schemes discover a range of achievements and difficulties, insights and dilemmas which are too often obscured by the theoretical and strategic questions discussed in the first part of this chapter. This section will highlight some of these practical issues as they have been experienced in one citizen advocacy scheme in the south-west of England.

Dorset Advocacy was founded in 1993. It develops citizen advocacy partnerships with people who have learning difficulties across the local authority areas of Dorset, Bournemouth and Poole. Around 80 advocacy partnerships are supported at any one time. The scheme is funded by the local health authority, although recently it has sought to diversify its funding base with approaches to social services departments and grant-making trusts. Those involved with Dorset Advocacy have reflected on a number of questions and themes since the early 1990s. Four of these themes will be examined here:

> success and failure in advocacy partnerships
>
> the two-way process of citizen advocacy

the balance between long-term and crisis partnerships

supporting citizen advocacy partnerships.

Each will be discussed in turn.

Success and failure in advocacy partnerships

The first section of this chapter outlined some of the core principles which guide citizen advocacy. None of these principles is easy to implement, as each involves something of a challenge to common assumptions about services, society and volunteering. Citizen advocacy schemes often have to work against a prevailing current of scepticism. In these circumstances, it is not surprising that the struggle to uphold citizen advocacy principles has consumed much of the movement's energy. This in turn has meant that success in citizen advocacy has tended to be defined solely in terms of how far a scheme adheres to the CAPE principles. The drawback of this approach is that it tends to obscure the very real achievements of citizen advocacy partnerships in helping people to make their lives better. There is now a real danger that in a funding environment that is increasingly (and even unhealthily) 'outcomes-driven', a citizen advocacy movement which speaks only of its principles and not of its impact will be misunderstood and marginalised.

If citizen advocacy schemes are to demonstrate their practical impact, they will need accessible and appropriate evaluation tools. Several evaluatory systems already exist, though none is yet widely used; this is an area which requires further development. But alongside this question of the formal evaluation of citizen advocacy sits another which is no less important: how, on a day-to-day basis, do schemes understand the aims of advocacy partnerships, and how do they distinguish success and failure in the pursuit of these aims? The principles of citizen advocacy are clear, if demanding, but what do schemes make of them in practice?

Once one adopts this more practical standpoint, the appearance of citizen advocacy changes dramatically, for whereas the principles of citizen advocacy are severe, even narrow, in its practice it is extremely diverse. There is no such thing as a typical, let alone an ideal, partnership. Advocates support people who have the mildest and the most profound learning difficulties. Their partners may be employed or unemployed; they may live alone, or with their families, or in residential care; they may be single, married or in relationships. Some will specifically have requested an advocate; in other instances the advocacy coordinator will have suggested the idea of advocacy to a partner.

What counts as success in this diverse field? Sometimes success is easy to discern:

> Mark asked for an advocate because he was unhappy with the residential home in which he lived. He was introduced to Ray, and Ray began to help him voice his wishes to the local social services. Within a year, Mark had moved to the home of his choice. He decided he no longer needed an advocate, so the partnership ended.

Mark was clearly happy with the result of his advocacy partnership. Ray felt satisfied that he had helped to make a difference in Mark's life, and that Mark now felt empowered enough to speak up without assistance. But what of an advocate who supports a partner who has little communication, and is also deemed to have 'challenging behaviour'? Over a number of years, the advocate spends one-to-one time with the partner, never finding it at all difficult. When the partner's residential service is faced with closure, the advocate suggests an alternative service which it is felt would be suitable. The partner moves there and appears to settle well. In this scenario, one cannot demonstrate exactly the impact of the partnership, or even prove conclusively that the advocate is acceptable to the partner. Yet it is possible that the advocacy partnership has given the partner a hitherto unavailable means to express themselves without recourse to anger, and that the advocate has had a decisive impact on the service provided to the partner. Citizen advocacy schemes are surely right to celebrate the unique commitment which underpins this kind of partnership; a commitment which may have even more far-reaching results than those highlighted in Mark and Ray's story.

This immense variety in citizen advocacy partnerships, and the fact that there is no single criterion of success, can make it difficult for schemes to give society at large a clear idea of their aims and achievements, or to 'sell' the idea of citizen advocacy to potential new advocates. Dorset Advocacy uses the following anecdote in the induction of new advocates, not because it represents an ideal, but because it captures something of the diversity of citizen advocacy whilst remaining a simple story of three people.

Paul and Sue are a couple who are jointly advocates for Barney. They wrote this of their partnership:

> We have been Barney's advocates for over four years now. It is hard to put into writing all that has happened in that time. There are two main ways we have tried to help:
>
> 1.   Raising awareness of Barney's needs and rights
> 2.   Being friends to Barney

Through meetings with Barney's care workers we have tried to ensure that he has a good home life, for example by asking that they help him to buy new clothes. We have campaigned for him to have the same choices others have.

We see Barney most weeks. Sometimes he comes for tea, sometimes we go to the pub. Because he cannot speak, Sue has learned Makaton signs, and now Barney uses these too – not always in the right context! He loves working with Paul in the garden or workshop, and this has increased his self-confidence.

Barney is part of our life, we aim to make sure his future is a good one.

There is a long tradition of using stories such as this to share experiences of citizen advocacy. They are a good (indeed, sometimes the only way) of showing the effectiveness of partnerships. Just as importantly though, they help to convey the 'feel' of a citizen advocacy scheme. Though principles may establish the boundaries of advocacy, much of its content can be understood only through participation. For this and other reasons, citizen advocacy is probably best viewed as a form of community development, rather than as an intervention or service. Whilst it can support people decisively in times of crisis (and more will be said of this later) there is about many citizen advocacy partnerships a deliberate open-endedness which is at odds with a 'systems' approach. Within such partnerships, specific goals arise from the relationship between advocate and partner; they are not stipulated at the outset.

So, alongside adherence to principles, citizen advocacy schemes also require a keen practical sense of what will be possible, useful and appropriate in their own areas. The way in which schemes address these issues will, as much as citizen advocacy principles, determine the identity of the scheme.

So far, attention has been given to the ways in which citizen advocacy schemes can aim for, and reflect on, their successes. But anything which is capable of success is also prone to failure, and citizen advocacy schemes are no exception to this rule. It is sometimes said, especially by care workers, that citizen advocacy is 'a great idea, but it doesn't work in practice'. A particular charge is that advocates sometimes simply walk away from a partnership, leaving their partner hurt, confused and, arguably, more devalued than ever. If citizen advocacy is to realise its potential, it must be open to this sort of examination, and honest when shortcomings are revealed.

How can schemes minimise this sort of failure in partnerships, where an advocate simply gives up, without letting their partner or the scheme know of their decision? There are no fail-safe answers here, but there are a couple of approaches which may help. The first is for schemes to be aware of the scale of the problem. If monitoring reveals that, over the course of a year, a large percentage of partnerships are ending in this way, then practice in selecting advocates, and preparing them for their role, probably need to be changed. Second, advocates can be encouraged to examine their own motivation:

> You don't need any special qualifications or experience to be an advocate. But before you volunteer, please ask yourself these two questions:
>
> > Do I care about justice and friendship for people who have a learning disability?
> >
> > Have I got the commitment needed to earn the trust of someone with a learning disability, and to carry on supporting them? (*Advocates' Handbook*, Dorset Advocacy)

It may be that the open-ended nature of citizen advocacy, which is a source of strength in the many successful partnerships that exist, can represent a difficulty to some advocates. To develop a rapport with someone who does not communicate easily, to try to identify the persons' needs and wishes, and then to voice those wishes to personnel who may in any case be sceptical of the advocacy role – all this can indeed appear daunting. In their selection and support of advocates, citizen advocacy schemes need to be alert to the possibility of their feeling overwhelmed. But this caution can be balanced by the knowledge that citizen advocacy has worked, and continues to work, in the most difficult circumstances. Citizen advocacy is never easy, and schemes need to demonstrate that they can identify, and learn from, failure; equally, however, they need to promote the diversity of their successes.

The two-way process of advocacy partnerships

It was stated earlier that citizen advocacy is better understood as a form of community development, rather than as an intervention or service, and this is reflected in the two-way nature of many citizen advocacy partnerships. The partner is not merely a recipient or service user; they are also a 'giver' who can contribute significantly to their advocate's life:

> It was during a week's Open University summer school that I first met and talked with disabled people. At the end of the week I took home with me a deeper understanding of the hurt and frustration felt by those who are excluded by society.
> It was this experience which led me to become an advocate. I have been Tracey's advocate for nearly a year now... What a year! It has been

> both challenging and rewarding, and Tracey has taught me a lot about myself. I hope I can return this gift by offering as many opportunities as I have had in life. I would recommend advocacy to anyone with time to spare. (Fiona)

In this partnership, it is the rapport between advocate and partner itself which has been rewarding for the advocate; it has been part of her personal growth. For other advocates, it will be the sense of having helped their partner to achieve something which gives them satisfaction in their role. A key part of the citizen advocacy coordinator's role, therefore, lies in identifying not just the partner's needs, but also the needs of the advocate and in using this information to create a successful advocate–partner match.

There are still other partnerships where the benefits for the advocate are unclear, or are not what the advocate thought they would be. These are the partnerships that are likely to require the most support from a citizen advocacy scheme. In the previous section, one possible cause of partnership failure was identified as the advocate's sense of daunting responsibilities which are not balanced either by a clear goal for their partnership, or by any sense of personal satisfaction. Where schemes are creating partnerships which are likely to make especial demands on the advocates' commitment or skills (for example, where the partner can give the advocate little positive feedback), the risk of failure can perhaps be reduced if advocates are given an honest assessment, from the outset, of what they are likely to gain from the partnership. If the difficulty of a particular role is acknowledged in this way, advocates can at least feel that they have made an informed choice when embarking on that partnership, and that their role is valued by the scheme.

It is important to reflect on the benefits for advocates, since their levels of motivation will have significant impact on both the duration and effectiveness of partnerships. The primary focus of the partnership, however, is the partner. How can their benefit from an advocacy partnership be assessed? There is an obvious paradox here: individuals who need an advocate to represent their interests may not be at all confident in speaking up about the quality of advocacy they receive. However, many schemes do have a body of evidence from partners, albeit limited in scope:

> I have found a very good advocate in Jill. Jill is a very understanding lady, very supportive, and has helped me wonderfully well even in the bleakest days. (Ian)

> I want to thank Dorset Advocacy for finding me a friend who does what he says he will. (James)

Asking partners wide-open questions about their advocacy partnership may not help them to give meaningful information: questions like 'How do you like your advocate?' or 'What has your advocate helped you to achieve?' could be perceived as quite intimidating. Asking more precise questions which do not require large-scale value judgements may gradually allow a picture of the partnership to emerge:

> Does your advocate keep their appointments with you?
>
> What sort of things do you like to talk to your advocate about?
>
> Are there other things you would like to talk to them about?
>
> Have you ever had any problems with your advocate?

The *way* in which the partner answers these sorts of questions, as well as the answers they give, will often help to convey an idea of how they view their partnership.

The balance between long-term and crisis partnerships

It is a distinguishing feature of citizen advocacy, as opposed to other forms of advocacy, that advocacy goals often emerge only over a period of time, and in the context of an ongoing partnership. In casework advocacy, the partner's initial aims determine the relationship with the advocate and the partnership ends when these aims are realised. In citizen advocacy, it may well be the relationship which determines the goals. For example, a citizen advocate may introduce the partner to an interest, such as cookery. The partner may develop this interest to such an extent that they wish to leave their day centre and study catering at college; the advocate then helps them to voice this wish.

This approach, which allows the relationship to come before any specific goal, can be of particular benefit to people with learning difficulties who have become institutionalised in restrictive care settings. Such individuals may have little or no concept of choice, and be accustomed to being surrounded by service workers whose role in their life is primarily instrumental. A freely given one-to-one partnership with a citizen advocate can help the partner to begin to have a sense of their own value; only where there is this self-esteem can meaningful choices start to be made. Thus the long-term nature of many citizen advocacy partnerships is central to the success of the model.

However, crises occur in the lives of people with learning difficulties as in the lives of everyone else (though accessing support in a time of crisis may be much more difficult for the former group). The situation facing numerous parents who have learning difficulties highlights this well. There often appears to be little appropriate antenatal help for this group. Then, when their child is born, a myriad of professionals descends on the maternity ward questioning the parents' ability and their right to bring up their child. The child protection process begins and there is a real possibility of the child being taken into care. The stress for the parents must be immense; having an advocate who can be introduced to them immediately gives them at least some chance of having their views heard.

It is with these and similar situations in mind that many citizen advocacy schemes recruit a pool of crisis advocates. Like casework advocates, crisis advocates help individuals through a particular difficulty to its resolution. Such advocates may be recruited for their skills in this field, or may undergo specific training by the scheme. The issues addressed by crisis partnerships are likely to be complex. More than long-term partnerships, they are also likely to be adversarial, involving complaints, appeals or even legal actions. The complexity of the role, and the fact that an advocate is often needed at very short notice, means that crisis advocacy can place a heavy demand on the resources of a citizen advocacy scheme, perhaps undermining its focus on the creation of long-term partnerships. This pressure is increased in a funding environment which tends to reward 'responsiveness' and to neglect the benefits of long-term support. How can schemes balance the two areas of work?

Part of the answer may lie in the concept of 'responsiveness' itself. Certainly, responsiveness means that crisis advocacy should be available at fairly short notice. It will also mean that advocates have a range of skills and knowledge appropriate to their role. But true responsiveness also means responding, not just to the crisis, but also to the person. Crisis advocacy is not simply about getting what the partner wants; it may also be about helping them express and work through their emotional reaction to the difficulties. Emotional articulacy is all too often denied to people who have learning difficulties, particularly at times of crisis, and this can lead to them being 'processed', rather than truly supported, by their services.

There is a strong argument, then, for suggesting that crisis advocacy with people with learning difficulties should draw on the values, practices and lessons of long-term advocacy partnerships wherever possible. This will mean that, whatever the exact ratio of long-term to crisis partnerships within a scheme, the scheme will ensure first of all that it secures the vigour, diversity and effectiveness of its long-term partnerships as the framework within which crisis advocacy can be developed.

Supporting citizen advocacy partnerships

Citizen advocacy schemes have three main aims in supporting advocacy partnerships. The first, as we have seen, is to ensure that both partners and advocates are happy with the progress of the partnership. Second, the scheme can provide a focal point for partnerships, helping them to feel part of a wider common endeavour. Schemes often celebrate the achievements of partnerships through social gatherings such as barbecues and skittles evenings, as well as in more formal settings such as annual general meetings. Third, partnership support entails schemes listening to, informing and encouraging advocates in order to help make their advocacy roles more effective. How can this be done whilst respecting the fundamentally independent nature of citizen advocacy partnerships?

Citizen advocacy schemes have traditionally fought shy of the idea of training their advocates. As we have seen, much of the force of citizen advocacy derives from the bond of natural loyalty between advocate and partner. Formal training might destroy this bond, leading advocates to see themselves as specialists, and their partners as 'cases'. On the other hand, it seems clear that some basic information on issues like negotiation and service structures would be very useful for some advocates; one cannot assume that because an advocate is committed to their partner they will automatically be able to negotiate successfully on their partner's behalf – they may even be unsure who to negotiate with. So some advocates at least will benefit from some kind of structured input from the scheme as they develop their role with their partner.

The *Advocacy in Context* series from the BILD pack *Pathways to Citizen Advocacy* (Brooke and Harris 2000) could be one useful resource for citizen advocacy schemes here. The series includes modules on issues such as:

Working with Professionals

Choice in Where to Live

Choice in Daytime Opportunities.

These can be delivered on a one-off basis or as part of a series. Alternatively, schemes may wish to develop their own information events, in the light of local conditions and the specific needs of partnerships. Over the years, Dorset Advocacy has run sessions on the benefits system, negotiating and relationships among other issues. Advocates could choose to attend or not, depending on whether the topic was relevant to their partnership.

Feedback from these information events showed that, whilst advocates valued factual inputs, they felt they derived most benefit from the opportunity to share news about the progress of their partnerships with each other. Developing this idea, in 2000 Dorset Advocacy set up local advocate get-togethers – opportunities for advocates in a given area to meet up every three months or so, to listen to and support one another. The meetings are confidential. Advocates can 'tell the story' of their partnership from their perspective, and then seek feedback and suggestions from the other advocates. The supportive atmosphere at these gatherings has been encouraging; they have underlined how dynamic and committed partnerships can be. The meetings offer one kind of balance between recognising the independence of partnerships from the scheme on the one hand, whilst offering advocates the opportunity to gain information, advice and support on the other.

Opportunities

There can be little doubt that the White Paper *Valuing People: A New Strategy for Learning Disability for the 21st Century* offers the best opportunity to date for the development of citizen advocacy in the UK (Department of Health 2001). This announced the government's commitment to 'developing and expanding advocacy services, particularly citizen advocacy and self-advocacy'. Significantly, it recognises that:

> Citizen advocates (i.e. volunteers) create a relationship with a person with learning disabilities, seeking to understand and to represent the person with learning disabilities' views. (Department of Health 2001, pp.45–46)

As we have seen, it is this stress on relationship which marks out citizen advocacy from other forms of advocacy. If the government honours this commitment it will therefore be a welcome reversal of the recent trend among local authority and other advocacy funders to fund only issues-based or crisis advocacy, neglecting the importance of cultivating relationships. Investment in citizen advocacy and self-advocacy holds out the prospect of appropriate advocacy for all people with learning disabilities who wish to take it up.

The White Paper will also lead to the establishment of a National Citizen Advocacy Network, 'charged with distributing funds to local groups in an equitable and open manner' (Department of Health 2001, p.47).

Such a network could prove a valuable resource for the many citizen advocacy schemes which are currently underfunded and isolated. The promise of funding from national government would also help citizen advocacy schemes to avoid the conflicts of interest that often arise where funding comes from local authorities; the same authorities that advocates will sometimes have to challenge or criticise. However, it appears that local authorities will still play a significant part in advocacy funding:

> Proposed Performance Indicator and PAF Indicator:
>
> The amount spent by each council on advocacy expressed as the amount per head of people with learning disabilities known to the council. (Department of Health 2001, p.124)

It is therefore to be hoped that the National Citizen Advocacy Network will at the very least draw up protocols to ensure that the conflicts of interest inherent in local authority funding of citizen advocacy are kept to a minimum.

No less important than the White Paper's commitment to the development of citizen advocacy is its insistence on person-centred planning:

> Given the importance of person-centred planning as a tool for achieving change, we will make supporting its implementation one of the priorities for the Learning Disability Development Fund and the Implementation Support Team. (Department of Health 2001, p.50)

What has prevented services from being person-centred hitherto? Two key factors have been the rigid boundaries between services (particularly health and social services) and the reluctance to create new services around individual needs. The White Paper addresses the first problem squarely, but will it also create a climate in which innovative services are the norm rather than the exception? This will require resources as well as commitment, and resources are rarely made available unless asked for and argued for. There may therefore be a significant role for citizen advocacy in helping to ensure that people with more severe learning difficulties in particular gain the attention, understanding and resources necessary to make person-centred planning a reality for them.

Finally, it is also to be hoped that the White Paper will lead to better understanding, and closer cooperation between the citizen advocacy and self-advocacy movements, without blurring the distinctive identities of either. Citizen advocacy schemes may need to be more including of people with learning disabilities, not only as partners, but also as advocates and committee members. It is hoped that those in the self-advocacy movement will also recognise that a freely given partnership can be an appropriate and effective means to represent and promote individual interests. The two movements should have much to offer each other.

Twenty years on, citizen advocacy is still here, still developing, still making a difference. This chapter has sought to identify some of the key ideas which inform citizen advocacy, and to draw out their implications. It has also suggested that principles alone cannot give us the whole picture of what citizen advocacy means, and it has tried to highlight some of the ways in which one scheme has developed its identity in practice. Readers may agree or disagree with the ideas presented; what is important is that the debate about good practice should continue. Finally, it has been suggested that the government's learning disability strategy offers real opportunities to citizen advocacy to become an established and accepted part of the life of the community. Though difficulties persist, the future of citizen advocacy looks promising.

References

Atkinson, D. (1999) *Advocacy: A Review.* Brighton: Pavilion.

Brooke, J. and Harris, J. (2000) *Pathways to Citizen Advocacy,* Parts 1 and 2. Kidderminster: BILD.

Department of Health (2001) *Valuing People: A New Strategy for Learning Disability for the 21st Century,* Cmnd 5086. London: Department of Health.

Dorset Advocacy (1999) *Advocates' Handbook.* Dorchester: Dorset Advocacy.

O'Brien, J. (1987) *Learning from Citizen Advocacy Program.* Atlanta, GA: Georgia Advocacy Office.

O'Brien, J. and Wolfensberger, W. (1979) *CAPE: Standards for Citizen Advocacy Program Evaluation.* Toronto: National Institute on Mental Retardation.

CHAPTER EIGHT

Self-Advocacy and Research

Dorothy Atkinson

Introduction

This chapter looks at recent research in relation to advocacy by, for and with people with learning difficulties. The focus is on research as it affects self-advocacy, as this raises many key issues about the nature of research, and of advocacy, and of the relationship between them. The interrelationship between research and (self) advocacy became apparent in the production and publication of the anthology, *Know Me as I Am* (Atkinson and Williams 1990). That book contained the life stories, many originally in oral form, of around 200 people with learning difficulties. The work of collecting and compiling the accounts of so many people, in such different circumstances, emulated a research process. The anthology allowed people to represent themselves, to 'speak up' for themselves. In this sense, it gave people a voice in a respected, published format. In so doing, it also encouraged self-representation or self-advocacy. At the same time, some of the stories were by self-advocates, reflecting on the importance of self-advocacy in their lives. The anthology, therefore, both drew on, and encouraged, the work of self-advocates and self-advocacy groups and has fed into subsequent research into advocacy.

The focus on self-advocacy is also prompted by the views of two people with learning difficulties whom I consulted prior to commencing work on this chapter. The extract below from the transcript of the consultation indicates the primacy of self-advocacy at least in their view (as advocates themselves) and, where self-representation is not possible, then peer advocacy is preferred to citizen advocacy – although neither term is used. The two people concerned are Mabel Cooper and Gloria Ferris, who are in other circumstances co-researchers with me in a life story research project (to which I return below). Here they are reflecting on what advocacy means to them:

Mabel: Self-advocacy is speaking for yourself. People First is a self-advocacy group. It's about people speaking for themselves. In our group there are three people who do not speak, they do not speak a word. No one is allowed to speak for them. Either they use signs or they draw pictures to tell other people what they want.

Gloria: I'm an advocate for Muriel. Advocacy is speaking up for somebody who can't speak for themselves, and if they need anything, you need to ask for them. When I visit Muriel, I first of all make her a cup of tea. I also feed her, wash her and do all sorts of things to help. I talk to her as if I'm talking to a normal person, and she responds – though she can't speak for herself very well.

She tries hard to speak. If you ask her if she wants tea or coffee she says 'oi' which means 'yes'.

Mabel: Muriel can't speak for herself, and she can't draw. Gloria can support Muriel because Gloria is another person with a learning disability. It has to be someone else with a learning disability.

The chapter will take as its starting point the generally accepted view of self-advocacy as articulated in the extract: 'Self-advocacy is speaking for yourself'. What does 'speaking for yourself' mean to people who are involved in the process? Addressing this question entails looking at research into self-advocacy. However, the chapter will also consider research by and with people with learning difficulties (participatory research) as that in itself can be seen as a manifestation of self-advocacy. Finally, research as advocacy and research as an empowering process will be considered.

Research into advocacy

Self-advocacy means speaking up for oneself (People First 1993a). The representation of one's own wishes and needs in this way is a fundamental aspect of human life. Self-advocacy, as I concluded elsewhere, 'has enabled people with learning difficulties to speak out; to have a voice, and to have the means by which that voice may be heard' (Atkinson 1999, p.6). The self-advocacy organisation, People First, London, says that self-advocacy means:

speaking for yourself

standing up for your rights

making choices

being independent

taking responsibility for yourself. (People First 1993a)

At an individual level, self-advocacy is seen to be beneficial for the people with learning difficulties involved. As well as enabling people to have a voice and be heard, self-advocacy is said to enhance personal identity, to raise self-esteem and to support self-determination (Mitchell 1997; Simons 1992, 1993; Sutcliffe and Simons 1993; Wertheimer 1990).

Self-advocacy, in practice, often means advocacy in a group, 'speaking up' with and for other people with learning difficulties. In these terms, it has been seen as part of the struggle of disadvantaged people for equality, equal rights and citizenship (Williams and Shoultz 1982). Similarly, self-advocacy in groups has been seen as helping to shift the balance of power between people with learning difficulties and the people close to them, such as parents and staff (Cooper and Hersov 1986). The capacity of self-advocacy to influence family relationships and routines has subsequently been called into question (Mitchell 1998). Nevertheless, advocacy outside the family setting does have an influence on policy and practice, to the extent that Whittell *et al.* (1998) have argued that self-advocacy has become a social movement which has given people with learning difficulties a collective as well as an individual voice. In that sense, self-advocacy is seen to be about people with learning difficulties as a group gaining power to speak up for their rights rather than wait for other people, including citizen advocates, to speak up for them (Walmsley and Downer 1997, p.36).

Self-advocacy is also about identity. In contrast to normalisation, where the emphasis is on conformity and denial of difference (Perrin and Nirje 1989), people in self-advocacy groups are more likely to acknowledge their identity as people with learning difficulties (Simons 1992; Walmsley and Downer 1997). This can be seen as a celebration of difference rather than a denial of difference – much in the way that other social groups such as women, black people and disabled people have developed and celebrated their identity (Walmsley and Downer 1997). Involvement in self-advocacy can bring its own sense of identity, where people's own personal history becomes intertwined with the history of the self-advocacy movement, and certain individuals become 'insiders' with 'insights into the first-hand experiences of self advocacy' (Goodley 2000, p.170).

Historically, self-advocacy emerged in Sweden, and then in the USA in the late 1960s, and found expression in the UK in a small way at first (Lee-Foster and Moorhead 1996). The organisation CMH (Campaign for People with Mental Handicaps, now known as VIA, Values into Action) hosted two participation events in the 1970s where people with learning difficulties spoke out publicly about their experiences in long-stay hospitals. Other initiatives followed such as Mencap's participation forum and the City Lit's adult education programme (Hersov 1996; Simons 1993). The movement became much more firmly established in 1984 when People First, London, was formed by people with learning difficulties who had attended a self-advocacy conference in the USA. The group's first newsletter appeared in 1985 and, since then, many local and regional groups have been formed (Simons 1993).

The capacity for self-representation, which self-advocacy promotes, has led to a number of publications created by, and developed for, people with learning difficulties. These include, for example, *Oi, It's my Assessment* (People First 1993b) and *Everything You Ever Wanted to Know about Safer Sex* (People First 1993c). In addition, a number of chapters have been co-written by people with and without learning difficulties (see, for example, Amans and Darbyshire 1989; Atkinson and Cooper 2000; Davis *et al.* 1995; Etherington, Hall and Whelan 1988). Conferences which address issues and concern to people with learning difficulties now almost routinely include people with learning difficulties themselves as speakers and delegates.

Self-advocacy has grown alongside research which sought to include the views of people with learning difficulties (Walmsley 1995). It has proved influential in research circles as well as itself being influenced by research. The self-advocacy movement demonstrated to researchers not only that people with learning difficulties wanted to 'speak up' but also that they were able to do so – and could be included in research as respondents and participants. At the same time as people with learning difficulties became more knowledgeable about research, and more confident in taking part, so some people emerged with an interest in being more directly involved in doing research.

Recent evidence suggests that speaking up in self-advocacy groups may lead to speaking up elsewhere – as consultants, advisers or co-researchers involved in research practice (rather than, or as well as, being the subjects of research). Just as self-advocacy itself can be empowering (Whittell *et al.* 1998) so can involvement in research (French and Swain 2000). In practice, the two may be intertwined – those who speak up in one context may be the people who take on research roles in another (Macadam and Townsley 1998; Rodgers 1999; Whittaker 1997;

Williams 1999). This is not to say that self-advocates tend to become researchers, nor that researchers – or those involved in research – necessarily become self-advocates, but to suggest there is a two-way link for some people. The link may well be found in empowerment; speaking up can be empowering, so too can researching.

Participatory research

Participatory research has become important in the learning disability field in recent years. This may be in part, as suggested above, because it links with, and supports (and on the whole is supported by) self-advocacy. In fact, throughout the 1990s learning disability researchers have sought ways to open up research so that people with learning difficulties could become active participants at all stages of the research process. In some instances this went beyond the involvement of people with learning difficulties as interviewees, seeing them instead as consultants, partners, interviewers and co-researchers (see, for example, Minkes *et al.* 1995; Mitchell 1998; Ward and Simons 1998; Williams 1999.)

Participatory research has been widely – though by no means universally – accepted in learning disability research. This is presumably because it has the potential to be inclusive, enabling and empowering through engaging people with learning difficulties in the various stages of research projects. This ranges from identifying the problem or focus, to designing and carrying out the fieldwork, interpreting the results and disseminating the findings. Participatory research changes the social relations of research and helps make it a partnership rather than a hierarchical relationship. The research process, and outcomes, are thought in this context to be empowering for participants (French and Swain 2000). The capacity of participatory research to encourage and support the empowerment of people with learning difficulties makes it an attractive option both for researchers and participants, and helps explain how it has become an 'important development for learning disability research' (Chappell 2000, p.41).

Participatory research is evolutionary rather than revolutionary. It builds on good practices drawn from qualitative research, including the notion of the 'sympathetic researcher' who works in partnership with people with learning difficulties to improve the quality of their lives (Chappell 2000). Participatory research is an inclusive approach which encourages and supports participation at all stages of the research process and, in that sense (as suggested above), supports self-advocacy, and the role of self-advocates as co-researchers. In a situation where research participants may have little knowledge or experience of research, it still provides a central role for the non-disabled researcher (Chappell 2000). This differentiates participatory research from the emancipatory research demanded by disabled people, where ownership and control of the research rests with disabled people (Oliver 1992, 1997; Zarb 1992).

Participatory research is finding favour in the learning disability field in part because projects are seen to have 'clear stages of development and specifiable outcomes' which make them potentially fundable (Kiernan 1999). Again, this is in contrast with emancipatory research which is more closely linked with political activism and which may not gain the same level of support from funding bodies which participatory research has done (Priestley 1999; Ward and Flynn 1994). Participatory research allows researchers to retain independence and rigour, and to avoid becoming the pawns of pressure groups (Kiernan 1999; Stone and Priestley 1996).

There is now a body of learning disability research literature on the participatory paradigm in relation to people with learning difficulties. Most of these publications are written by non-disabled researchers (see, for example, Cocks and Cockram 1995; Lynd 1992; Northway 1998; Ramcharan and Grant 1994; Riddell, Wilkinson and Baron 1998; Rodgers 1999; Stalker 1998; Ward and Flynn 1994; Whittaker, Gardner and Kershaw 1991). A number of publications are, however, research accounts told by the research participants or co-researchers, albeit with the support of non-disabled researchers (March *et al.* 1997; Palmer and Turner 1998; People First 1994). Not surprisingly, the latter publications are written by people involved in self-advocacy as well as research; their route into research was through self-advocacy, underlining the two-way link between the two activities suggested above.

Participatory research may have many advantages, but it also has potential pitfalls. The closeness of the research relationship is itself problematic when participants are vulnerable and isolated (Booth 1998). The extended time and space required for doing it well, especially with people inexperienced in research, sit uneasily alongside the pressures on researchers to find funds and deliver outcomes as quickly as possible (Minkes *et al.* 1995; Riddell *et al.* 1998; Ward and Simons 1998). Research with people with learning difficulties takes time, it also often demands different kinds of publication and dissemination (Goodley and Moore 2000).

Research as advocacy

It is at least in part through the emergence of self-advocacy that people with learning difficulties have begun to speak up about their lives and experiences; to tell their life stories. In this context, people with learning difficulties have started to articulate their experience of being labelled, or categorised, as different. As a result, alongside the growth of the self-advocacy movement has been a steady stream of autobiographies by people with learning difficulties, where people have told their own stories with or without the help of a facilitator (see, for example, Barron 1996; Burnside 1991; Cooper 1997; Deacon 1974; Hunt 1967). The interest in their own, and other people's, life stories has led some people, including self-advocates, into life story research where 'lives' are compiled from oral and documentary sources (Rolph 1999).

Life story research was made possible through self-advocacy, and the interest of people within the movement in telling their stories. Although people with learning difficulties are able to articulate their experience, and to reflect on it, through the telling of their life stories, theorising from their experience has proved more problematic (Chappell 1997; Riddell *et al.* 1998). On the whole, this means that non-disabled people are still needed as allies in the research process in learning disability, although this view is contested by Aspis (2000). This is in contrast to emancipatory research where the demand is for the research to be owned and controlled by disabled people (Finkelstein 1999; Zarb 1992).

My current research project involves life story research with people with learning difficulties, some of whom, including Mabel Cooper and Gloria Ferris, who were quoted at the outset, are also self-advocates. Their interest in researching their own life stories, and the stories of other people with learning difficulties, was prompted by their involvement in self-advocacy, and their capacity – and confidence – to speak up about themselves and their lives. Just as self-advocacy is about self-representation, so too is the recounting of the life story. It enables people not only to make sense of their own lives but also to understand their lives in relation to those of other people. Where people tell their own stories, they are inevitably more complex than the stories told about them by others. They are more likely to cast themselves as fully rounded human beings rather than the perpetrators of social ills, as the eugenicists portrayed them in the early years of the twentieth century, or as victims of an oppressive system, as the proponents of normalisation saw them in the later decades of the century.

Life story research treats people as 'expert witnesses' in the matter of their own lives (Birren and Deutchman 1991). This is in contrast with the more usual view of people with learning difficulties as 'sources of data' for researchers' own narratives, rather than as people with personal stories to tell (Booth and Booth 1996). Being the author of their own story can be especially important for those people with learning difficulties who, because of their segregated lives, have none of the usual 'stock of stories' from family and friends, nor the everyday documents, photographs and memorabilia of family life, from which to draw in order to make sense of their lives (Gillman, Swain and Heyman 1997). This makes the telling of their own story even more compelling – and empowering. Life story research provides the time, space and context in which history can be told and, in so doing, it gives people back their past and 'also helps them towards a future' (Thompson 1988, p.265). Life stories can thus become 'treasured possessions' for people with learning difficulties (Gray and Ridden 1999, p.15).

In the participatory life story research project in which I am currently involved, the life historians are people who have lived for many years in long-stay hospitals. They include Mabel Cooper and Gloria Ferris. As well as spending time on the process of telling, recording and compiling individual life histories, we have also spent time on reflecting on the meaning of the life stories for the people concerned. The extract below is taken from the tape transcription of one such reflective discussion.

Dorothy: What have you got out of telling your stories? What has it meant to you?

Mabel: I think it's been great, from the word go, and knowing. I'd rather know than not know. I think if you don't know then it isn't fair, it's not the same as knowing. So for me, I'd rather know.

Gloria: It makes you wonder what you've done in your life now that you're older.

Mabel: It's because of all the things that you do now that you didn't have the chance to do when you were younger. It gives you that and, OK, you've got it, you've got it for life, and it tells you everything. (Cooper, Ferris and Coventry 2000, pp.183–184)

It has been argued that people who lack a history, and an identity, are likely to have an identity imposed upon them (Gillman *et al.* 1997; Sutcliffe and Simons 1993). The objectification of people with learning difficulties as 'other' is due in part to this lack of history (Ramcharan *et al.* 1997). Seen as an homogeneous group, they are defined by their learning disability and their behaviour in their case records in a 'ritual of exclusion' (White and Epston 1990). It is in this context where self-advocacy provides the drive, and life story research provides the means, for people with learning difficulties to tell their stories – to claim a history

– and to have it recorded. Again in a reflective discussion, Mabel Cooper made the link between self-advocacy and life story research:

> My story and a lot more will help people with a learning difficulty, and I hope it will learn them to tell their story of what happened to them... I'm involved in People First, I'm chair of Croydon People First. Before that I was chair of London People First, for four years, helping people with learning difficulties to speak up; enabling people to speak up, and educating other people to make that happen. Now I'm encouraging other people to tell their stories. I think it's good, and I think it teaches the public that people with learning difficulties are not going to hurt anyone and all the time we can get people to write their story and tell what happened to them, and publish it, or do a book for themselves – like Doris [a friend] wants to do – then it helps everyone. And Doris wants to show her book to other people, when it's done, so she can say, 'Look, this is what I've done, and this is what it's all about'. (Atkinson and Cooper 2000, pp.23–24)

Life story research has demonstrated the resilience of people with learning difficulties in the face of adversity (Goodley 1996). In the recounting of their stories, they do not portray themselves solely as victims but as people who showed resistance against the forces of oppression. From their own accounts, they resisted, they fought back and they mocked the people and the systems which sought to control them (Goodley 1996; Potts and Fido 1991; Rolph 1999; Sibley 1995; Stuart 1998). Fighting back is one way of becoming a 'border crosser' from a segregated life to an inclusive one in the mainstream of society (Ramcharan *et al.* 1997; Rolph 1999).

Mabel Cooper, for example, expressed her resistance to the regime of St Lawrence's Hospital, in Caterham, Surrey, through a deliberate policy of remaining silent during much of her 20-year stay there. Although her case notes described her as timid and shy, her own account made clear that her silence was a form of protest:

> I never said anything in the hospital because there was no point. Nobody listened, so why speak? If you spoke they told you to shut up, so I stopped saying anything. I didn't talk, it was a protest really rather than anything else. I only said two words, 'yes' and 'no', and mostly I only said 'no'! (Atkinson 2000, p.22).

Life story research both draws from, and contributes to, the self-advocacy movement, and can be seen to be empowering for the people concerned. Is research in a wider sense empowering? The final section of the chapter will consider the possible claims of research to be empowering.

Research and empowerment

The question 'Can research empower people?' was posed by Stalker (1998). Although she concluded that the most likely beneficiary would be the researcher, others have attributed to research the potential for empowering those people involved in it whilst also promoting their interests (Ward 1997). Not all research can be empowering, it is not intended to be. However, participatory research makes claims to be empowering, especially where the researcher and participants work and learn together over an extended period of time (Northway 2000). In the participatory research paradigm, the researcher is expected to show commitment to the project and the participants, and to be sympathetic to the aims and outcomes (Chappell 2000; Hall 1979). The researcher works from an explicit value base, according to Cocks and Cockram (1995). This entails being engaged rather than detached and developing a close partnership with the research participants (Knox, Mok and Parmenter 2000; Northway 2000; Ward and Simons 1998).

What do people with learning difficulties themselves say about being involved in research? Do they find it empowering? One group of researchers said: 'We are part of a self-advocacy group in England, out to do some research work' (Palmer and Turner 1998, p.12). Another group said: 'We are research people. This article is about how we planned a research project. The research is about self-advocacy and families' (March *et al.* 1997, p.77). Although the word 'empowering' is not used, links are made between self-advocacy and research. According to Williams, in relation to her research with a self-advocacy group, her co-researchers not only saw research as a process of finding information, but also saw it as a process of taking action to bring about change (Williams 2000). The process and outcome may be beneficial, but so too may be the role of 'researcher' as this is a valued social role (Walmsley 2001) and a 'powerful way of self-presentation' (Williams 2000).

Self-advocacy can be empowering – but so too can research (Palmer *et al.* 1999). Life story research involves people telling the story of their own life – this can include the part that advocacy has played in it. Research in this context supports self-advocacy in enabling people to represent themselves, but it also provides a forum in which the accounts by self-advocates of their experiences of advocacy may be heard. In Mabel Cooper's case, her life story included her account of becoming a self-advocate:

> I joined People First two or three years ago, when Isabel asked me would I like to join. There were about ten people when it first started in Croydon, now there's loads. I didn't join in very much at the first time or for a

couple of weeks, something like that. Then one of the men what was chairperson, he didn't turn up so they asked me would I take it on. So I said, 'Oh, all right, I'll take it on for one week'. And one week got more weeks than ever...

I think being in a group teaches you you've got to learn to say what you want to say and not what everybody else wants you to say. The others feel the same. We've stopped the children, for starts. We've stopped them calling us names, the children don't do it so much. They used to call us horrible names, some of the names you would never dream of. They stopped it, even in Purley, and the teachers go with them now...

I'm more confident since I've been in the People First group. You do what you want to do and not get anybody else to do something for you. I'm chairperson, but it's just the same as anybody else. You just help the people what can't do it for themselves. (Cooper 1997, pp.32–34)

In Gloria Ferris's life story, her account of advocacy is as a citizen advocate for her long-standing friend, Muriel:

I've known Muriel for over 40 years, since 1956, when we were both in St Lawrence's Hospital. Of course, she was quite young when I took her on, 9 or 10, I can't remember just what age she was...

In 1994 I became an advocate for Muriel. And that was the year she left St Lawrence's and went to Whitehill House to live... I go to see Muriel two days a week, Wednesday and Thursday. When I first arrive her face lights up!...

It's what I really like doing, I like being with Muriel and people like her. It's what I am. I like to help, and I like to mix with other people. I'm part of Muriel's family now. I always thought she was special. She looks forward to it, too, and I think she must miss it when I'm not there. If you've got a tongue in your head to speak for yourself then you can speak up. Like Muriel, she can't speak, so I speak for her and ask for the things that she needs done for her. That's what they call 'being an advocate'. Doing the things that she needs and what she wants. I love it. I love life as it is now. (Cooper, Ferris and Coventry 2000, pp.190–193)

Although, again, Gloria does not use the term 'peer advocacy', this is what she is describing. Although, like citizen advocacy, peer advocacy involves a partnership between two people, it is on a very different basis from the former. Gloria is an 'insider' in relation to Muriel, and in the know through her own experience as a person labelled as having a learning difficulty. She can draw on that experience to make sense of Muriel's life and to represent her wishes and needs. In the extract which opened this chapter, the view was expressed that only people with learning difficulties can represent other people with learning difficulties. This view links with similar views expressed by survivors of the mental health system and disabled people. Some disabled people, for example, see citizen advocacy in its pure form as potentially a devaluing process. This is because the basis of citizen advocacy is the partnership between the 'ordinary', 'valued' advocate and their 'devalued' partner.

Although the relationship between advocate and partner is intended to be supportive and empowering, the fact that it is between a 'valued' and a 'devalued' person suggests a fundamental inequality. Even the language of 'partnership' is problematic. Partnership suggests a two-way relationship, but in practice advocacy partnerships may be quite one-sided (Simons 1993; Walmsley 1996). In this context, self-advocacy and peer advocacy, as described by my co-researchers above, are seen to be of central importance for people with learning difficulties.

Conclusion

There is a two-way link between advocacy and research. Self-advocacy makes research possible – but at the same time research supports self-advocacy. Life story research, which has informed this chapter, demonstrates the two-way link. It contributes to self-advocacy both at an individual and at a social level. At an individual level, life story research involves people in telling the story of their own life. This involves a life review, and enables the story-teller to emerge as a person rather than as a 'case'. The capacity of people to remember, and recount, who they have been, and to know where they have come from, helps shape their sense of self or identity in the present (Thomson 1999). People with learning difficulties who have been involved with me in telling their story attest to the positive affirmation of identity which this has given them:

> We are self-advocates who are running workshops on 'telling your life story' for people with learning disabilities. We have both been supported to write our own life stories and want to help others to do theirs. (Able and Cooper 2000)

At a social or collective level, the life story research involved people with learning difficulties in research roles – for example, as historical witness, as critical commentator and as research partner. Research roles can be empowering (Palmer et al. 1999; Ward 1998). However, the process of 'bearing witness' to the social and political oppression of oneself and others is the ultimate means of representing oneself and others – of being an advocate.

References

Able, J. and Cooper, M. (2000) 'Mabel Cooper's and John Able's Stories.' In *Self Advocacy Stories*. London: Mencap.

Amans, D. and Darbyshire, C. (1989) 'A voice of our own.' In A. Brechin and J. Walmsley (eds) *Making Connections: Reflecting on the Lives and Experiences of People with Learning Difficulties*. London: Hodder and Stoughton.

Aspis, S. (2000) 'Researching our history: who is in charge?' In L. Brigham, D. Atkinson, M. Jackson, S. Rolph and J. Walmsley (eds) *Crossing Boundaries: Change and Continuity in the History of Learning Disability*. Kidderminster: BILD.

Atkinson, D. (1999) 'An old story.' In S. French and J. Swain (eds) *Therapy and Learning Difficulties: Advocacy, Participation and Partnership*. Oxford: Butterworth Heinemann.

Atkinson, D. (2000) ' Bringing lives into focus: the disabled person's perspective.' In D. May (ed) *Research Highlights in Social Work: Transitions and Change in the Lives of People with Intellectual Disabilities*. London: Jessica Kingsley.

Atkinson, D. and Cooper, M. (2000) 'Parallel stories.' In L. Brigham, D. Atkinson, M. Jackson, S. Rolph and J. Walmsley (eds) *Crossing Boundaries: Continuity and Change in the History of Learning Disability*. Kidderminster: BILD.

Atkinson, D. and Williams, F. (1990) *'Know Me as I Am': An Anthology of Prose, Poetry and Art by People with Learning Difficulties*. London: Hodder and Stoughton.

Barron, D. (1996) *A Price to be Born*. Huddersfield: H. Charlesworth.

Birren, J. and Deutchman, D. (1991) *Guiding Autobiography Groups for Older Adults*. London: Johns Hopkins University Press.

Booth, T. and Booth, W. (1996) 'Sounds of silence: narrative research with inarticulate subjects.' *Disability and Society 11*, 1, 55–69.

Booth, W. (1998) 'Doing research with lonely people.' *British Journal of Learning Disabilities 26*, 4, 132–134.

Burnside, M. (1991) *My Life Story*. Halifax: Pecket Well College.

Chappell, A. L. (1997) 'From normalization to where?' In L. Barton and M. Oliver (eds) *Disability Studies: Past, Present and Future*. Leeds: Disability Press.

Chappell, A.L. (2000) 'Emergence of participatory methodology in learning disability research: understanding the context.' *British Journal of Learning Disabilities 28*, 1, 38–43.

Cocks, E. and Cockram, J. (1995) 'The participatory research paradigm and intellectual disability.' *Mental Handicap Research 8*, 1, 25–37.

Cooper, D. and Hersov, J. (1986) *We Can Change the Future: Self-advocacy for People with Learning Difficulties*. London: National Bureau for Handicapped Students.

Cooper, M. (1997) 'Mabel Cooper's life story.' In D. Atkinson, M. Jackson and J. Walmsley (eds) *Forgotten Lives: Exploring the History of Learning Disability*. Kidderminster: BILD.

Cooper, M., Ferris, G. and Coventry, M. (2000) 'Croydon lives.' In D. Atkinson, M. McCarthy, J. Walmsley, M. Cooper, S. Rolph, S. Aspis, P. Barette, M. Coventry and G. Ferris (eds) *Good Times, Bad Times: Women with Learning Difficulties Telling their Stories*. Kidderminster: BILD.

Davis, A., Eley, R., Flynn, M., Flynn, P. and Roberts, G. (1995) 'To have and have not: addressing issues of poverty.' In T. Philpot and L. Ward (eds) *Values and Visions:*

Changing Ideas in Services for People with Learning Difficulties. Oxford: Butterworth Heinemann.

Deacon, J. (1974) *Tongue Tied.* London: National Society for Mentally Handicapped Children.

Etherington, A., Hall, K. and Whelan, E. (1988) 'What it's like for us.' In D. Towell (ed) *An Ordinary Life in Practice: Developing Comprehensive Community-Based Services for People with Learning Disabilities.* London: King's Fund Centre.

Finkelstein, V. (1999) 'Doing disability research' (extended book review). *Disability and Society 14,* 6, 859–867.

French, S. and Swain, J. (2000) 'Good intentions: reflecting on researching the lives and experiences of visually disabled people.' *Annual Review of Critical Psychology 2,* 35–54.

Gillman, M., Swain, J. and Heyman, B. (1997) '"Life" history or "case" history: the objectification of people with learning difficulties through the tyranny of professional discourse.' *Disability and Society 12,* 5, 675–693.

Goodley, D. (1996) 'Tales of hidden lives: a critical examination of life history research with people who have learning difficulties.' *Disability and Society 11,* 3, 333–348.

Goodley, D. (2000) 'Collecting the life stories of self-advocates: crossing the boundary between researcher and researched.' In L. Brigham, D. Atkinson, M. Jackson, S. Rolph and J. Walmsley (eds) *Crossing Boundaries: Change and Continuity in the History of Learning Disability.* Kidderminster: BILD.

Goodley, D. and Moore, M. (2000) 'Doing disability research: activist lives and the academy.' *Disability and Society 15,* 6, 861–882.

Gray, B. and Ridden, G. (1999) *Lifemaps of People with Learning Disabilities.* London: Jessica Kingsley.

Hall, B.L. (1979) 'Knowledge as a commodity and participatory research.' *Prospects 9,* 4, 393–408.

Hersov, J. (1996) 'The rise of self-advocacy in Great Britain.' In G. Dybwad and H. Bersani Jr (eds) *New Voices: Self-Advocacy by People with Disabilities.* Cambridge, MA: Brookline Books.

Hunt, N. (1967) *The World of Nigel Hunt.* Beaconsfield: Darwen Finlayson.

Kiernan, C. (1999) 'Participation in research by people with learning disability: origins and issues.' *British Journal of Learning Disabilities 27,* 2, 43–47.

Knox, M., Mok, M. and Parmenter, T.R. (2000) 'Working with the experts: collaborative research with people with an intellectual disability.' *Disability and Society 15,* 1, 49–61.

Lee-Foster, A. and Moorhead, D. (1996) *Do the Rights Thing! An Advocacy Learning Pack.* London: Sage.

Lynd, M. (1992) 'Creating knowledge through theater: a case study with developmentally disabled adults.' *American Sociologist 23,* 4, 100–115.

Macadam, M. and Townsley, R. (1998) 'Who chooses? Involving people with learning difficulties in staff selection and recruitment.' In L. Ward (ed) *Innovations in Advocacy and Empowerment for People with Intellectual Disabilities.* Chorley: Lisieux Hall.

March, J., Steingold, B., Justice, S. and Mitchell, P. (1997) 'Follow the yellow brick road: people with learning difficulties as researchers.' *British Journal of Learning Disabilities 25,* 77–80.

Minkes, J., Townsley, R., Weston, C. and Williams, C. (1995) 'Having a voice: involving people with learning difficulties in research.' *British Journal of Learning Disabilities 23*, 3, 94–97.

Mitchell, P. (1997) 'The impact of self-advocacy on families.' *Disability and Society 12*, 1, 43–56.

Mitchell, P. (1998) 'Self-advocacy and families', unpublished PhD thesis, Open University, Milton Keynes.

Northway, R. (1998) 'Engaging in participatory research: some personal reflections.' *Journal of Learning Disabilities for Nursing, Health and Social Care 2*, 3, 144–149.

Northway, R. (2000) 'Ending participatory research?' *Journal of Learning Disabilities 4*, 1, 27–36.

Oliver, M. (1992) 'Changing the social relations of research production?' *Disability, Handicap and Society 7*, 2, 101–114.

Oliver, M. (1997) 'Emancipatory research: realistic goal or impossible dream?' In C. Barnes and G. Mercer (eds) *Doing Disability Research*. Leeds: Disability Press.

Palmer, N. and Turner, F. (1998) 'Self-advocacy: doing our own research.' *Royal College of Speech and Language Therapy Bulletin* August, 12–13.

Palmer, N., Peacock, C., Turner, F. and Vasey, B. with Williams, V. (1999) 'Telling people what you think.' In J. Swain and S. French (eds) *Therapy and Learning Difficulties: Advocacy, Participation and Partnership*. Oxford: Butterworth Heinemann.

People First (1993a) *Self-Advocacy Starter Pack*. London: People First.

People First (1993b) *Oi, It's my Assessment*. London: People First.

People First (1993c) *Everything You Ever Wanted to Know about Safer Sex*. London: People First.

People First (1994) *Outside not Inside... Yet*. London: People First.

Perrin, B. and Nirje, B. (1989) 'Setting the record straight: a critique of some frequent misconceptions of the normalisation principle.' In A. Brechin and J. Walmsley (eds) *Making Connections: Reflecting on the Lives and Experiences of People with Learning Difficulties*. London: Hodder and Stoughton.

Potts, M. and Fido, R. (1991) *A Fit Person to be Removed: Personal Accounts of Life in a Mental Deficiency Institution*. Plymouth: Northcote House.

Priestley, M. (1999) *Disability Politics and Community Care*. London: Jessica Kingsley.

Ramcharan, P. and Grant, G. (1994) 'Setting one agenda for empowering persons with a disadvantage within the research process.' In M.H. Rioux and M. Bach (eds) *Disability is not Measles: New Research Paradigms in Disability*. Ontario: Roeher Institute.

Ramcharan, P., Roberts, G., Grant, G. and Borland, J. (1997) 'Citizenship, empowerment and everyday life.' In P. Ramcharan, G. Roberts, G. Grant and J. Borland (eds) *Empowerment in Everyday Life: Learning Disability*. London: Jessica Kingsley.

Riddell, S., Wilkinson, H. and Baron, S. (1998) 'From emancipatory research to focus group: people with learning difficulties and the research process.' In P. Clough and L. Barton (eds) *Articulating with Difficulty: Research Voices in Inclusive Education*. London: Paul Chapman.

Rodgers, J. (1999) 'Trying to get it right: undertaking research involving people with learning difficulties.' *Disability and Society 14*, 4, 421–433.

Rolph, S. (1999) 'The history of community care for people with learning difficulties in Norfolk 1930–1980: the role of two hostels', unpublished PhD thesis, Open University, Milton Keynes.

Sibley, D. (1995) *Geographies of Exclusion.* London: Routledge.

Simons, K. (1992) *Sticking Up for Yourself: Self-Advocacy and People with Learning Difficulties.* York: Joseph Rowntree Foundation.

Simons, K. (1993) *Citizen Advocacy: The Inside View.* Bristol: Norah Fry Research Centre.

Stalker, K. (1998) 'Some ethical and methodological issues in research with people with learning difficulties.' *Disability and Society 13,* 1, 5–19.

Stone, E. and Priestley, M. (1996) 'Parasites, pawns and partners: disability research and the role of non disabled researchers.' *British Journal of Sociology 47,* 4, 699–716.

Stuart, M. (1998) 'Mothers, sisters and daughters: an investigation into convent homes for women labelled as having learning difficulties', unpublished PhD thesis, Open University, Milton Keynes.

Sutcliffe, J. and Simons, K. (1993) *Self-Advocacy and Adults with Learning Difficulties.* Leicester: National Institute of Adult Continuing Education.

Thompson, P. (1988) *The Voice of the Past: Oral History,* 2nd edn. Oxford: Oxford University Press.

Thomson, A. (1999) 'Moving stories: oral history and migration studies.' *Oral History 27,* 1, 24–37.

Walmsley, J. (1995) 'Gender, caring and learning disability', unpublished PhD thesis, Open University, Milton Keynes.

Walmsley, J. (1996) *Working Together for Change (Workbook 3). K503, Learning Disability: Working as Equal People.* Milton Keynes: Open University.

Walmsley, J. (2001) 'Normalisation, emancipatory research and inclusive research in learning disability.' *Disability and Society 16,* 2, 187–205.

Walmsley, J. and Downer, J. (1997) 'Shouting the loudest: self-advocacy, power and diversity.' In P. Ramcharan, G. Roberts, G. Grant and J. Borland (eds) *Empowerment in Everyday Life: Learning Disability.* London: Jessica Kingsley.

Ward, L. (1997) *Seen and Heard: Involving Disabled Children and Young People in Research and Development Projects.* York: Joseph Rowntree Foundation.

Ward, L. (1998) 'Voices and choices: innovations in advocacy and empowerment – an overview.' In L. Ward (ed) *Innovations and Empowerment for People with Intellectual Disabilities.* Chorley: Lisieux Hall.

Ward, L. and Flynn, M. (1994) 'What matters most: disability, research and empowerment.' In M.H. Rioux and M. Bach (eds) *Disability is not Measles: New Research Paradigms in Disability.* Toronto: Roeher Institute.

Ward, L. and Simons, K. (1998) 'Practising partnership: involving people with learning difficulties in research.' *British Journal of Learning Disabilities 26,* 4, 128–131.

Wertheimer, A. (1990) *A Voice of our Own: Now and in the Future.* London: People First.

White, M. and Epston, D. (1990) *Narrative Means to Therapeutic Ends.* New York: Norton.

Whittaker, A. (1997) *Looking at our Services: Service Evaluations by People with Learning Difficulties.* London: King's Fund Centre.

Whittaker, A., Gardner, S. and Kershaw, J. (1991) *Service Evaluation by People with Learning Difficulties.* London: King's Fund Centre.

Whittell, B., Ramcharan, P. and Members of People First Cardiff and the Vale (1998) 'Speaking up for ourselves and each other.' In L. Ward (ed) *Innovations in Advocacy and Empowerment for People with Intellectual Disabilities.* Chorley: Lisieux Hall.

Williams, P. and Shoultz, B. (1982) *We Can Speak for Ourselves: Self-Advocacy by Mentally Handicapped People.* London: Souvenir.

Williams, V. (1999) 'Researching together.' *British Journal of Learning Disabilities 27*, 2, 48–51.

Williams, V. (2000) 'Participatory research: the two worlds of discourse.' Paper presented at the Learning Disability Foundation Seminar, London, 14 April.

Zarb, G. (1992) 'On the road to Damascus: first steps towards changing the relations of disability research production.' *Disability, Handicap and Society 7*, 125–138.

CHAPTER NINE

The Role Of Self-Advocacy

Stories From a Self-Advocacy Group Through the Experiences Of its Members

Fred Spedding, Elizabeth Harkness, Louise Townson, Andy Docherty, Niall McNulty and Rohhss Chapman

'What they want – yes, but what we want – bugger us!'

Fred Spedding, Director, Carlisle People First

In the past I was too frightened to speak my mind because I was scared stiff I'd be hit. I know it's shocking to say that, but the truth is it does go on, in the home and in places that are caring for people with special needs. I've been hit myself in the past. Not all of the staff working with special needs people behave as you might expect.

When I was young I used to get blamed for everything at home. Once somebody chucked me in a bath of scalding hot water, to get me to admit to stealing some money I hadn't stolen.

In fact all of my life people have made decisions for me about where I would live and what I would do. They didn't even ask me how I felt about big decisions like that, they just told me. How would you like that? Can you imagine how frustrating that is for an adult? How would people like to be in my shoes?

I feel a lot happier these days but I've had a lot of upsets over the years. Now I'm living in my own flat in Carlisle, I work at People First, I get a Direct Payment, I employ my own carers, I even visit them at their home and we do a lot of things together.

In the past I've had no end of trouble with carers, some even locked my biscuits away from me in my own home! I've had a carer who dropped me and broke my tibia, carers who would not help me get up to go to the toilet in care.

Then they would sleep in all morning anyway. They have stolen from me, kept my keys when they left and one even tried to kill herself when she was in my flat. Why did I get sent carers with all these problems?

Over the past few years I have complained about things that have happened to me, but a lot of the time people don't want to hear the complaints or think I am just aggressive, or think I should accept things. I was very unhappy and in a lot of pain when my hip was replaced. I had to stay in hospital for ages and I felt threatened with losing my flat, with all the problems over money and benefits and not being able to pay for the care I needed. All my life I have wanted to live on my own and have my own place and now eventually I have that. But sometimes in the past, especially since I needed 24-hour care, even though I had my own flat it didn't feel like it was mine, because of carers living there and trying to make all the rules.

Now things are a little different with the Direct Payment. I'm flying to Canada with my carers later this week. I went to the International Self-Advocacy Conference in Toronto in 1993 and I met a woman called Norma; we spent all our time together. We have stayed in touch all of these years and now I'm going back to see her. Actually I'm only thinking about the trip, and looking forward to seeing her really. I'm not thinking about when I get back at the moment; all I want to do now is go off and enjoy myself!

'I used to keep my feelings to myself'

Elizabeth Harkness, Training Group member and Co-researcher, Carlisle People First

I think disabled people should speak up for their educational rights. Statemented education only lasts for the time you are in school but I think it should go on for life. People may start at 3 years old and at the moment state education stops at 19 years old. But what if they want to go onto university and they can't? I have been talking to self-advocacy groups over the world on the Internet and we are all looking at setting up a People First University. I think it's a right that people should be able to go on learning for life. People First can speak up for education and write to their MP and ask what they will do about it.

I'm a financial director for the training group at People First so that means I get all the money in for the training group from the people we train. I'm also on the Citizens' Advice Bureau Committee and I'm going on the Community Health Council to represent People First. I go to self-advocacy meetings when I can but sometimes there's a clash if I'm going to college. I'm on the Mencap group and

I'm talking about going to be on the National Assembly for Mencap. In the daytime I work in a canteen at a special school and also I do some work in the People First office.

All my jobs are important but I'd like to learn more about money, counting is difficult as I missed a lot of my education as I had a speech difficulty when I was younger and didn't go to school until I was 7. I went away from 10 to 19. The first training work I ever did was when I lived in St Stephen's Hostel in 1996 and I worked in the kitchen. That place has closed now.

Work is very important – it gives me my own satisfaction of being able to do things. To do things well I think you need to be able to speak up for yourself. I would like to do more at Carlisle People First if I could get released from my other job to work there. I need to speak to them about it.

Some people don't want change to happen because they don't know how to go about it but it helps if you are involved in People First because there are other people there to support you. By speaking up and voting for an MP it also helps disabled people if they are going to do things for us.

I used to keep my feelings to myself but now I say to other people that they should all learn to speak up for themselves and join a group. For instance the people in a big residential home here haven't been able to speak up for themselves and talk about where they want to go when it closes down.

People First can help by going and telling them about self-advocacy and what it is and what it could do for them. Will people that run the home listen though? That will be the problem, will they let us in? But we ought to go and try. I know quite a few people there as my mother used to live there too. People don't speak up because they are scared of what's going to happen to them, they think they maybe would get put out earlier than they should and not get the right support, I think this can happen, I think if we didn't get involved it might happen.

I think people can be scared because some are going to be sent back to Newcastle and they don't want to go. Lauren and Julia don't want to go but they may be made to go by the people who run it. They should be allowed to choose where they want to live, I mean they may want to carry on with their course at the college here and so on. People should be allowed to choose where they live with minimal support not where the head ones want them to go.

I don't think people with learning difficulties should live in the outside community together all next to each other; they should live in ordinary houses. They sometimes get told there is nowhere else but nowadays you can go to ordinary houses run by housing associations, not stuck with others in a community. They should be able to mix with retired people and lots of other people.

I got into my house by saying what I wanted through a housing association. I went there because it was near where I went to church and work and near my friends. If someone told me I had to go and live in Newcastle it wouldn't work as my friends live here and I can please myself.

'There are bigger fish to fry'

Louise Townson, Administrator and Co-researcher, Carlisle People First

I was born here in Carlisle. I went away to school in Newcastle because I had visual difficulties. Dad was going to get a job transfer and move my sister out of school and go to Newcastle with me but the social worker said it would be better not to and to let me go.

For the first year I was only 4 and obviously I was distressed – I used to spend half the week away at school until the Wednesday. Then I would go back home for the other half of the week. This happened for a year and then I settled in. I was in my school in Newcastle for eight years. Then I went to a school in Liverpool, which was my secondary school, and I was there until 1986. That school was OK: it was practically run by the nuns so it was very, very strict. I can always remember once when I was there the housemother of my dormitory, one of the nuns, she only let you watch TV if what was on was 'clean' as she would put it. One night I was watching *Brookside* and there was a lot of shouting and swearing and somebody was being drunk and she said to me, 'Well I'm surprised your mother lets you watch this at home!' I just turned round and said, 'Well my mother watches this herself,' and the nun didn't actually know where to look!

I went to a further education college in Birmingham; I was there from 1986 to 1989. My schooling and my college and the education that I had was really good. This is important to me because a lot of people I have come across with learning difficulties – well, I have been absolutely amazed at the amount of people that are not able to read and write. It was something that I learned to do and was given the opportunity to do; some didn't have that opportunity at all. I am quite appalled in a way at the lack of education that some people have had. They just got written off.

I left college in 1989 and then I came back to live at home. I will admit that being away from home for fifteen years of my life off and on was the best thing that could have happened to me. I have seen a lot of people in People First whose parents are very, very protective. I mean they see a night out, as coming to pick them up at 10 o'clock, which even my mother said is not a 'night out'! I'm quite grateful to them for allowing me to go away to school for if they hadn't I don't think I would have been able to do a lot of the things that I have done and I'm doing now.

I used to work voluntary for the WRVS (Women's Royal Voluntary Service), and I did that till about 1995 or something, then I had to give it up because everything become more computerised and it became difficult for them to show me how to do the things they wanted me to do. After I left college I went into Cumbria Training Company – that was a bit boring because there wasn't much to do. Somebody used to bully and intimidate me quite a bit. For example at dinnertime there was a Portakabin and we all went in there for our lunch. A crowd of them used to have a game of cards during the lunch break but if this girl was there she would never let me join in with them. If she wasn't playing then the rest of them were actually happy for me to join in but if she was there – for some reason she had taken a dislike to me. It did bother me for a bit but then I just thought, well if that's the way she wants to be then that's the way she wants to be.

The early days of People First in Carlisle

I joined People First in February 1993. My friend was involved at the time and she asked me if I wanted to come to one of the meetings. The first description from my friend was that we would just go and talk. So to start with I did think twice about going but my mother said, 'Well if you want to go, give it a go, and if you don't like it you needn't go back.' The first meeting I ever went to was the Monday night self-advocacy meeting at Greystone Community Centre, and we had a talk on rights with Joanna Leith from Age Concern. She was one of our advisers. In September 1993 I actually enrolled on a course that was organised by the advocacy group along with Charlotte Mason College in Ambleside. I did a few things on that course with the advocacy worker from People First and that was when I really got to know her.

In December 1993 we won the Avis Akighir Award for innovation and good practice so that was a great honour for the advocacy group. We were in the paper, on the radio and given a statue. Also in 1993 I went on my first self-advocacy conference to Swanwick. The conference itself was good, and we met loads of people but a facilitator who didn't like you having a giggle ran the workshop I was in. She used to tell you that there was time for that after sessions. A lot of us think people with learning difficulties should run the workshops.

In 1994 we got some funding and moved into our first office on Earl Street in Carlisle. Later I started working at the office. Since then I have been the administrator for Carlisle People First.

Things are not always easy and the group has had its fair share of problems what with staffing issues and funding issues and what have you. Sometimes these crises have taken their toll on the support workers and members of the group but we have all come through it because we're all good friends rather than just a group of people. We actually support each other through these things. I'm not saying that everyone in the group agrees all the time and we do have times when we disagree, but we only ever fall out with each other for a fraction of a second and then it's all over and forgotten because there are bigger fish to fry.

For instance, we were involved with the consultation for the Department of Health White Paper, which was very good. The Department of Health Task Group of London People First came up to Carlisle and talked to our members about their experiences and ideas. Complaints were made about the terrible experiences people had had to go through here. There were lots of examples of where people had not being treated fairly and I can tell you some of the ways people have been treated has been appalling. In fact some things that I have heard have actually made me feel physically sick, not to put too fine a point on it, but a lot of it is confidential. But through this work investigations were carried out and improvements have been made. This would not have happened without the self advocacy group and that is the important thing.

I've also been involved as a facilitator on the Workers' Committee at the Adult Training Centre (ATC). The advocacy group started up there with a volunteer in 1990 but it was difficult for them so when the group moved from there to meet in the community we set up a Workers' Committee at the ATC. This had representatives from every workshop that would meet weekly and deal with issues purely to do with the ATC. We've done research about the dispersal of the ATC and how workers felt about it as well. I started to get involved with that about six months after I started at People First. Andy asked me if I wanted to go to the committee and take the minutes. So I did that for a while and then I actually co-facilitated the group with the advocacy worker and that was the first facilitation work I had done. The drawback was when she was not there, the way I was treated as a facilitator and the way she was treated by people was actually entirely different. I could give you loads of examples but I'll narrow it down. The worst thing that happened to me at the ATC was when the advocacy worker was finding committee members in the workshops and one of the staff wanted to speak to a committee member already in the meeting room. We explained we were about to start a meeting. So she said to me, 'Oh, well you can shut the bloody door then can't you?' Well I was actually quite furious that she spoke to me like that and then she slammed the door. So I made a complaint, I got an official form to fill in and all that and I got called to a meeting with the member of staff I had complained about and another senior member of staff. The advocacy worker said she would support me but I decided to do it on my own.

At that meeting the senior member of staff asked me to repeat my complaint to the person's face, which I did. But she turned round to me and said, 'Well actually I did not swear at you and I only meant to nudge the door but it slammed'. I was annoyed because after the member of staff said that, it was just swept under the carpet, even though there were at least half a dozen witnesses of people with learning difficulties to what she had actually said. They were not even questioned. Just because the member of staff said she hadn't sworn at me, nobody was interested in what I had to say. This is typical of what happens and I'm just pleased I never had to go to a place like that because I don't think I could have lasted five minutes basically.

In People First I have done quite a lot of talks and run workshops at different places, which I really enjoy. People ask do I get nervous when I'm giving a workshop and I say actually no because it's just water off a duck's back to me now. I've done it for so long that I can just do it. I've even spoken on a platform with [then Minister] John Hutton when he came to launch a new post here in Cumbria. I've also been to Gibraltar to do a Circle of Support workshop. It was absolutely fantastic because that was the first time that I had been abroad with People First.

I used to do some work at an institution in Cumbria called Dovenby Hospital. I was doing some of the advocacy work there helping people have some choice over where they were going to go when the place closed. I think it closed in about 1996. A few of the women were in there because they had a kid outside of marriage. Once the babies were born they were taken away, never to be seen again. That is so awful. They should never have been put there in the first place because you're talking about the 1940s and 1950s when people were called mentally handicapped and shoved away to rot.

I can remember a number of things that we have watched. One was the Macintyre investigation and I was absolutely disgusted by what I saw. I had it on at home and my Dad said, 'What are you watching?' He had come in the room in the middle of it. My Dad said to me (and excuse the language), 'Well it's absolutely bloody disgusting this!' He said, ' I've never seen so much ill treatment of anybody in my entire life'. With not having much to do with it I don't think he realised that type of thing went on and to be honest neither did I. Some of the things that I saw in that documentary really made my stomach turn over and I had quite a crusade in the group about this programme – I went on about it for months after it had been on because I felt so sick and so disgusted that people could have been abused in that way.

Another documentary that I saw with the group was a thing called *Stolen Lives* where an officer of an institution was actually getting kids off the street when they were walking home from school, if they were called feeble minded or imbeciles or whatever. This was in the 1920s and 1930s. He used to pick them up off the streets and take them to Meanwood, which was an institution in Leeds for 'medical defects' as they called them. They wouldn't be allowed to see their parents for ages. It was heartbreaking. You saw them being interviewed now on the TV, some of these people were in their eighties and to think that they actually had their lives stolen like that was an absolute disgrace.

Since I've been at People First I've seen a lot of people who come and go. It's opened my eyes and I think it has given a lot of people the confidence and the strength to move on if they are unhappy and say to people, 'Look, I do not want to be treated in that way, you cannot talk to me like that,' and that sort of thing. I think it's actually opened my mum's eyes as well to see what's going on because she didn't have a clue about half the stuff that's happened in people's lives until I told her.

People First has helped me personally through quite a lot of things in my life since I became involved eight years ago. I do think that advocacy and People First has come on a long way if you are talking about even 20 or 30 years ago. I do think it has because a long time ago 'learning difficulties' was a dirty word, it was a case of – put them in hospital and forget about them. I think everybody with learning difficulties has such a lot to offer and can live the same life and can have just as much a fulfilled life as anybody who has not got a learning difficulty.

'From pillar to post'

Andy Docherty, Project Director and Co-researcher, Carlisle People First

I was in hospital in Scotland since I was a baby of 5. I went to Challenger Lodge until I was 13, then to Lennox Castle and then to a place called Gogarburn. I've been from pillar to post.

I can tell you all about what hospital life is like. There were only two hospitals I liked. My best was Challenger Lodge as I was put there when I was 5 years old. It was good – I liked Christmas then! They used to put toys in your pillow, they said if you didn't go to sleep you would get a bunch of holly! They used to pull a wardrobe back and thought the noise was Santa coming down the chimney! I would go swimming every Thursday and Friday; you got bathed every night except the two nights you went swimming, as that was your bath on those nights. I liked that place and I was sorry to leave it actually. I didn't know I was leaving until the day before I went...it was terrible.

When I went to Lennox Castle I was too far away from my Mum for her to visit every week and so I missed her a lot. In hospital they didn't have bedrooms it was all dormitories and so you couldn't be alone. On a Saturday and Sunday the ward was closed and you could only get out if you had visitors. So this was difficult for me because it was hard for my Mum to get there. If you didn't have visitors then you were stuck inside the day room and would just sit and watch tele or listen to a radio programme, you weren't allowed outside the gates. Inside was your territory because they would say you were out of bounds outside the gates. So on a Saturday or Sunday afternoon it was like a prison.

I remember in Lennox Castle they used to give you medicine to go to toilet all the time! If people had seizures they took their medicine twice a week. And then there was the castor oil – I got that every Tuesday morning, ugh!

Once at Lennox Castle they took me to this part where you got admitted to be assessed. It was a Saturday and my Mum came to see me but she didn't know where I was. Do you know when she found me it was 6 o'clock at night because no one told her I had been transferred! When she got to the ward and found me she was soaking. They never even offered her a cup of tea or anything.

Some of the staff were nasty. There was one – he was really nasty. One day we got transferred to different wards, my friends went off to a different place and I couldn't go because I couldn't walk on my own. So I went back to the ward and this chargeman threw me to the floor and dragged me through to the day room. He was the charge nurse of Hut G. He was often nasty to the patients. There was nothing you could do but I told my Mum when I got transferred again. She came to see me not long after Christmas and she said she would write to the head doctor. Whether she did I don't know but in any case he was still nasty.

I got put into Lennox Castle when I was 13; I had no choice. When I got to be 20 I was transferred to Gogarburn. That wasn't too bad you could get out on a Saturday afternoon, but even then you couldn't do your own thing.

We had this doctor called Dr Bailey, I wasn't there but my friend Jimmy told me what happened. If he saw you with a woman he would send you to your bed for a month! There was this guy who went with a lass called Mary. They were in the back of the warehouse having it off and Dr Bailey said right you two! They both had to be put to bed for a month, no day clothes, no anything. When he was let back out he did the same thing again! The doctor told the staff to put him to bed for another month. These were adults!

They used to sit in their nightshirts and watch the tele; it was Dr Bailey's orders to have all the clothes locked up. They were worried the boys would go in with the girls. Even when the pictures were on every Wednesday in the wintertime the girls were separated from the boys – they were on one side and we were on the other. This even happened at the dance on Friday nights. Oh God…it was like a concentration camp! Then once Dr Bailey left we got someone called Dr Pilkington and he said all the girls and boys could mix now.

Sometimes things happened that the papers got hold of, like when a man got out and raped a woman in her own bed. At Gogarburn you had to watch what you were doing…mind you half the stuff that was going on at Gogarburn the papers didn't know. It was like Colditz! Most of them wanted out. People were there because of their condition, if you had epileptic seizures, if you were off your head, people who couldn't speak. There was a Ward 5 where every time you passed there would be a broken window or something smashed through temper. So they put unbreakable glass in but it still broke.

What I didn't like about Ward 5 was, they had this doctor – and if a patient had managed to get out but then they were put back in, the patient was made to tell everyone why they were dropped back. I don't think that was right. If they asked me I would say I'm not saying nothing.

Some doctors were good and some were bad. Some doctors always wanted to know everything. We had this very good doctor on Ward 9; he used to listen to what you had to say. There was another doctor; she used to have spyglasses and she used to spy on the patients and go back and tell Dr Bailey what happened.

In those days you couldn't stand up for things. They would always say, you do what we say, not what you say, oh aye…if people stood up for themselves they got put to bed. They wouldn't be able to do it nowadays – it would all be knocked on the head. If I went back now I would be able to speak up for myself and say 'you can't do that' and they would listen. They would have to.

My mother was my first advocate

Since I've joined People First I speak out for myself – I'm not afraid to speak my mind now.

How it started was one day a volunteer came up to the Adult Training Centre to talk about self-advocacy and I was asked if I would like to go to this meeting. This was after I had moved to Carlisle. Then one weekend the advocacy group went down to Oxford to a conference. I had £5 to spend on myself so on the Sunday night after the conference I got back to the house and I was told they were after my blood. I was asked 'What did you spend my £5 on?'… I said I got a

Madonna tape and they said: 'Who told you to get that with my money?' But you see it was my money. Because of that my suitcase was left unpacked and I couldn't get any help. It started to get nasty then.

When I went to this first conference in Oxford people were talking up for themselves and I thought, I think I'll start doing that, and I did – and I haven't looked back. Now every meeting that I go to I'm not frightened to speak up anymore I just get on and do it. I know now there's nothing in it. Let's put it this way, I try not to boast about it, but it makes me feel grand when I can speak up. When my mother was alive she used to say it's time I was speaking up for myself. She said 'What do you think you've got a tongue in your head for?' But I wouldn't, I was frightened. So. It's got easier, I even speak up to my own care worker now I've moved on and got my own flat.

The person that used to be my care worker would say: 'Oh you can't do this, you can't do that'. I don't think my girlfriend Lou will mind me telling you this, every Monday when Lou came to my house to see me, the care worker used to say: 'Oh you're here, I'll come back round another time'. You see I think she didn't want to say anything to me in front of Lou who would be my witness. There had been times before when she had changed what she said and I'd wished I'd had a recorder. Anyway, once there had been some confusion. She had gone to let the cat out but it had got locked up again and made a mess, so she said: 'I think you will have to get rid of the cat'.

I thought I would have to. But I woke up the next morning and I knew I didn't want to get rid of the cat. Lou said: 'Well, good for you!' So on the Wednesday I had to phone the care worker and she said to me: ' Er…have you decided about the cat?' I said: 'I am keeping it' and she replied: 'Well you've got to think of Lou stepping in the litter box!' You see, she really didn't care about me and how I felt. Lou, when I told her, said: 'I've got a good mind to ring her up and say don't use my name to try and get what you want!'

It's all since I've started doing more with People First. You see it takes time I think for people to speak out, some people are frightened to speak out. They've just got to learn how to do it. Even some of the parents are barriers to their daughters or sons; they say, 'I don't think you should go there tonight, I don't think you should risk it'. I know a lass, I can't mention her name, but she lives in Carlisle and her mother won't let her go anywhere. She goes to bed early, gets up early and does everything. But we know and we are there for her.

I go to a lot of meetings and conferences and next month I'm going down to London for a seminar for the Research Group. I like travelling; I know I can come back and that I'll enjoy it.

I think talking about the past can help people. People need to know what's happened. That's what needed. People need to speak up for their rights. If they don't do it now they might never do it. People should try and do this for themselves – I mean no one's going to give them a row for their rights, that's what they've got a tongue for. People know I won't let them get away with things. I used to let people walk all over me but I won't let them now. I don't get treated badly now. People respect my position as Project Director with People First, which I am very pleased about. I really didn't think I would see a day when I could speak up for myself. If my mother could see me now she would say to herself, 'I don't believe it, why could he not do that years ago?'

'What sort of support are we giving?'

Rohhss Chapman, Volunteer and Co-researcher, Carlisle People First and Open University

This chapter launches straight into the heart of what self-advocacy is about and in this way the stories speak for themselves. However, I am writing a part here to explain the process of how these stories were produced and then some analysis of what I think are recurrent themes which can usefully be taken up by support workers in working with people in self-advocacy groups.

Many self-advocacy groups involve or employ support workers and that has been my role with Carlisle People First since 1990. I began as a volunteer, was later employed by the group and have now gone full circle to being a volunteer again. As part of my support work I facilitated a Research Group and so when I left for the Open University to take up a research studentship around self-advocacy, we agreed that it would be not only appropriate but also essential to continue working together because of the topic. Now the Carlisle People First Research Group is undertaking research around the history of the self-advocacy movement from the members' perspective and we are working together as co-researchers. My own research is focusing on the role of support workers within the movement but in such a way that the two can be linked.

When the opportunity arose to write a chapter for this book we decided to produce it in partnership. This involved talking about the plan for the whole book and discussing how our chapter would fit. We realised our chapter was likely be one of the few where the voices of people stood out, so we decided it should be filled in exactly that way.

Lou and Andy put their thoughts on to tape, expressing their views about life, life history and self-advocacy. The work with Fred's contribution was based on his thoughts on a newspaper article written about him in 1994. This brought back memories of a number of past events. I also spoke to Fred on the phone after his holiday in Canada and went over drafts of what I had written. As far as possible I have written word for word what he said. I then edited the draft at his request.

Andy's tape was added to at a later date through his support worker Niall asking specific questions about the past, or his views, and probing further on some of the points Andy came up with. Niall interviewed Elizabeth in a similar way but you will notice that I have left out Niall's questions, which perhaps makes the account flow very quickly.

Lou gave me her initial tape to listen to, which I transcribed. This was about her life history so I asked her to say a bit more about her role with the self-advocacy group. Both Lou and Andy's stories are direct transcriptions with minor editing. They feel this translates as a genuine record of their spoken words. In addition, everyone wanted to keep his or her own name. The group is being paid for their efforts, which was one of the stipulations put forward at the beginning. Everyone has said that the process was enjoyable and we are waiting to see it in print.

As I mentioned earlier these personal narratives provide a stark reminder of the importance of self-advocacy in people's lives and why it is such a powerful tool for invoking change. In addition these stories tell us about the changing nature of personal understandings of self-advocacy. They also intertwine references to the development of the organisation. In providing some context, Fred's story is a clear example.

Fred invited a reporter to interview him at his home on the evening the office had opened in 1994. He was asked about his life, the organisation and why he had become involved in self-advocacy. The story he told the paper was obviously similar to the account he expresses here.

Fred's story hit the local paper later that week. Almost instantly the self-advocacy group was condemned and ostracised by staff working in local statutory services. Even community leaders who had previously shown some support to the group phoned to complain. 'How could you let Fred say those things?' we were asked, as if Fred's voice was under central control. No one complained directly to Fred and actually no one questioned his story. That the story was awful seemed to be irrelevant; the 'problem' was Fred had allowed it to become public.

The story in the paper and the reaction of other people proved to be a significant learning exercise. It informed the group of the struggle people would have simply to tell the truth about their lives let alone to try and change things. It contrasted with the empty 'buzz' words about respect and equality that were being exchanged within services at that time. It made clear that People First needed to be strong enough to stand on its own and not to rely on the 'goodwill' of other people who may take offence at members speaking out.

So in a wider sense, the group development until that point, which had so far been about personal stories and experiences, developed a broader perspective. Self-advocacy was no longer simply about speaking up by individual members over personal issues but also about the oppression faced by people with learning difficulties in general. As this happened the group began to focus more on group issues, ran issue-led workshops, focused on the rights people had (or not) in law and later developed a campaigner's post. Lou's and Elizabeth's stories capture the broader themes about people's rights around abusive treatment and education.

This is an important point for support workers as it allows them to take stock of the sort of support they are providing. In tracing the history of individuals and a group with its members, opportunities arise to make open and clear these shifts from the personal to the political aspects of self-advocacy work. This then provides a wider framework for supporters to act within that links directly into the social model of disability. So, for example, instances of not being listened to (Andy about the doctors at Gogarburn; Fred with his carers; Lou making her complaint at the Adult Training Centre), hinge on more than the individual short-comings of a particular staff person. If this link is not made then advocacy work will remain locked into an ever-revolving wheel of personal issues so wider chal-lenges to service systems and government will fail to be made.

Likewise the network of the different self-advocacy groups have been and still are important for learning, the exchange of ideas and bringing self-advocacy out into a broader arena through the exchanging and gathering of stories. Our regional group, North-West People First involving Liverpool, Manchester, Tameside, Crewe, West Cumbria and Carlisle, has been particularly active and produced a number of joint working events. Joining together regionally is only a few steps away from joining together as a national movement.

In looking back, the early days of Carlisle People First were a struggle to get the group and its ideas taken seriously within the locality. When the group began the idea was new to our county despite groups already existing in other parts of the UK. Meeting up with these other groups provided enormous support. There were several local incidents where self-advocates had their group meetings derided or patronised by professionals. They assumed the meetings were simply 'unrealistic', or aimed to incite members to irresponsibly challenge the authority of service staff. However, being new to self-advocacy, the group sessions covered all sorts of topics such as discussing life in general through people's experiences, skill building, and learning about rights and possible routes for change. In this way the group was involved in an initial extensive process of consciousness-raising.

The group moved out into the community after a year or so. It was a time of instability, as some members' parents did not 'allow' them to attend in the evenings. The group faced a lot of challenges about room renting and transport issues and how to keep everyone's confidence up about the future. The need to have an office base came to the fore. The self-advocacy group gradually reformed and moved on in numbers and strength, fortified by obtaining funding, setting up the office base, incorporating as a company and employing support workers and members. All of the new skills required for these developments had to be learned from the beginning by everyone involved. The enormity of this is present in Andy's narrative where he remarks how people respect his role as Project Director. Nobody was a professional or an expert but everyone was united in the aims of the organisation.

The core members have been the real powerhouse of the organisation. People have acted as role models for newcomers who, in hearing the struggle of moving on from difficult situations to ones of independence and freedom, have obviously felt inspired to begin looking at change within their own lives. There is a life-changing concept: 'If they can do that then so can I'. Andy felt empowered to move on because he had observed the success of Fred's fight for a place of his own.

There are implications here for support workers. The development of Carlisle People First, like many other self-advocacy groups, has been very focused on the process of exactly how people come together and work in an inclusive way. Through people's stories and experiences supporters can point out how personal problems can become shared group issues and how individual concerns pave the way through networking to the development of ideas about self-advocacy as a national movement. The group is constantly dynamic because new members arrive, others leave or more poignantly die, support workers change and new volunteers become involved. For all the flux that takes place in the organisation it can be made clear that society is the place that needs to be changed, not the people within.

CHAPTER TEN

The Neglected Dimension
Advocacy and the families of children with learning difficulties

Nick Pike

Introduction

The first reaction to being asked to contribute a chapter on advocacy with families is to ask 'What is there to write about?' Unlike the wider world of advocacy, there is little in the way of coherent tested models; little in the way of published research; few examples of good practice. On reflection though, this in itself offers a good rationale for writing. Given the importance attached to advocacy in other spheres, why is there no similar established tradition in relation to children with learning difficulties and their families?

In tackling this question, the chapter will seek to explore several different dimensions:

> core assumptions about the key role played by family members in advocating for their own children

> the history of specific service developments that have included an element of advocacy

> the service incoherence and conceptual confusion that has resulted from piecemeal developments

> the implications for the practice of advocacy.

Throughout, the chapter will be earthed in the everyday experience of advocating for and with families, drawing on the author's continuing research into the experiences of children with tuberous sclerosis and their families, and his experience as a Named Person (Independent Parental Supporter) under the Special Education legislation.

Advocacy: a key responsibility for families?

Marian Barnes (1997) in her discussion of empowerment and family life, draws upon Barrett and McIntosh's (1991) *Anti-Social Family* to identify three key assumptions about the nature of family life that underpin societal expectations for family members:

> families provide emotional security not easily available elsewhere
>
> the family is the most supportive environment in which to bring up children
>
> families are, in some sense, 'natural'.

While it is obvious that all three of these claims are to a degree ideological in nature, it is easy to see how such assumptions lead inexorably to the view that advocating for one's children is an essential core task of any parent. It is, arguably, only an extension of protecting one's child in an otherwise hostile world.

In a longitudinal ethnographic study of children with tuberous sclerosis (TS)[1] all participants reported the need to take on new roles *vis-à-vis* the external social world, particularly the world of professional services. Becoming an advocate was the most important of these new roles. Respondents described the need to advocate in respect of all the major decisions affecting their children: medical care; appropriate education and family support.

Participants also reported advocacy as being the most stressful and demanding role that they had to undertake. Respondents reported themselves as having to develop new skills of assertiveness, negotiation and persistence that were, with few exceptions, reported as requiring significant changes in self-concept.

A number of respondents reported themselves as having become 'pushy'. One, describing her insistence on inviting herself to key meetings from which she had been excluded, and shouting down the telephone to make her point, said, 'I do not like the person I have had to become'. Many respondents indicated that they felt themselves to have become experts in understanding the needs of their child, while expressing the view that relevant professionals found this hard to accept.

The role of advocate in this study was found to be highly gendered. With one exception, the lead role was always taken by the female partner, with male partners, where they existed, being lined up to support positions at key meetings.

Intriguingly, older siblings also adopted the role of advocate, although here, this was with respect to enabling an affected child to participate in school or community. This, too, appears to be strongly associated with gender, with female siblings starting young as advocates (as young as 7), with the role strengthening as the sibling matured. In the case of male siblings, there are clear examples of younger siblings taking on an advocacy role, but this seems to peter out during adolescence (or in one case delegated to the next youngest male sibling). Advocacy amongst siblings was highly represented where the child with tuberous sclerosis attended the same mainstream school as the sibling, less so where the TS child was in a special needs school.

As Burke and Cigno (1996) suggest, the need to take on an advocacy role arises because:

> many families lack basic good advice. Their experience is of being pushed from service to service, having to 'fight' for the needs of their children, or else they 'give-up'. It is apparent that there is not one professional person with the time and commitment to listen, understand and explain to parents how to access services or to find the level of support they require... Typically, parents seem to exist in a day-to day state of uncertainty and stress which is seemingly connected with not being understood or heard. (Burke and Cigno 1996, p.128)

Hubert (1991) also describes this sense of isolation and of a protracted battle to obtain support in her study of 20 young people with challenging behaviour:

> Despite all these support systems the twenty families without exception, see their experiences to date as an uphill struggle, mainly because they have had to fight a constant battle to get adequate help and support from local health and social services. They feel that much of the help and support they have received has been disorganised, unreliable and thus far from adequate. At all levels, and in most contexts, these parents feel that they are fighting a battle which is all the harder because they know that the professionals they work with generally consider it to be a losing battle. (Hubert 1991, p.13)

Beresford (1995) agrees, suggesting that dealing with service providers is consistently identified as the most stressful part of bringing up a disabled child, and going on to identify three basic sets of enduring difficulties between parents and service providers:

> a discrepancy of opinions between parent and professional about the parent's and child's needs, and an unwillingness on the part of professionals to acknowledge parents as experts in the care of their child

a confused relationship between parent and professional.
Professionals can view parents as a resource for statutory services, as
co-workers and as clients in their own right. Because of this,
professionals find it hard to develop appropriate ways of working
with parents

a lack of coordination between services – a problem compounded by
the fact that numerous professionals tend to be involved with these
families. (Beresford 1995, p.24)

The tuberous sclerosis study referred to earlier produced similar results. Parents,
especially mothers, in this study were often very knowledgeable – supported as
most of them were by the Tuberous Sclerosis Association, which provided both
written information and telephone helpline support. They spoke very highly of
their encounter with knowledgeable professionals. Whether these were medical
practitioners at specialist TS clinics, or professionals who had built up a working
knowledge of TS over many years (as for example in the big urban hospitals),
their advice and guidance was respected.

Parents were equally happy to work with less knowledgeable professionals
who were willing to respect the expertise of parents, admit their lack of specialist
knowledge and work in partnership. There were a small number of encounters,
though, that were described where neither condition prevailed where inexpert
professionals appeared to decry the knowledge of parents and all respondents
found such encounters stressful and unsatisfactory. One mother of a 4 year old
said:

It's certainly been a fight, and I just wish the professionals would listen to
you. You're the child's best advert, you know their needs more than
anyone and sometimes they over-block that and say 'No, I'm the
professional here'.

Respondents spoke warmly of those service providers who sought to work in
partnership with parents. Such encounters were characterised by transparency
(parents understood what decisions were being taken, why they were being
taken, and were fully involved in the decision making process) and equality.

Far from advocacy, then, being a natural extension of family caring, it may be
a survival skill acquired by family members in the face of uncoordinated services
and unresponsive professional helpers. But is that the whole of the story?

Sociologists like Margaret Voysey (1975) and Walter Jaehnig (Baldwin and
Carlisle 1999, p.349) have argued for a central place in our understanding of

family life with a disabled child of the meaning that parents (and other family members) construct for themselves.

> One of the important insights [this approach] delivers is the extent to which coping is linked to success in 'normalising' the child's upbringing – finding a way of parenting 'which maintains habitual or expected child-rearing practices or customary goals'. (Philp and Duckworth 1982, p.38)

Underpinning this particular coping strategy is the set of assumptions referred to earlier about the nature of the family in contemporary society. This set of assumptions – which Dalley (1993) refers to as a 'familist ideology' (in Burke and Cigno 1996, p.128) – emphasises the centrality of self-support and mutual caring within the boundaries of the family. Family life is essentially exclusive. Care is offered within the boundaries of the family group. The responsibility for meeting the challenge of nurturing a disabled child is one for family members, and outsiders, whether lay or professional are admitted only on the family's terms.

This sense of 'normality' is not specific to families of disabled children. But Voysey (1972), who refers to the basic concept as 'coping splendidly', sees the acquisition of this understanding of their task as both a successful adaptive strategy for family members and a goal of intervention by health and social care professionals. This sense of normality is part of the wider thrust towards the maintenance of a moral order. Ball (1970), drawing on Garfinkel's (1976) ethnomethodological approach to sociology writes:

> In a series of studies Garfinkel has demonstrated ethnomethodologically that for members, *'moral'* as social reality *equals normal*: to be perceived-to-be-normal means appearing to be conventionally situated or placed in the natural-order-of-persons-taken-for-granted, to be socially located in the 'of course' environment of non-reflective everyday/anyday life. Thus to be accorded such placement is to be deemed to be normal, and this location is a moral one: normal = moral, and therefore to be respectable one must appear to be normal, must be received as such, confirmed as such (for example, through deferential or respectful responses from others), and thereby socially demonstrate one's moral worth. It is in a sense close to this that some sociologists conceive of society itself as a moral order – that is, as a set of normally, and thus morally, ordered locations of positions and roles realized in symbolic communication...it is a basic property of respectability that it is actively sought in social transactions, just as the appearance of its antitheses...is actively avoided... respectability or the attribution of normality and thus moral worth and its recognition seems for Everyman a necessary precondition to ordinary social conduct, to the pursuit of goals and the favourable experiencing of self. (Ball 1970, pp.332, 336, 359, original emphasis)

In other words, in times when there are marked discrepancies between life as it is actually experienced, and life as it is anticipated, there is a process of approximation, of 'normalisation' (not in its Wolfensbergian sense), in which taking the familist ideology as a baseline and constructing a new identity, a new sense of 'normal' family life forms a core element.

This sense of the 'normal' is then continually refined and redefined in the interaction with others in daily life: in the workplace; at the school gate; in dialogue with extended family members; in engagement with service providers and other professionals. This is the process identified by Nolan, Grant and Keady (1996, p.45) as 'constructive care', something that they see as a common process in the lives and experiences of the families of children with learning difficulties.

So far, then it has been suggested that there are two major barriers to the development of advocacy services for children with learning difficulties and their families. The first of these is the necessary response of family members to an incoherent and unresponsive service system. While this in itself would suggest a valuable place both for service co-ordination and effective advocacy, the prevailing ideology of family life and the way that this is constructed in the lives and experiences of families tends to prevent the development of services that might be seen to detract from the primary responsibility of parents for their own children.

Dale (1996) makes this point in her discussion of the relative strengths and weaknesses of advocacy and enabling in service responses to the families of children with special needs. She writes:

> If advocacy is distinguished from enabling, the professional wishing to empower a parent will have to decide between either process. Which is more useful to a parent depends on individual circumstances, but the following points are worth noting. (Dale 1996, pp.271–272)

In some cases, enabling is preferable because:

> it does not undermine the parent's confidence or make the parent dependent on the particular professional; the parent is facilitated to make decisions and to take action and/or negotiate with the professional

> it is less likely that the professional will be trapped between conflicting pressures from the parent and the professional network system or the professional's employing agency.

In some other circumstances, advocacy may be desirable because:

the parent is unable to communicate for themselves (lack of English, illiterate, disabled slow/learning, unable to be present at case conferences)

expert representation is needed to present the parent's case in a legal dispute; e.g. independent professional advice is needed for appeal to SEN [Special Educational Needs] Tribunal, a solicitor for a court hearing

the parent has been actively marginalised and disempowered. If other professionals refuse to listen to the parent's viewpoint or to involve the parent, the parent may have no option but to seek representation in order to be heard. (Dale 1996, pp.271–272)

The tenor of Dale's argument is clear. All things being equal parents are expected to advocate for their own children, and the role of the service professional is to enable and empower. Advocacy runs the risk of taking away that key responsibility from family members, and should be reserved for highly specific circumstances.

This is a core theme of policy development in support services for children with learning difficulties and their families, as the history of service development (to which we now turn) clearly demonstrates.

Keyworking and advocacy

References to a role for an independent person to guide and assist the families of children with learning difficulties can be traced back as far as the Court Report of 1976:

parents...find the existing pattern of services confusing... [They] are faced with a conglomeration of professionals, the majority working in separate uncoordinated services with limited roles and limited communication with each other, and few of whom are specially trained to work with children. Not all are equally accessible, and parents often do not know to whom to turn for help... So parents fail to obtain the ready help and support for which they constantly and desperately feel the need. (Court Committee 1976, paras 4.45–4.46)

Here the primary issue was identified as the need for coordination of services, and the provision of independent advice to families. The Court Report recommended the establishment of district handicap teams and the allocation of individual *keyworkers* to families. Although the recommendations were never implemented wholesale across the UK, there were a number of experimental schemes set up designed to test the effectiveness of the Court model, of which the Exeter

Honeylands project was perhaps the best known (Brimblecombe and Russell 1988).

Despite these attempts, when the Warnock Committee reported in 1978, they addressed the same problem and proposed their own solution:

> there is a clear need for one person to whom the parents of children with disabilities or incipient special needs can turn for advice on the different services available to meet their child's needs. This should be someone who is well known to and accepted by them. The principle holds whether the children are under five, of school age, or making the transition from school to adult life. (Warnock Committee 1978, paras 5.12–5.13)

The Warnock Committee called this role the 'named person' and saw it as central to the development of partnership practice in both education and child welfare services. A number of influential schemes have been set up to test the idea, the best known of which have been the Named Worker scheme developed at the KIDS family centre from 1983 to 1988 (Dale 1996) and the Resource Worker project set up by the York University Social Policy Research Unit in the early 1980s (Glendinning 1986).

Advocacy was clearly and explicitly identified as a key responsibility of resource workers in the York project. Their tasks were identified as:

maintaining regular contact

giving information

offering advice

counselling parents and other family members

liasing and improving communications

coordinating the delivery of services

acting as an advocate on the family's behalf.

This idea, that advocacy is but one role amongst a bundle of responsibilities for a named person, has been a very influential one. In the written report of the York project (Glendinning 1986), clear links were made between the multiple roles of the resource worker and the parallel developments in what was then known as *case management* (now more familiarly described as *care management*). The suggestion at this stage in the research literature was that 'case managers' would themselves act as professional advocates for the families that they worked with. This idea formed the core of the then Conservative government's opposition to the full implementation of the Disabled Persons (Services, Consultation and Representation) Act 1986. They argued that the new care managers established under the NHS and Community Care Act 1990 would take on the role of advocacy and representation, and hence the legal rights to advocacy enshrined in the earlier Act would be redundant.

Intriguingly, the KIDS Family Centre project from 1983 (although very similar to the York project in other respects) had serious reservations about the inclusion of advocacy in their Named Workers' brief. We have already seen Dale's (1996) general reservations about advocacy as an intervention strategy, but she also makes some sensible points about confusion of roles. Prospective advocates are encouraged to

> be clear how advocacy fits in with their other responsibilities towards the child and family

> ensure that advocacy does not conflict with their responsibilities to other families or to your employing agency

> be prepared to represent the parents' view without trying to influence or change it. The advocate needs to act impartially and be willing to represent the parent whatever his or her own viewpoint.

She ends by pointing out that in some situations it is advisable that the professional is independent, if they are to be an effective advocate (Dale 1996, p.278).

However, the notion of advocacy as a role independent of all other responsibilities has been very much a minority theme in working with learning disabled children and their families, with the multiple role keyworker being a much more common recommendation. The most recent manifestation of this has been the Joseph Rowntree Foundation's keyworking project (Mukherjee, Beresford and Sloper 1999; Sloper et al. 1999). In this project, although an explicit advocacy role was not included, it emerged as a key task for keyworkers and is at least implicit in the six key elements of keyworking that emerged from the project:

> proactive regular contact

> a supportive open relationship

> a family-centred approach

> working across agencies

> working with families strengths and ways of coping

> working for the family as opposed to working for an agency.

Evidence from all the projects referred to in this section, and others not discussed all point to high levels of parental satisfaction with dedicated keyworking systems (Read and Clements 2001, pp.45–48) and while such systems are in place only in limited parts of the UK, and to a minority of children (Beresford *et al.* 1996), it has been a very influential model and may well have been a brake on the development of formal, independent advocacy schemes.

While the multi-role, keyworking professional has been the dominant theme of research and policy literature since the mid-1970s, there have been other developments that are worth noting.

Named persons and special education

Of these, the earliest derives from the Warnock Report and the development of the process of statementing in special needs education. The Warnock Committee had strongly recommended the creation of a role for a named person to coordinate all services for families of disabled children. The English and Welsh legislation to implement the recommendations of the Warnock Report ignored this advice, unlike the Scottish response which identified two key roles – the Named Officer and the Named Person. The Named Officer was an identified officer of the education authority who was responsible for the preparation of the Record of Needs (the Scottish equivalent of the Statement of Special Educational Needs), and was to be available to parents during the assessment, planning and implementation of the Record. The Named Person, by contrast was an independent individual nominated by parents and appointed by the education authority 'to support parents [and] to help parents express their views most effectively in matters to do with their child's education and to give advice' (Kerr, Sutherland and Wilson 1994, p.13). While the role is not identified specifically as an advocacy role, the advocacy element is strong as the following list of tasks demonstrates:

> to listen to parents and encourage them to be confident in expressing their views
>
> to help parents draw up a profile of their child
>
> to make telephone calls on behalf of parents
>
> to accompany parents on visits to schools, especially the first visit
>
> to sit in on meetings, ask the questions that are difficult

to listen at meetings, take notes and then discuss with parents what was said

to give a second opinion

to offer constructive criticism

to help parents to understand the assessment process, the roles of the various professionals, jargon, and so on.

to get information from other agencies

to accompany parents to appeal hearings (though not necessarily acting as their legal representative)

to keep records of meetings and correspondence

to help write letters to officials

to help fill in forms

to explain official documents including the Record of Needs.

Unlike the professional keyworkers referred to earlier, or the Named Officers, Named Persons are assumed to be people who are acting independently, and in an essentially voluntary capacity, although many will be professionals in allied fields. The relationship was intended to be one that would last throughout the child's educational career.

Introduced in Scotland in 1980, the scheme was not similarly introduced into England and Wales until 1994. That did not mean that the new SEN systems did not throw up a need for specialised advocacy. The formal nature of the statementing process, the role of appeals tribunals, and the possibility of appeals to the Secretary of State all generated a demand for specialised advocacy. The gap was filled by a hotchpotch of schemes, some of which were on an ad-hoc local basis, others more formally structured.

Some were essentially parental self-help groups such as those facilitated by Contact-A-Family (Hatch and Hinton 1986) or the larger voluntary learning disability and child care organisations. Others included the specialists groups like the Avon scheme Supportive Parents for Special Children (Mallett 1997), Network '81 (Paige-Smith 1997) and IPSEA – the Independent Panel for Special Education Advice (Simmons 1997).

While there are individual examples of excellent work from all of these sources, the overall result was of a very localised and patchy access to independent advocacy in the special education arena.

Government was persuaded at a late stage in the development of the Code of Practice on the Identification and Assessment of Special Educational Needs (1994) to emulate the Scottish experience by beefing up its commitment to parental support by formally requiring (and funding) the development of Parent Partnership schemes in all local education authorities (LEAs).

The definition of the Named Person in the Code of Practice is a thin one. She or he is someone who:

> in future can give the parents advice and information about their child's special educational needs
>
> the parents can trust. He or she should be capable of giving accurate information and advice
>
> is independent of and who is not employed by the LEA.

LEAs were encouraged to 'consult local voluntary organisations, parents' groups and relevant professionals in order to identify individuals who are willing to act as Named Persons'. As in Scotland, the role is essentially a voluntary one, with training and support being provided by the LEA.

The scheme to date has been patchy. Numbers of Named Persons recruited have varied enormously from authority to authority – from a few hundred to a handful. Recruitment has reflected definition – large recruitments have focused on the importance of friendly support, with parents being encouraged to nominate their own Named Person from amongst their family and community networks, while smaller recruitment has reflected a more 'professional' understanding of the role. Dropout from schemes has been high, and training and support variable. Some authorities have had very clear job definitions, with contracts, appraisal and formal training. Others have not (Furze and Conrad 1997).

Since 1997, there have been several attempts in Department for Education and Employment (DfEE) publications to clarify and define the role of the Named Person and in the draft revised Code of Practice (out for consultation at the time of writing), the role is replaced by the new one of Independent Parental Supporter (IPS) who is defined as someone who:

> can support parents' meetings or reviews and provide a wide range of information on special educational needs
>
> enable parents to make their contribution to both the assessment and the statement and to understand the implications of any objectives set within the assessment process

has no connection with the LEA or the child's school

is fully informed about local and national policies and procedures around special educational needs and feels confident to work with parents in a variety of different situations. (DfEE 2001)

This role clearly edges towards the 'professional' definition of a Named Person identified above, and this is indicated by the guidance (though not requirement) to LEAs to enter into partnership with voluntary organisations to provide IPSs.

It is, of course, much too early to see how such a revised scheme will work, although it probably comes closest to a pure definition of advocacy of any of the approaches to family support that we have discussed so far.

Advocacy for children?

Up till now, we have been discussing approaches to assisting and supporting parents or whole families, and given the ideological position set out earlier, this is, perhaps, not surprising. However, as Kagan (citing Brandon, Brandon and Brandon 1995, p.49) points out:

> it will not always be in the disabled person's best interests to have their family members advocate on their behalf. Some relatives have different concerns from their disabled members and they are not always able to disentangle them. More importantly families can be a source of oppression depending on the sorts of relationships people have developed and their understanding of the meaning of disability. (Kagan 1995, p.5)

So what scope is there for independent advocacy or representation for children and young people with learning difficulties? The answer is precious little. Marchant (2001) points out that 'advocacy on behalf of children has a relatively short history; in particular rights-oriented advocacy with children is in its infancy' (Marchant 2001, p.216).

And if this is true for all children, it is crucially true for children with learning difficulties. While there is some evidence of local schemes of both self-advocacy and citizen advocacy, such schemes are usually small-scale, experimental and short-lived. Apart from the work of Young People First, there is no self-advocacy network.

While the Children Act 1989 made provision for independent representatives for children being accommodated away from home, few of the schemes for representation have addressed the needs of children with learning difficulties (except the work of Voice of the Child in Care), despite the large numbers of children with learning difficulties who spend all or part of their lives being 'looked after'.

Rights-based organisations like the Children's Legal Centre have undertaken some legal advocacy work, and there is some evidence that other organisations developing children's rights have begun to recognise the need for advocacy. One of the few groups to have done much work in this area is the Who Cares Trust, which began as a self-advocacy and pressure group for children in care. Its Disabled Children's Reference Group called recently for a network of advocates who would:

> be independent
>
> find out what the child needs
>
> have the sole aim of supporting the child
>
> treat the child as an equal
>
> have the power to sort out problems.

While endorsing this position, Corker and Davis (2000, p.235) point out that there is as yet neither the legal nor practical basis for such a network. The absence of such a network 'continues to add to widespread abuses of the human and civil rights of disabled children, and the silencing of their voices, rendering them "invisible under law"'.

Implications for practice

The foregoing discussion has suggested that there are a number of major obstacles to the development of formal and informal advocacy for children with learning difficulties and their families. First amongst these is the socially constructed notion that the family is the primary advocate for the child. We have seen that this distorts the reality of many families, poses exceptional strain on family members and prevents the needs of the child as an individual being addressed.

For prospective advocates, it puts a primary emphasis on the support and empowerment of the family, rather than on a clearly articulated advocacy role, either for the child or the family. This is compounded by the fact that families do have clearly identified needs for support. We have noted the observations about the lack of parental support which go all the way back to the Court and Warnock Reports. The same plethora of professionals; the same confusion of roles; the same lack of information (Beresford 1995) still exists for families, and anyone acting as an independent person in any one capacity will rapidly become involved in others.

As an example, as a pastoral carer based in his local church, the author became involved with a family with two children on the autistic spectrum. Although his role was specifically pastoral, he rapidly became involved as an adviser and advocate in obtaining an appropriate assessment under the Code of Practice, and in seeking support from the local social services department, who in turn tried to use him to coordinate local voluntary support to the family.

A second example derives from working as a Named Person for the author's local LEA. Working with one particular child, the author began as an adviser in the later stages of statementing, took on the role of advocacy with the LEA supporting a family's desire for inclusive education, and ended up advising on the completion of Disability Living Allowance (DLA) claim forms.

In reality, the lack of a coordinated and focused support service for families ensures that any independent professional ends up playing multiple roles, and this is not beneficial for maintaining a clear advocacy focus.

As a result, the focus of one's energy goes into representing families, rather than into representing the child. Alongside the pervasive assumption of family responsibility, the lack of coherent family support structures makes this inevitable, although it is far from desirable. Where families feel abandoned and unsupported, any interest from an independent person is welcomed and used to the full. It then becomes very difficult to identify ways of separating out the needs of the child from the needs of the family and to represent and advocate for the needs of the child.

Finally, the sheer lack of an advocacy tradition poses problems of its own. The absence of straightforward models of practice or examples of organisational frameworks or evaluated schemes mean that the prospective advocate, or advocacy service is left with little in the way of guidance. This is particularly clear where issues such as ensuring independence, developing funding strategies, designing contracts and clarifying roles is concerned. Although Dale (1996), based on the KIDS Family Centre model, sets out some sensible guidance, there is little alternative to inventing one's own systems and procedures. This is a marked difference from other fields of advocacy where well-tried models and systems exist which can be utilised as a starting point.

Thus, when one local LEA set up its Named Person scheme in 1994, the training materials specified the independence of the Named Person, and the responsibility to represent the child's parents in equalising the balance of power between parent and professional. The trainer, on the other hand, saw a Named

Person as being a mediator retained by the LEA to 'explain LEA decisions' and persuade families of their rightness!

Conclusion

This chapter has argued that advocacy for children with learning difficulties and their families is the 'neglected dimension' in the support network for such children and families. The reasons for this have been suggested to be:

a pervasive 'familist ideology' that puts the responsibility for advocacy firmly onto the shoulders of parents, even at considerable personal cost

a lack of a coherent framework for family support

a consequent plethora of models of service and practice, with little in the way of clear roles and frameworks to build on

a lack of a clear conceptual and organisational model for advocacy development.

How then might we go forward? All the issues raised above suggest that the core problem is to develop first a coherent framework of family support services. This is neither a new nor a radical suggestion, but until families as a whole feel engaged and supported in the task of caring, then the prospects of developing advocacy will remain slim.

The existence of the developing Independent Parental Supporter framework in all LEAs could be the basis of such a service (as the Warnock Report suggested back in 1978!), but it would need to expand its brief to cover all aspects of the childhood disability network.

However, Dale's (1996) reservation about confusing family support with advocacy is a sensible one. If we are to meet the basic criteria of the Who Cares Trust, set out above, we must avoid incorporating advocacy within the wider brief of family support. Instead we should be looking to develop a network of disabled children's advocates, perhaps by extending the brief of existing children's rights schemes, or by extending the terms of reference of citizen advocacy schemes.

At the moment, the patchwork of incoherent services is working in no one's interest and advocacy remains a neglected dimension.

Note

1 Taken from the author's doctoral research programme 'Tuberous Sclerosis and Family Life' being conducted under the auspices of the School of Health and Social Welfare at the Open University.

References

Baldwin, S. and Carlisle, J. (1999) 'Living with disability: the experiences of parents and children.' In G. Allan (ed) *The Sociology of the Family*. Oxford: Blackwell.

Ball, D.W. (1970) 'The problematics of respectability.' In J.D. Douglas (ed) *Deviance and Respectability: The Social Construction of Moral Meanings*. New York and London: Basic Books.

Barnes, M. (1997) 'Families and empowerment.' In P. Ramcharan, G. Roberts, G. Grant and J. Borland (eds) *Empowerment in Everyday Life: Learning Disability*. London: Jessica Kingsley.

Barrett, M. and McIntosh, M. (1991) *The Anti-Social Family*. London: Verso.

Beresford, B. (1995) *Expert Opinions*. Bristol: Policy Press.

Beresford, B., Sloper, P., Baldwin, S. and Newman, T. (1996) *What Works in Services for Families with a Disabled Child?* Ilford: Barnardo's.

Brandon, D., Brandon, A. and Brandon, T. (1995) *Advocacy: Power to People with Disabilities*. Birmingham: Venture.

Brimblecombe, F. and Russell, P. (1988) *Honeylands: Developing a Service for Families with a Handicapped Child*. London: National Children's Bureau.

Burke, P. and Cigno, K. (1996) *Support for Families*. Aldershot: Avebury.

Corker, M. and Davis, J.M. (2000) 'Disabled children: (still) invisible under the law.' In J. Cooper (ed) *Law, Rights and Disability*. London: Jessica Kingsley.

Court Committee (1976) *Fit for the Future : Report of the Committee on Child Health Services (Court Report)* Cmnd 6684. London: HMSO.

Dale, N. (1996) *Working with Families of Children with Special Needs: Partnership and Practice*. London: Routledge.

Dalley, G. (1993) 'Familist ideology and possessive individualism.' In A. Beattie, M. Gott, L. Jones and M. Sidell (eds) *Health and Wellbeing*. London: MacMillan.

Department for Education and Employment (DfEE) (2001) *Draft Revised Code of Practice for the Identification and Assessment of Special Educational Need*. London: DfEE.

Furze, T. and Conrad, A. (1997) 'A review of parent partnership schemes.' In S. Wolfendale (ed) *Working with Parents of SEN Children after the Code of Practice*. London: David Fulton.

Garfinkel, H. (1967) *Studies in Ethnomethodology*. Englewood Cliffs, New Jersey: Prentice Hall.

Glendinning, C. (1986) *A Single Door*. London: Allen and Unwin.

Hatch, S. and Hinton, T. (1986) *Self-Help in Practice*, Social Work Monographs. Sheffield: Joint Unit for Social Work Support, University of Sheffield.

Hubert, J. (1991) *Home-Bound*. London: King's Fund Centre.

Kagan, C. (1995) *Agencies and Advocates: Experience in the North West*. Clitheroe: North West Training and Development Team.

Kerr, L., Sutherland, L. and Wilson, J (1994) *A Special Partnership*. Edinburgh: HMSO with Children in Scotland.

Mallett, R. (1997) 'A parental perspective on partnership.' In S. Wolfendale (ed) *Working with Parents of SEN Children after the Code of Practice*. London: David Fulton.

Marchant, R. (2001) 'The assessment of children with complex needs.' In J. Howarth (ed) *The Child's World*. London: Jessica Kingsley.

Mukherjee, S., Beresford, B. and Sloper, P. (1999) *Unlocking Key Working*. Bristol: Policy Press.

Nolan, M., Grant, G. and Keady, J. (1996) *Understanding Family Care*. Buckingham: Open University Press.

Paige-Smith, A. (1997) 'The rise and impact of the parental lobby: including voluntary groups and the education of children with learning difficulties or disabilities.' In S. Wolfendale (ed) *Working with Parents of SEN Children after the Code of Practice*. London: David Fulton.

Philp, M. and Duckworth, D. (1982) *Children with Disabilities and their Families*. Windsor: NFER-Nelson.

Read, J. and Clements, L. (2001) *Disabled Children and the Law: Research and Good Practice*. London: Jessica Kingsley.

Simmons, K. (1997) 'Supporting parents at the Special Educational Needs Tribunal.' In S. Wolfendale (ed) *Working with Parents of SEN Children after the Code of Practice*. London: David Fulton.

Sloper, P., Mukherjee, S., Beresford, B., Lightfoot, J. and Norris, P. (1999) *Real Change not Rhetoric*. Bristol: Policy Press.

Voysey, M. (1972) 'Impression management by parents with disabled children.' *Journal of Health and Social Behaviour 13*, 80–89.

Voysey, M. (1975) *A Constant Burden: The Reconstitution of Family Life*. London: Routledge and Kegan Paul.

Warnock Committee (1978) *Special Educational Needs: Report of the Committee of Enquiry into the Education of Handicapped Children and Young People*. (Warnock Report) Cmnd 7212. London: HMSO.

CHAPTER ELEVEN

Advocacy with People with Communication Difficulties

Janet Scott and Janet Larcher

Introduction

Advocating for someone who has significant limitations in their ability to communicate can present enormous challenges; it can also be very rewarding; what is not in question is that it is extremely important.

A communication difficulty is an invisible disability, resulting in its not being apparent until the person tries to speak. Each time the person tries to speak the listener is made aware of that individual's difference and limitations. A communication difficulty, by its very nature, may significantly interfere with how the individual is able to interact with people around them and with society at large, and, as such it can be very obtrusive (Goffman 1963). One of the greatest barriers facing people with significant communication difficulties is how they are perceived and valued by others.

The non-politically correct term 'dumb' originally meant 'non-speaking'; use of the term then spread to include people who appeared to have a degree of cognitive impairment or who were behaving in an unexpected or 'stupid' manner.

> my first memory was one of frustration, frustration with not being understood – and, because I was not understood, being treated differently – treated as if I was not intelligent or worse again treated as if I was stupid. (McFadden 1995, p.11)

Lack of speech is often seen as signifying a lack of intelligence, of rendering the person 'mentally incapable' (Jenkins 2000). People with a learning disability are already at risk of being 'stigmatised' and marginalised – having an additional

communication disability magnifies this risk many times over. Having a communication difficulty is likely to mean that the person has had even fewer opportunities to voice their opinions, to make choices and to be assertive than a person with
similar cognitive abilities but without this additional problem. When the person
is given the opportunity to make choices and decisions about their life – how do
we know that the choice is a real one and that the decision made is based on an
accurate knowledge and appreciation of the facts? Language and communication
are how we share our experience of the world around us with others. Without an
ability to express ourselves how can other people understand our own particular
view, how can our misapprehensions be understood?

In a recent discussion about independent living options with a young woman
with cerebral palsy, one of the authors was surprised to find that the young
woman thought that able-bodied people regularly went to the cinema several
times a week. At the start of the conversation the young woman indicated that she
did not feel that she would want to be able to go to the cinema. However, more
than an hour into the general discussion, she suggested that maybe she would like
to be able to go – but only two or three times a week, not every day! This young
person had spent all her life living in segregated accommodation, children's
homes and hostels for people with disabilities. She had little experience of
growing up in a family context, of taking part in 'normal' social activities. The
discussion about independent living options and the hiring of personal assistants
had been based (wrongly) on the expectation of a shared understanding about
what someone might want to do in their spare time. She uses a highly sophisticated electronic communication aid very effectively and so was able to show her
misconception of 'normal' life. Without that means of communication how
would the conversation have progressed? Decisions and choices made might have
been based on a false understanding of what might be possible, of what might be
desirable.

Advocacy can have a significant role to play in empowering people with
communication problems. To be an effective advocate for someone with communication difficulties it is important for the advocate to know about the different
types and degrees of communication difficulty, the impact these might have on
the person and the resultant effect on that individual's communication partners.
The advocate will need to be aware of, and to develop skills in, different techniques used to augment and facilitate non-speech communication – and to know
how to access more specialist help and advice.

The focus of this chapter is to provide the reader with an insight into the
world of communication disability and how it might impact on the advocacy

process, highlighting the challenges posed as well as illustrating some of the very positive benefits. Practical suggestions and possible methods for developing a means of communication will be discussed. Sources of further information on this topic are also provided.

Communication and advocacy

Communication – being able to understand each other, at least to some extent – is the basis for being an advocate. Highlighting the need for advocacy services not to exclude those individuals with the most profound disabilities, Jackson (1999) has argued that it is possible to represent people and defend their rights, even if that individual is unable to communicate their wishes independently. While agreeing with that position, we would argue that there is a need for the advocate to try and establish a channel of communication between him or herself and the person for whom they are advocating. Communication is possible even in the most extreme of situations. 'If it's important, you'll find a way to tell me, and I'll find a way to understand' (Hulme 1983, p.71). However, it can take a long time to develop an effective communication partnership, it takes time to develop an ability to be aware of and understand 'unusual' communication modes, the rate of communication exchange itself is likely to be slower than between two speaking people. As Jackson (1999) points out, time is not a commodity that is usually found in abundance in advocacy services. However, to be an effective advocate for someone with a communication difficulty, it is important to try to find that time. It is important not to use a lack of time as an excuse for inaction.

Meaning of communication?

In the twenty-first century the term 'communication' has many different meanings. At its most basic communication can be seen as a two-way process involving a transmitter and a receiver. In the current context communication is interpersonal, between two or more people, and involving someone in a 'speaking' and at least one person in a 'listening' role. In a traditional conversation the person speaking is actually doing just that – using primarily spoken language to express him or herself. The person listening (the communication partner) is as important as the person speaking. Both are responsible for making the conversation successful.

Communication is more than just speech. We communicate with each other in many different ways, facial expression, gesture, touch, and body posture for example. We usually use a range of these non-verbal communication modes as well as speech. Sometimes these non-verbal communications can reflect more accurately what the person is trying (or trying not!) to say. For full communication to happen these non-verbal signals need to be noticed and understood.

Communication can be fleeting or long-lasting, it can be face to face or over a long distance, private or public. As well as using speech we can also use other communication tools, the telephone, email, fax, pen and paper, tape/video recorder, photographs, painting, sculpture, and so on, to express ourselves and to get our meaning across. Again, the power of the communication is totally dependent on the ability of the receiver to understand the medium.

We usually take the ability to communicate for granted; most people are not aware of the complexity of the process until something goes wrong. If there is a problem with one half of the process, then there is likely to be a breakdown in communication. When talking with a person who has a significant limitation in their communication ability there is more onus on the communication partner to play an active role in maintaining and extending the conversation. Instead of simply *listening* the communication partner has to use a technique of *active* listening – interpreting every movement, gesture and vocalisation, and giving these meaning. 'Is his face really that easy to read, or am I just looking harder because he can't talk?' (Hulme 1983, p.21). The meaning of the interaction has to be jointly co-constructed between the speaker and the listener.

Meaning of communication difficulty?

A 'communication difficulty' is not a discrete entity – there are degrees of difficulty, elements of the communication process can be affected differently in different individuals, reaction to having a communication difficulty is different from person to person. For a particular individual, their communication difficulty may be restricted to certain situations and/or types of people. Perhaps their family and close friends have little difficulty understanding their speech, the main problem being when they are required to talk to people unused to how they pronounce certain sounds, or who are not prepared to wait while they get out the words they want to say. Alternatively the person with the communication difficulty may have no speech at all; they may understand most of what is said to them but have no ability to communicate independently. People who know them well may be able to interpret some facial expressions and body movements, but they are highly dependent on what other people think they are trying to communicate. Some people may use disruptive and 'challenging' behaviours as their main means of communication – for someone with profound cognitive limitations, dual sensory impairment and a physical impairment for instance, spitting, scratching, screaming or head banging may be the only way they have to express unhappiness, to call for attention, to escape from a situation, and so on.

The American Speech-Language-Hearing Association (ASHA) describes an individual as having a 'severe communication disorder' when their 'gestural, speech, and/or written communication is temporarily or permanently inadequate to meet all of their communication needs' (ASHA 1991, p.10). This definition allows the person to have a limited amount of speech, but which is inadequate to meet their varied communication needs. People with a severe communication disorder may have congenital or developmental disabilities, such as those associated with a learning disability, autism or cerebral palsy, or may have an acquired disability, following a stroke or head injury, or as a result of motor neurone disease for instance. Just as communication involves more than just the speaking partner, so a severe communication disorder may involve not only the person's ability to make themselves understood via speech but also their ability to understand what others are saying. This may be especially true if the severe communication impairment is associated with a learning disability, where the individual has a limitation not just with the motor (or physical) process of articulating/speaking but also with linguistic aspects.

What would it be like to have a significant communication difficulty?

People who are able to speak relatively easily have little idea what it must be like to be someone with a severe communication difficulty.

The nearest comparison, perhaps, is to imagine how you might feel living in a country where you do not speak the language. You may have problems understanding what people are saying to you, you may not be able to ask for things, explain things, let other people know what you are thinking – how would you feel?

Some people who have significant limitations in their spoken communication skills may use special techniques and/or technologies to supplement their spontaneous attempts at communication. These techniques and technologies are referred to as Augmentative and Alternative Communication (AAC).

Augmentative and alternative communication

Augmentative and Alternative Communication is the term used to describe methods of communication which can be used to supplement the more usual methods of speech and writing when these are impaired. The idea behind AAC is to use the person's abilities, whatever they are, to compensate for their difficulties and to make communication as quick, simple and effective as possible when speech alone does not work. Although we all use aspects of AAC from time to time, e.g. waving goodbye instead of saying it, pointing to a picture or gesturing to make yourself understood in a foreign country, some people rely on AAC all of the time.

What does AAC include?

AAC is a whole range of different activities – there is not just one type of AAC. AAC includes facial expression, eye pointing, gesture, signing, graphic symbols, spelling out a message on a letter board or computer, electronic speech output aids, and so on.

AAC includes four interlinking strands (Royal College of Speech and Language Therapists (RCSLT) 1996). Having an awareness of these different aspects of AAC is important when communicating with someone with a significant communication difficulty as it helps to clarify the processes involved.

THE COMMUNICATION MEDIUM

Basically this refers to the method of information transfer. This can be 'unaided', where nothing other than the person's body is used to convey the message. Speech is an unaided form of communication, as are gesture, body posture and facial expression. Examples of unaided forms of AAC are Makaton™ and Sign Along™ signing systems, as well as individualised methods such as blinking once for 'yes', twice for 'no', and so on. The communication medium can also be 'aided', involving the use of additional equipment; writing a letter is a mainstream example of aided communication. Aided methods of AAC may be low-tech or high-tech. Both low- and high-tech systems can be used by people who are unable to spell or read, as well as by people who are highly literate.

Low-tech communication systems may take many forms and are basically anything you can use which does not need a battery to function. Low-tech communication systems include a pen and paper to write messages, alphabet charts, charts and books with picture symbols or photos, and tangible symbols. High-tech communication systems are devices requiring at least a battery to operate. High-tech communication systems range from simple high-tech (e.g. single message devices; pointer boards; toys or books which speak when touched, and so on) to very sophisticated systems (e.g. specialised computers and programs, electronic aids which speak and/or print).

Most people who use AAC use a combination of unaided and aided methods. 'Low'-tech does not necessarily imply a simpler, more basic communication system. Low-tech communication systems can be just as sophisticated and flexible as many high-tech systems – for some people and in some situations low-tech systems can be more functional. With a low-tech communication system the balance of communication can be more evenly shared between both partners – both are actively involved in working at the meaning of the message. Electronic communication aids put more of the communication responsibility on the shoulders of the person using the system; their meaning tends to be taken more literally. For instance, if someone points to a picture of a television using this as a clue to what they want to convey, the communication partner is left to guess the accurate meaning: 'Do you want to watch TV?'; 'Did you watch TV last night?'; 'Do you want to talk about a TV programme?'; and so on. However if the person is using a high-tech aid and transmits a pre-programmed message: 'I want to watch TV', then the listener is likely to take that as the intended meaning rather than realise that it may be only a clue. Many people using communication aids with pre-programmed messages will not have access to everything they might want to say – they may well use existing phrases to clue the listener in to what they actually are meaning. However, the power of speech is such that the listener is more likely to assume that the speaker means what they are saying if the message is conveyed by a spoken phrase than if it is merely indicated by pointing to a picture or spoken word

A MEANS OF ACCESS TO THE COMMUNICATION MEDIUM

Many people who use AAC have severe physical disabilities. The physical act of speaking involves the complex interplay of various groups of muscles in the tongue, larynx, diaphragm, and so on. People using AAC need to use different physical processes to access (or control) their communication medium. Use of a signing, gestural system of communication requires a degree of fine motor control and manual dexterity. People using aided methods of AAC will require different physical skills. There are two main methods of 'accessing' an aided AAC system: *direct* and *indirect* selection. Direct selection is the most obvious method and one that is the easiest for people unfamiliar with AAC to understand. We are all familiar with this method of access – pointing at a picture, or touching the keyboard to type out a message or to dial a telephone number. Some people who need to use an AAC system to communicate may have enough physical ability to use this direct form of access. Others may be able to point or to type using a differ- ent part of their bodies, e.g. a fist instead of a finger, using their toes to point, or maybe using a technique called eye pointing. For computers and some high-tech communication aids there are also a range of different 'pointing devices' which some people can use, such as tracker/roller balls or infrared pointing devices such as HeadMouse™. Indirect access methods such as scanning with a switch may be the best option for some people with very severe physical limitations as well as a communication difficulty. The user needs to be able to activate either a single switch or a number of switches connected to the communication aid or computer. The person selects what he or she wants to say by activating the switch to control a moving cursor on the screen. Scanning is a difficult skill to learn and most people are not able to use their communication aid or computer immediately without having a period of training and practice. Switch users have to learn when to press the switch, when to release it, what to do if they make a wrong selection, and so on.

A SYSTEM OF REPRESENTING MEANING

When people speak or write, the words used act as symbols, meaning is represented by the written or spoken word. For instance, if you see the sign EXIT above a door, you know that you are allowed to leave by that door; if someone says, 'I've just bought a new car', you have a picture in your head of a shining new car: something you sit in, something which usually has four wheels, something made of metal and something which will be expensive to keep going! People who are unable to speak (or whose speech is not sufficiently clear to be generally understandable), who are not able to use words in a traditional sense, need some other symbol system to get their message across. Some people with a severe speech and communication difficulty may be able to use spelling and the written word as a means of self-expression, however there are many for whom that may not be a reliable or feasible option. There are a number of different symbol systems available, some are graphic (i.e. drawn two-dimensionally), others are gestural or based on hand movements and shapes, and others make use of three-dimensional objects. Each symbol system has its own strengths and weaknesses (see section on symbol systems). Choice of one particular symbol system over another should be based on the needs and abilities of the potential user. The importance of providing someone with a severe communication difficulty with an alternative system for representing meaning should never be underestimated. Several years ago, one of the authors was teaching a young man a basic vocabulary of pictorial (graphic) symbols. She was confused by the man's consistent selection of the symbol for 'wheelchair' when asked to find the symbol for himself, while at the same time being able to identify the symbol for 'woman' for her, the symbol for 'man' for his brother, the symbol for 'dog', and so on. Listening to the language used in this young man's environment made everything clear. He was used to hearing phrases such as: 'Line the wheelchairs up by the door', 'The wheelchairs go in the bus first' or even 'The wheelchairs have their lunch first. They take longer to eat.' Despite taking many photographs of him out of his wheelchair, photographs of wheelchairs with no one sitting in them, pictures of other people sitting in wheelchairs, and so on, working on his own identity apart from that of him associated with his wheelchair, there was still confusion and doubt in his mind. Over the years he had developed an idiosyncratic meaning reference to both the spoken word 'wheelchair' and, by association, its graphic symbol. This association did not seem to be negative in his mind – just different. However it was only when he was provided with a symbolic system for expressing himself, for communicating his view of the world, that anyone else could appreciate what he was thinking. No two people's life experiences are the same, however some people's experiences are very different. Not being able to move around independently, never having had the opportunity to ask questions in a way that other people could understand, never having had a chance to have your confusions clarified – is likely to give you a very different view of the world. When talking with someone who has significant communication difficulties it is always important to try and ensure that both parties are working from some degree of common understanding, it is important not to assume that we all mean the same by the words (and other symbols) we use. This is especially so in an advocacy role where the advocate is required to represent the interests of another person, as if they were their own (Wolfensberger 1975).

STRATEGIES FOR INTERACTING

Having a conversation is a balancing act; both parties are involved in keeping it going, usually the 'control' of the interaction is shared fairly evenly, silences or gaps in the conversation tend to be kept to a minimum as these are regarded rather negatively in western culture. People who are able to speak relatively easily learn from a very early age about taking turns in a conversation, how to interrupt, how to ask a question, how to start up a conversation and how to close it. The experience of talking can be very different for someone who is using AAC: they may not have had the same opportunities for learning the communication interaction skills in childhood; they may not be used to people giving them a chance to speak; they may be unsure of how to say what they want to say using their AAC system. Because of the differences between AAC and vocal spoken communication, different skills are required to maintain a conversation. Conversations are usually much slower; people using AAC take longer, in general, to initiate a communication attempt, their rate of message production is usually slower and it can take longer for the communication partner to understand what is being communicated. Both parties need to learn how best to accommodate this slower rate of communication. For instance, the person using AAC might find it helpful to have a pre-stored message explaining this and suggesting what the communication partner should do, e.g. 'It will take me some time to answer, please just wait' or 'I know I can take a long time to say things, if you think you can guess what I am trying to say before I am finished, I don't mind if you guess – as long as you check with me that you are guessing correctly!' Communication partners of people using AAC need to learn to take things more slowly than usual: allowing a gap of at least 10 seconds between questions or comments gives the person using AAC a chance to respond. Misunderstandings are much more common – it is important that the person using AAC knows how to indicate to their communication partner when they have not been understood correctly, communication partners need to be alert to misunderstandings and to be aware of techniques to try and repair the communication breakdown. Murphy and Scott (1995) highlight a range of communication strategies relevant to both parties in AAC conversations.

Symbol systems
USING OBJECTS

Real objects can be used to encourage people to choose, e.g. holding up a bottle of Cola and a bottle of orange to give someone a choice of drink. Objects can be used to let an individual know what is going to happen, e.g. letting someone feel the swimming costume before putting it in a bag might let that person know that he or she was going swimming. Objects used in this way are sometimes called 'objects of reference' or 'tangible symbols' (Rowland and Schweigert 2000). If you are using objects of reference as a means of communication you need to think about how that object will make sense to the person you are using it with. If you are not able to see, a toy car bears little resemblance to the experience of going in a car – if you cannot see that the toy car is a miniaturised version of the real thing it will be meaningless as an object of reference. It does not feel like a real car, it does not sound like one, smell like one, or feel like it does when you are motoring along. It would be better to use some other aspect of the real car as the object of reference e.g. a piece of material which feels similar to the car seat or to the seat belt, or maybe to use a car key as the signifier. You will have to teach the person that these objects have a meaning e.g. that they are going for a ride in the car.

USING PHOTOGRAPHS

Photographs can also be used in a symbolic manner; they can be used as 'tangible symbols'. Photographs can be used in exactly the same way as objects of reference: to let the individual know what is going to happen, to let them choose what they want to do, to let them tell you something. You might start with giving the person a choice of two photographs, and gradually increase the number available for choosing between.

GRAPHIC SYMBOLS

We see examples of graphic symbols all around us everyday. Traffic signs are examples of pictorial symbols – some are more obvious and more pictorial than others are – but they all convey a message visually. At airports there are symbols to show you where the departure and arrival gates are, public toilets usually have a picture of a man or a woman on the door to let you know which one you should go into and so on. In the field of communication disability, there are a number of graphic symbol systems in common use in the UK. The most frequently used are Picture Communication Symbols™ (PCS™), Rebus™, Makaton Symbols™ and Blissymbols™. There are also some graphic symbol systems associated with specific high-tech communication aids, e.g. Minsymbols™ and Dynasyms™. Some symbols systems are more pictorial than others are. However, abstract language is always difficult to convey in a pictorial way – how can you draw 'through', 'tomorrow' or 'wan', and so on ? Some of the more pictorial symbols have a lot of detail which can be distracting for some people. Every symbol system has to be *taught* to its users.

SIGNING SYSTEMS

Signing (like speaking) is an unaided form of communication in that it does not need the communicator to use another object or piece of equipment to get their message across. It can therefore be a very spontaneous and immediate form of communication. Of all the forms of AAC it is the most like speech – you do not have to communicate via an aid. The main difficulty with signing and gesture systems is that everybody has to learn the system. If an individual tries to communicate through signs and gestures to people who do not know the system then they are not likely to be very successful, as their communication partners possibly will not understand them. For someone to learn to communicate by signing and to value it as a method of communication everybody in his or her environment needs to sign for at least part of the time.

A word of caution: AAC alone is not the magic answer!

Although AAC has the potential to allow the person to say what they want, when they want to, by itself it does not necessarily improve communication. People using AAC are much more dependent on their communication partners' reaction to and acceptance of their communication method than someone who is able to speak. Talking with someone who uses AAC is different for the listener than talking with someone who is able to speak naturally. The person using AAC is likely to be 'speaking' much more slowly, they may use a synthesised voice which might take the listener some time to tune in to, they might not be speaking in the traditional sense at all – they might need the listener to read what they are pointing to on a chart or a screen.

AAC is a method of compensating for an inherent disability, it is not a cure. Communication ability is intertwined with a person's underlying cognitive and linguistic skills – these are not altered by the provision of an AAC system. If someone has nothing to talk about, perhaps because their experience of life has been very impoverished, simply giving them an AAC system will not improve this – they will still have nothing to talk about! If given sufficient support, AAC can enable a person to communicate up to his or her inherent potential. Different AAC systems are required to meet people's different abilities and needs.

The individual's method of augmenting their natural communication may not be adequate for all situations. Balandin (2000) suggests that AAC systems which support communication in the everyday environment may not be sufficient for the very specific communication requirements presented by more formal, legal type processes. Relevant vocabulary may be missing from the person's communication aid, either low-tech or high-tech. Murphy *et al.* (1996) found that even users of quite sophisticated AAC systems did not have the appropriate vocabulary available to allow them to open and close a conversation. How much less likely are they to have the vocabulary at their disposal to say what they feel about changing where they live, to interview care staff, to make a complaint about how they have been treated? The stressful nature of more formal situations such as attending a review meeting, going for a job interview or reporting an incident to the police, may result in the individual not being able to provide the necessary information even though they have the relevant vocabulary at their disposal. They may find it more difficult than usual to physically control or to access their communication system, and may fatigue rapidly in a highly stressed situation. Factors specific to many AAC conversations such as the active involvement of the communication partner to co-construct meaning and rate of message production may not be acceptable in a formal situation, especially where there are legal implications. How independent is the communication?

There is a common misconception that simply providing people with a symbol system will make communication possible. However, to the uninitiated, pictorial graphic symbols can be just as confusing as the spoken or written word. Look at Figure 11.1 showing six Picture Communication Symbols™, and try to work out what you think they mean.

Figure 11.1 Symbols without accompanying text

(Picture Communication Symbols, 1981–2000, Mayer-Johnson Co., PO Box 1579, Solana Beach, CA 92075, USA)

Now turn to Figure 11.2 at the end of this chapter – how many did you get correct?

We usually see symbols with the meaning written above them. Because we are able to read the accompanying text and can therefore see what the symbol is representing, we assume that the pictorial symbols themselves are equally obvious. What is important to remember is that the person that we are likely to use these symbols with may well have problems reading and understanding the text. For them trying to work out the symbol's meaning may be guesswork and chance.

Techniques for developing a means of communication
IDENTIFYING HOW THE INDIVIDUAL INDICATES YES AND NO

This may seem very obvious but is often overlooked. Some people may have very idiosyncratic methods of indicating 'yes' and 'no', others may have no clear method at all. If it is unclear, then a direct approach is required! Say to the person: 'Show me how you say yes', 'Show me how you say no', negotiate an agreed yes/no response which is as clear and unambiguous as possible. Identifying a yes/no response is the most basic communication strategy. If a person can indicate 'yes' and 'no' reliably they can answer carefully phrased questions. In interview type situations the emphasis is usually on open questions rather than closed 'yes/no' type questions. However the use of open questions relies on the other person having the means to respond. Some people with a significant communication problem will not have the communication skills or the means available to give a more full response. If using 'yes/no' questions, however, it is important to ensure that the questions are as unbiased and as 'free' as possible. Often 'yes/no' questions are used for confirmation or denial of an assumed fact, e.g. 'You want to move into your own home, don't you?' rather than 'Do you want to move into your own home?' The 'do you?' and 'don't you?' tags are a clue that the question is weighted; their use is liable to result in acquiescence.

USE OF VISUAL REFERENTS

People who find abstract concepts difficult to understand, or who have problems remembering things find having some visual referent very useful. The nature of the referent will be dependent on the needs and abilities of the individual, as well as the nature and topic of the item being referred to. Time is an abstract concept, for example, and one that many people find hard to understand. Simply drawing a time line featuring events important to the individual may be all that is required. 'Waiting' (for something to happen, and so on) can also be difficult to grasp – a 'short wait' might be depicted as a drawing of a single clock or egg timer, a 'long wait' as perhaps five clocks or egg timers. The meaning behind these drawings will need to be explained, but having something visual does help. Sometimes it can be useful to remove, or cover the symbols or pictures from the time line as the waiting progresses – similar to an Advent calendar. If the person is familiar with a graphic symbol system such as Makaton Symbols™ or PCS™, then these should be used. Computer programs are available which can produce text and symbols simultaneously, which can then be printed. These programs need to be used judiciously – symbolising every word on a page of text will *not* make that text easier to read. Using symbols to highlight the key elements of the message, however, *can* be a very useful technique – provided that the individual is familiar with the symbols used. Photographs, video and audio recordings can be very powerful. Remnants – a cinema ticket, a shell from a visit to the beach, a birthday card, and so on – can be useful memory joggers and provide a focus for conversation. If the person is using objects of reference as a way of understanding the environment around them or as a means of making choices these same objects can be used in an advocacy context.

TALKING MATS

This is a specific technique of using graphic symbols to allow people to express their views. It is also a form of visual reference. The Talking Mats framework was developed by Murphy and has been widely used (Brown, Dendy and Murphy 2000; Cameron and Murphy 2001; Murphy 1998a, 1998b, 1999, 2000). Talking Mats can be used across ages and abilities. It seems to help people process concepts and separate the enmeshed strands of issues, as well as giving them time to consider and change their mind. The technique avoids direct confrontation and reduces the risk of acquiescence. Talking Mats is not an augmentative communication system in itself, but has been used frequently to supplement the person's existing communication system. People who have significant physical impairments find the Talking Mats approach easy to use.

FEEDBACK

It is important to provide the individual with feedback – to check that you have understood them correctly and to give both parties an opportunity to correct misunderstandings as they occur. Feedback may be in the form of a digital photograph of the person's Talking Mat, it may be a rephrasing for clarification of what the person has said using their AAC system, it may be echoing each word as the person points to symbols on a chart.

Where to go from here?

Advocating for someone with significant communication difficulties can be a challenge. It can be difficult to know what the person's wishes are, it can be more difficult to develop rapport and to establish a bond – however it is the authors' belief that it is precisely because of these difficulties that advocacy is important. It is vital that people with communication difficulties have the same opportunities to make choices and decisions about how they live and what they want to do. A general principle behind the Adults with Incapacity (Scotland) Act 2000 is that the wishes and feelings of the person should be taken into account 'so far as they can be ascertained by any means of communication, whether human or by mechanical aid (whether of an interpretative nature or otherwise) appropriate to the adult' (Scottish Executive 2000). Advocacy is seen as one means of helping people to express their views and to exercise to the full what capacity they have.

The aim of this chapter is to provide the reader with an overview of the implications of communication disability and to highlight the techniques available to overcome at least some of these difficulties. It is impossible to cover all aspects of communication impairment in a single chapter and to equip the reader with all the skills required to facilitate communication. Advocates should be aware of their own limitations and should know how to access additional help and support.

Many people with significant communication difficulties will be known to their local speech and language therapy service. Speech and language therapists know about communication impairment and would be able to give specific advice on how best to communicate with an individual, and whether or not AAC might be appropriate. They can be contacted through any local hospital or health centre. There are also specialist AAC assessment and resource centres throughout the UK. Contacts are provided in the Resources section near the end of this chapter.

Figure 11.2 Symbols with accompanying text

(*Picture Communication Symbols, 1981–2000, Mayer-Johnson Co., PO Box 1579, Solana Beach, CA 92075, USA*)

Resources
Training materials

Larcher, J., Dennett, G., Hunter, A., Jans, D., Masterson, G., Millar, S., Scott, J. and Warrington, M. (1998) *Speaking Up, Speaking Out: Pathways to Self Advocacy.* Oxford: Communication Matters.

This package consists of a handbook and a practical guide, and is aimed at anyone who works with, or supports, individuals with severe communication difficulties. It contains detailed information about advocacy and communicating with people with severe communication difficulties, including people who use AAC.

Murphy, J. and Scott, J. (1995) *Attitudes and Strategies towards AAC: A Training Package for AAC Users and Carers.* Stirling: University of Stirling.

This package provides a ready-to-use resource for training people who need to speak to individuals using AAC. It is workshop based and focuses on attitudes to AAC and strategies used in AAC conversations. The package enables AAC users to be directly involved in training other people how to communicate with them.

Murphy, J. and Scott, J. (1996) *Talking to People with Severe Communication Difficulties: An Introductory Training Video.* Stirling: University of Stirling.

This video has been designed specifically for care staff and others who have day-to-day contact with people who have severe communication disabilities – particularly those who use communication aids and other forms of AAC. It has been designed to be used either on its own or as part of an induction programme for new and existing staff.

Murphy, J. (1998) *Talking Mats: A Low-tech Framework to Help People with Severe Communication Difficulties Express their Views.* Stirling: University of Stirling.

Talking Mats is a framework which uses picture symbols to help people with severe communication difficulties communicate about particular issues relevant to them. It has potential for a wide range of people, both children and adults. It provides them with a means of expressing their views more easily.

Symbol software

BoardMaker™
Cambridge Adaptive Communication
8 Farmbrough Close
Stocklake
Aylesbury
Buckinghamshire HP20 1DQ

Clicker4™
Crick Software
35 Charter Gate
Quarry Park Close
Moulton Park
Northampton NN3 6QB

Writing with Symbols 2000™
Widgit Software Ltd
26 Queen Street
Cubbington
Leamington Spa CV32 7NA

Organisations

Communication Matters
c/o ACE Centre
92 Windmill Road
Headington
Oxford OX3 7DR
Tel: 01870 606 5463
Email: admin@communicationmatters.org.uk
Website: www.communicationmatters.org.uk

Communications Forum
Carnelford House
87–89 Albert Embankment
London SE1 7TP
Tel: 020 7582 9200
Website: www.communicationsforum.org.uk

Royal College of Speech and Language Therapists
2 White Hart Yard
London SE1 1NX
Tel: 020 7378 1200
Website: www.rcslt.org

References

American Speech-Language-Hearing Association (ASHA) (1991) 'Report: Augmentative and Alternative Communication', *ASHA 33* (suppl. 5), 9–12.

Balandin, S. (2000) 'Witnessing without words.' In T. Shaddock, M. Bond, I. Bowen and K. Hales (eds) *Intellectual Disability and the Law: Contemporary Australian Issues*, Monograph no. 1, 41–48. Callaghan, NSW: Australian Society for the Study of Intellectual Disability Inc., University of Newcastle Union.

Brown, L., Dendy, M. and Murphy, J. (2000) 'Respite review: obtaining the views of the users.' *Communication Matters 14*, 25–26.

Cameron, L. and Murphy, J. (2001) 'Views of young adults at the time of transition.' *Communication Matters 15*, 31–32.

Goffman, E. (1963) *Stigma: Notes on the Management of Spoiled Identity*. Harmondsworth: Penguin.

Hulme, K. (1983) *The Bone People*. London: Picador.

Jackson, R. (1999) 'Learning disability and advocacy: obstacles to client empowerment.' *Journal of Learning Disabilities for Nursing, Health and Social Care 3*, 50–55.

Jenkins, C. (2000) 'Mental incapacity: new millennium – new law?' *RCSLT Bulletin 573*, 15.

McFadden, D. (1995) 'AAC in the community: a personal viewpoint.' In S. Millar and A. Wilson (eds) *Widening the Perspective*. Edinburgh: CALL Centre.

Murphy, J. (1998a) 'Helping people with severe communication difficulties to express their views: a low-tech tool.' *Communication Matters 12*, 9–11.

Murphy, J. (1998b) 'Talking Mats: speech and language research in practice.' *Speech and Language Therapy in Practice* Autumn, 11–14.

Murphy, J. (1999) 'Enabling people with motor neurone disease to discuss their quality of life.' *Communication Matters 13*, 2–6.

Murphy, J. (2000) 'Enabling people with aphasia to discuss quality of life.' *British Journal of Therapy and Rehabilitation 7*, 454–457.

Murphy, J. and Scott, J. (1995) *Attitudes and Strategies towards AAC: A Training Package for AAC Users and Carers*. Stirling: University of Stirling.

Murphy, J., Markova, I., Collins, S. and Moodie, E. (1996) 'AAC systems: obstacles to effective use.' *European Journal of Disorders of Communication 31*, 31–44.

Rowland, C. and Schweigert, P. (2000) 'Tangible symbols, tangible outcomes.' *Augmentative and Alternative Communication 16*, 61–78.

Royal College of Speech and Language Therapists (RCSLT) (1996) *Communicating Quality 2: Professional Standards for Speech and Language Therapists*. London: RCSLT.

Scottish Executive (2000) *Adults with Incapacity (Scotland) Act 2000*. London: Stationery Office.

Wolfensberger, W. (1975) *Citizen Advocacy for the Handicapped, Impaired and Disadvantaged: An Overview*. Washington, DC: US Government Printing Office.

CHAPTER TWELVE

Some Observations on the American Advocacy Scene

Michael Kendrick

Introduction

The United States advocacy 'system' for persons with developmental disabilities (as they would use the term) is quite developed at the beginning of the twenty-first century, and offers many instructive strengths and challenges. The sheer scale and complexity of the US advocacy scene defies any brief and generalised treatment of it, so this chapter will deal only with some notable but selective overall strengths and some very instructive issues. The intent will be to draw out some of the more central issues that will help define the state of development of the advocacy sector in that nation in the years to come.

In this era, it is increasingly hard to treat any nation as distinct and apart from other nations, as we are all increasingly interconnected. Similarly, the ease of communication and contact between countries has helped underline and accentuate much of what is universal to all human activity. It is no different in regards to advocacy, in that issues in advocacy are remarkably similar from place to place. Thus, there needs to be caution about too easy generalisations concerning a nation as diverse and nuanced as the USA is. Still, the effort to capture the broad characteristics is valuable nonetheless.

The US advocacy scene for developmental disabilities covers a variety of advocacy 'types' such as citizen advocacy, legal advocacy, family advocacy, peer advocacy, individual and systems advocacy, advocacy coalitions, self-advocacy, voluntary advocacy membership associations, mandated state protection and advocacy programmes, grassroots insurgencies, and various hybrids of these main types. It functions at the local, regional, state and national level and roughly parallels the governmental and quasi-governmental authorities it monitors and watchdogs.

Brief description of some strengths of the US advocacy scene

Apparent cultural acceptance of advocacy as a social institution

Though it is always a matter of degree what is accepted by a culture as its own, it seems safe to say that the Americans have come to expect that there will be organised advocacy for persons with disabilities *and that this is a good thing*. This seems to be partly rooted in the American cultural and political ethos of rights, countervailing balances to public authority and the general propriety of self and collective freedom of expression.

It has also been helped by the increasing public recognition that living with a disability legitimately does bring with it many disadvantages that ought to be taken into consideration. On occasion after occasion, the public has witnessed the authorities conceding to these kinds of claims of disadvantage, discrimination, violation of rights and so forth. This has helped give to advocates the advantages of both precedence and standing. Were the public less tolerant of such claims it would undoubtedly make the task of advocating much more difficult.

What now gives advocacy its institutional status is its routine presence *vis-à-vis* existing authorities and processes associated with them such as the preparation of legislation, the conduct of legal processes, the management of services, access to the media, the ability to question professional conduct and so forth. In these and many other instances where matters affecting the well being of persons with disabilities are under consideration, it would now seem odd to most people that some measure of advocacy participation would not seem appropriate and fair. Thus, the public's value placed on fairness provides a cultural and legal basis for the legitimacy of advocacy.

Scale and diversity of advocacy types

As a matter of perspective, it is hard to imagine another nation, at the present moment, that has so extensively developed an advocacy 'infrastructure' quite as extensive as that of the USA. While the US system does have its biases towards particular advocacy types such as legal advocacy, especially class action litigation, it is nonetheless notable for the wide varieties of advocacy that have emerged. The scale of these is also significant, given that there are no regions of the nation that lack advocacy of various kinds, notwithstanding the remarkably non-uniform character of the interstate differences within the country.

The types of advocacy involved have already been mentioned, but what has not been highlighted is the extent to which these types of advocacy work together to create an overarching effect when they coalesce. An instructive example of this is the success the advocacy community has had in the past generation in establishing and expanding the enforcement of a right to inclusive education. This has involved persons with disabilities, families, legal advocates, voluntary advocacy organisations, citizen advocates, dissident professionals and their advocacy organisations and so on. What should not be lost is that each contributed to this outcome but from a quite different base.

In-depth experience with the conduct of advocacy

Given the scale and scope of advocacy within the USA, it is not surprising that there exists extensive opportunities for people to become quite proficient at the tasks involved. This is even truer when one considers that many of these advocacy entities have been in existence since the early 1970s. This is not meant to suggest that advocacy practice is all routinely of good quality, but rather to point out the general depth of experience that it is possible to amass with such a huge set of ongoing opportunities.

This depth is best appreciated not only from the perspective of the years of existence of the many advocacy programmes, but also from the dimension of the 50 or more states within which this experience has been gained. The matrix of these two facets of advocacy combines to give the field a tenure and breadth that is unmatched, at present, in terms of advocacy. There are larger countries, to be sure, than the USA, but there are none that has hosted an advocacy movement in this field for so long and covering so much ground. Conceivably the expanded European Union zone is comparable in size, but certainly has had a far less pronounced period of development of advocacy even when measured collectively.

Enduring and expanding affirmation of the rights and interests of persons with disabilities

If one took just the reductionist measure of the formalisation of rights into laws, codes, practices and entitlements as a kind of social indicator that the advocacy was having an effect, then the US advocacy scene has produced effects that are measurably in favour of the rights and interests of persons with disabilities.

It is also very obvious that the advancement of community prospects for persons with disabilities in favour of greater social inclusion and citizenship have been largely beneficial even using crude statistics like regular school attendance, persons leaving residential institutions, numbers of self-advocacy groups. The USA is no utopia in this regard but it does have 'on the ground' social statistics that are tangibly advantageous in terms of the broad well-being of persons with disabilities. It is also notable that this trend has not yet relented and therefore might be properly thought of as a reasonably enduring accomplishment.

Strong alliances across the political ideological spectrum

Though it would be tempting to credit only social progressives with solidarity with persons with disabilities, the actual reality in the USA is far from this stereotype. The advocacy community has been able to forge alliances along a broad spectrum of political and ideological constituencies from right to left. In fact, if one looks at indicators as to who supported the now well-known Americans with Disabilities Act, one can see prominent politicians from both the (dominant) Republican and Democratic parties.

It is also true that if one looks at the states that have eliminated their reliance on institutional care (and were in the vanguard of doing so), one sees states with both strong conservative bases (e.g. New Hampshire, Wisconsin, New Mexico, and so on) and states with more progressive electoral histories (e.g. Vermont, Rhode Island, Pennsylvania, and so on). In each case one would find that the advocacy groups in the state were integral to these outcomes, and thus provide an instructive benchmark for the capacity of advocates to work with both right- and left-leaning authorities to achieve their ends.

Establishment of recurrent and diverse funding sources for advocacy

Though it is common in many countries for there to be some dependable security of funding for advocacy from governments, it cannot be said that this is true for funds that come from other sources. The USA has been remarkable in its diversity of advocacy financing sources going beyond that of obtaining funds solely from public authorities. In fact, the advocacy community in the USA is rather opportunistic in having been able to acquire funds from such diverse sources as local, state and national fundraising, grants from foundations, corporate contributions, fees, memberships, donations, statutory allocations, damage awards, 'pro bono' or 'in kind' services and so on. These are also present in many countries but the sheer scale and diversity of these is worth pointing out.

This does not mean that people are universally well served by advocacy in the USA, but it does mean that the Americans have left few stones unturned in scouring the landscape to find ways to keep advocacy viable. It is also notable that they have gained in the process a measure of separation of advocacy functions from the state itself, thereby making more probable the holding of states to account for their conduct. This has been particularly noticeable in the domain of human services, bureaucracies and legislatures that are regularly held accountable by independent advocates. Again, this is not unique to the USA but it is neverthe-less an intrinsic accomplishment of their system.

Presence of strong local, state, regional and national networks of advocates

As has been indicated earlier, the US advocacy movements rarely operate solely on their own, and are quick to coalesce into formal and informal coalitions when their interests are met by doing so. This is greatly facilitated by the often unher-alded, but nonetheless effective networks of informal and formal personal contacts that exist throughout the advocacy world at local, state and national levels. The formal organisations of advocates do not reveal the web of personal relationships that lie behind the façade that these formal organisations present. This networking is not unique to the USA, but it is nevertheless an asset when it comes to any number of functions that prop up advocacy.

Through these networks comes practical help in locating talent, information, good examples, best practices, problem solving, funding, allies, concepts and so forth. On top of this would be all manner of emotional and moral supports of a collegial kind. If the scene operated in a more isolated manner, then these largely non-financial 'resources' would not be available to the advocacy world and it would be poorer for it. A further, and usually untabulated benefit, would be the consensus building function that such networking provides by way of crystallising emergent viewpoints as to the positions advocates 'ought' to take on many matters. When this works well it gives people courage, and when the message that is communicated is defeatist, it can breed depression and defeat.

A culture of learning

The US advocacy scene is sufficiently established and developed, to now involve thousands upon thousands of individuals both entering and leaving the scene. This is quite apart from the many who have stayed with it, often for a quarter century or more. This scale has created the need constantly to orient and reorient these vast numbers of people. Additionally, it has created a predictable need for people to disseminate all manner of breaking news and information in a nation that is as nearly as large internally as Europe is in its entirety. Despite these obstacles, the US advocacy scene, through a complex arrangement of conferences, networks, consultancies, technical assistance, evaluation, publications, bulletins, newsletters and seminars does a quite remarkable job of keeping people informed and alert to wherever the 'edge' may be.

A good example of this can be seen in the case of the National Association of Protection and Advocacy Systems. This umbrella group of state advocacy organisations provides one of the key national networks for advocacy in the USA. It has for years provided all of the above functions plus very targeted special training initiatives on various needs as they have arisen. This has been done as a largely 'private' and independent initiative even though considerable amounts of public funds have been sought and obtained to further this work. What may be remarkable about this continuing and almost 'routinised' investment in learning and education is that it is so 'built in' that it escapes observation as being the overall systemic advantage that it is. Were it to suddenly disappear overnight, it would be devastating to the productivity of advocacy. However, it is likely to be rather quickly reinvented and reinstalled given how reflexive the orientation to an infrastructure of ongoing learning is embedded in the culture of the advocacy world.

Some instructive issues within the US advocacy scene

Despite the preceding recitation of some of the virtues of the US advocacy scene, it would be very unwise to conclude that all is well. One just has to look at any number of the often-alarming statistics on the well being of people with disabilities to know that much remains to be done. If advocacy were effective as a potent counter to social devaluation and mistreatment, then more and enduring amounts of advocacy would be the appropriate remedy. However, things are rarely that simple and this is no exception. What follows here, is the presentation of a selection of several key issues that help capture some of the more prominent and important dilemmas of the US advocacy scene. Like any selection, it leaves out many matters that might well have been better to include. It is important to keep this in mind.

Limited sources of sufficiently independent funding for advocacy

The advocacy world has long noted that all money comes with strings attached to it, and that 'he who pays the piper plays the tune'. Advocates are well aware that their 'structural' independence is highly dependent on advocacy groups or individuals not placing themselves into worrisome conflicts of interest. One key source of such conflict may often be in the very funds that sustain the work. The crucial test is whether these funds bring with them any kind of inhibition about the kind of advocacy that could be attempted.

The principal sources of funding for US advocacy groups are funds that come directly from statutory mandates, those that come through class action litigation related mandates, those that come from purchase of service arrangements with government agencies, and those that come from 'private' sources such as fundraising, foundation grants, and even fees and settlements. The statutory sources are often the most independent, if viewed from the vantage point of the legitimacy of the advocacy, and the freedom to conduct the advocacy with governmental blessing. Nonetheless, the statutes creating such advocacy may contain within them various limitations on the advocacy group's activities that might make them ineligible for funds if these provisions are violated.

The classic examples of some of these are the tax related restrictions placed on not-for-profit organisations being involved in political lobbying, the various constraints on whom might be eligible for advocacy support and various requirements for reporting that may be in place. These sorts of restrictions do, nevertheless, underline whom it is that is calling the shots. On the whole, these constraints have not produced onerous burdens for the advocates and, in fact, have tended to insulate them from many political pressures, at least to some degree. This has resulted in legislated advocacy being able to combine a fair degree, though not absolute degree of independence, with ongoing sustainable funding. Even so, there is always the risk of defunding that lingers particularly if the advocacy is publicly divisive. There is also the risk of inadequate funding, and the possible conflicts that may be present if the agency doing the funding is also funding organisations that are targets of advocacy.

In the instance of class-action-related mandates to provide advocacy, the advocacy is usually available only to class members, only for the duration of the case, and possibly may contain other kinds of limitations. In this sense, it is a reasonably independent source of funding in that the funder, while still being the defendant, usually does not have the ability to limit the advocacy. This option to evade the demands of the advocates is usually forfeited by defendant systems via the mechanism of court supervised 'consent decrees' that typically authorise these.

Standing back from these kinds of cases, it is important to note that only a small percentage of persons with disabilities are actually benefited by such a specialised form of advocacy, given that such cases touch only a small number of people due to the narrowness of the legal 'classes' of recipients that are eligible. This is in contrast to the coverage involved in legislated advocacy, which is typically cast to enable a broad based wrong to be righted, thereby making advocacy much more widely available.

The third source of funding is where the funding agency 'buys' advocacy as being just another of the services it renders. Such arrangements are usually fraught with the most intense conflicts of interest because the same funder is typically also deeply in relationship with the various agencies, professionals and interests that the advocates are supposed to 'keep honest'. The advocates do indeed have to 'bite the hands that feed them', and are thus at risk constantly of alienating their funders and thus possibly undermining their future viability, quite apart from whatever damage is brought to their integrity.

The fourth source of funding is what might be called 'private'. This can, in theory, include sources of funds that are largely outside of governmental control, and thereby deliver to the advocates a degree of independence to pursue matters that are well beyond the bounds of the political constraint and discipline of majorities and consensus. One would think that such funds would be highly desirable, in that one is seemingly not constrained.

This appearance is quite illusory, if in order to obtain funds one has to stop doing advocacy for periods of time so that one's energies can go to fundraising. It is also a bit naive to imagine that the private sources of funding do not have their own politics and strings attached. For instance, foundations and donors have agendas that are every bit as demanding as that found in the public arena. The American 'United Way' funding organisations are a good example of this, in that while these are 'private', they are organisations with huge political pressures and interest groups to contend with.

More crucially, it is important to note that, while the USA comparatively relies more heavily than does other nations on private funds for advocacy, these account for only a minor element of available advocacy funding at a given point. Thus, advocacy 'coverage' in the USA is biased well towards public financing, with the bulk of it coming not from the more protected and independent legislated advocacy, but from less independent public sources.

The strategic significance of this pattern is obvious. Much of the advocacy that is undertaken in the USA, and that is done independently in the ethical sense, owes a measure of its capacity to do this to the good faith of legislators, and to a degree, public bureaucrats that essentially respect the need for advocacy to be independent. Were this to erode, as was witnessed in the USA, in the case of the legislated prohibitions placed on legal aid lawyers to pursue public litigation targets while receiving public monies, it becomes clear that securing more conflict free funding is strategically advantageous.

This issue has managed to evade much scrutiny up to the moment because the public, by and large, has supported much of the more prominent elements of the advocacy agenda for people with disabilities. This support should not be taken to be a permanent 'given', and thus much thought needs to be invested into what can be done to ensure that a ready supply of needed 'unrestricted' advocacy funding is available when the advocacy cause slips into the netherworld of being unpopular and unwelcome. This will be a solid test of whether the modest amount of independent funding available will really be sufficient to protect people.

Bias towards a reliance on 'paid' or professionalised advocacy

The US advocacy 'scene' is often thought by the people involved to be solely the organisations or professions that prominently conduct advocacy. Many of these are typically almost entirely reliant on the use of hired advocates. Consequently, if the funding were to disappear, so would the advocates, and possibly the organisations themselves. If this sort of eventuality did occur, it is certainly true that most formal advocacy would decline. This is a real limit of professionalised solutions, in that nothing is normally done unless it is paid for. Similarly, it inevitably sets as a 'given', the 'necessity' of placing all one's emphasis on professionals and organisations. In so doing, it relegates to a kind of invisibility other quite viable forms of advocacy.

However, the USA, going back even to the days of Alexis de Toqueville's astute observations of the character of American society and culture, has long enjoyed a rather robust tradition of partisan grass roots involvement and advocacy. This has involved many 'causes' including female suffrage, civil rights, prohibition, child welfare, environmental improvement and so forth. This 'popular' variety of advocacy is quite different in character to that of what we see today in formal 'paid' advocacy. Perhaps the most notable difference is that it relies most heavily on its membership for its fundamental sustenance, rather than 'funders'. This variety of advocacy is not quite the creature of its funding source that present-day advocacy programmes are. In this sense it is *voluntaristic* at its core. Commonly its organisational form is that of voluntary associations.

It is notable that virtually only a tiny percentage of advocacy funds are devoted to changing and inspiring *citizens* to rally around and stand up for their *fellow citizens* who are facing hardship and mistreatment. Advocacy of that type is much more one of building solidarity and social movements, more than it is being yet another bureaucratically supported 'representation' programme. Yet, the potential for social movements to advocate for and mobilise people can be prodigious. Its dynamism derives from its own distinct 'currency' of passion, commitment, inspiration and courage, all of which need constant propping up. Thus, it would be unwise to elevate this expression of advocacy to a panacea, even if it does offer a valid path that is *in addition to* the present bias towards advocacy being a new expert occupation in the service economy.

More important for the long term, would be the careful appraisal of whether the 'advocacy guild' that has established itself over the past generation, might be unwittingly undermining the possibility of citizens' movements of alliance and defence of person's with disabilities, even as it strengthens their interests in other ways. While there is much talk of 'community' and its place in people's lives as a goal for society as a whole, there seems scant attention to the possibility that advocacy might become a duty of ordinary citizens for each other. It is not surprising, therefore, that there is so little distinct advocacy component of this quite viable societal ethic.

In many ways 'paid' advocacy displaces unpaid citizen advocacy. This occurs because the ordinary citizen comes to believe that this is no longer an option for them, and ought to be undertaken by some sort of societal authority. This kind of attitude in turn convinces ordinary citizens that becoming an ally or defender of other people is something that they are not legitimately entitled to do. This, of course, undermines social solidarity and thus deprives 'at risk' groups of what might have been 'natural' allies. The balance is achieved in not permitting the quite valid task of representation to obscure the value and contribution of *personal* social and moral alliances. The more of these, the less that disadvantaged people are cast to the societal sidelines.

Ambiguity as to what is good advocacy

It is a bit of a paradox that, in a society with such an abundance of advocacy as the USA currently enjoys, there is so little said about worthy and unworthy forms of advocacy. While there is widespread agreement that people ought to have advocacy, the quality of it is either assumed to be adequate or at least acceptable, or it is perhaps seen as being of minor significance. Nonetheless, the quality of advocacy is an important issue, given that resources for it are always at a premium, and poor advocacy is in some ways 'wasted advocacy', if the person's or group's interests are not well served.

To be fair, it is not that there is no recognition of the issue of quality, or that people do not care about it. Rather, it has not been an issue that has resulted in any major national initiatives *of a sustained character* to pin down the essential substance of the subject. The interest in the question has tended to be episodic. There does exist, within some advocacy circles, a measure of peer review, some worthy advocacy principles, and even a tradition of external and quasi-external evaluation. For instance, in citizen advocacy circles, there are several evaluation tools in use to assess the quality of programmes, and a long history of independent external teams carrying these evaluations out. At the same time, the overarching ideological principles that might serve as a broad basis of consensus to guide the entirety of the advocacy world remain to be charted and agreed upon.

This may be the result of pragmatism, in that the quality of advocacy must come behind the issue of simply getting access to advocacy for most people. Nevertheless, it is a curious lapse that the very people, who most criticise others for the lack of quality of their efforts, are so coy when it comes to appraising their own. It may also reflect a certain intellectual and reflective incapacity in the institution of the advocacy world itself. By this it is meant that its own internal institutional interests are not well served by too much scrutiny of the quality question.

Attention to quality might predictably arise in the context of criticisms of the advocacy world, and it is understandable that this is not always welcomed, at least in the more public dimensions of the advocacy world's existence. This omission, of a fuller and more prominent attack on the definition of advocacy quality, is regrettable given the richness of the advocacy experience available to draw upon. It should not be equated with a failure to achieve quality in practice, nor should it be taken as being indifference. The notable feature is the apparent reluctance to advance the waiting debate as to what is optimal advocacy.

Actual effectiveness of advocacy priorities

It is of paramount importance that advocacy be effective. As was taken up in the comments on quality, advocacy should be judged by the extent to which it benefits those it claims to aid. Yet if this standard were used with some measure of rigour, a key question would be why so many things can occur in American society that are largely unchallenged by advocates for long period of times.

A good example of this would be the very quiet and largely hidden build up of nursing homes as a kind of back door or alternative to the public institutionalisation of people. It was not until the very late 1990s that this issue resulted in a major (albeit still symbolic) challenge to government practice with the *Roland v. Celluci* consent decree in Massachusetts. By contrast, during the 1980–2000 period, there were innumerable actions of all kinds to limit public institutions, while private ones largely, though not entirely, escaped notice.

What instances like this reveal, is the underlying difficulty facing all advocacy initiatives, of having to settle on priorities. In the process, it becomes quite possible for advocates to 'succeed', only if particular measures of success are used. In the example just given, the advocates had succeeded impressively in achieving an overall decline in the use of public institutions. However, some of this was achieved, paradoxically, by ignoring other transgressions against people with disabilities such as their placement into nursing homes, either in lieu of public institutionalisation, or as a consequence or component of public deinstitutionalisation.

Also noticeable, in the example of the public institutions, is the widespread practice of advocates agreeing to community placements of people out of public institutions, that amount to the creation of the next generation of mini-institutions. While all this is done with the best of intentions to help people be part of their communities, it is also undeniable that we have seen this become the creation of the next generation of target programmes for concerned advocates, i.e. inferior or dated community services. This is all too evident when one looks at the huge numbers of people being (curiously involuntarily) placed in them. Whether these mini-institutions come in standardised packages of three, four, eight or whatever amount of persons, misses the point. The point is, is this really what is desirable from advocacy and its priorities? Put another way – are the priorities the right ones?

Challenge of ideological vision

Ideology is in many ways a kind of quagmire for advocates. Questions of ideology invariably shape the assumptions of what advocates believe they should aim for. This foray into ideology takes them well out of the more instrumental questions of winning or losing, to the more prior metaphysical and values matters that underlie the struggle itself. Nonetheless, human well-being and its defence, cannot be taken up without addressing values and affirming or denying their importance.

Advocacy as a kind of civil function is one thing, but the direction that it should take is rarely as easily camouflaged in a kind of utilitarian pragmatism. One of the core dilemmas facing advocates, and the advocacy community overall, is the specifics of the vision that is to be advocated for in the coming years. In this, the American advocacy scene faces quite predictable challenges in terms of settling on some sort of ideological consensus. It faces these large questions from within a period in which there is not anything approaching a unifying vision of what life *should be like* for people with disabilities within American society.

The now somewhat receding debate concerning the fate of public institutions, and the access of people to community, has had to gradually give way to highly specific matters concerning the quality of community life, as it is within the community that most lives are now lived. However, this has opened up a predictable range of views as to what a good life in the community could look like. With the disappearance – perhaps only temporarily – of the institutions there no longer exists quite the same unifying ideological convenience that this concern has provided the advocacy community for these past few decades.

There are many rival ideological successors to the 'community living' consensus. These typically arise from the emphasis being placed on one or another aspect of personal well-being. This would include common aspects of life such as social inclusion, self-determination, personal relationships, home ownership, employment, individualisation and so forth. Sometimes, these get translated and distilled into a preference for particular practices such as person-centred planning, supportive living, individualized funding and so on. In some cases, these practices and the *idée fixe* ideological 'fragments' they derive their authority from, serve as a kind of rudimentary answer to, the question of vision.

A closer and more indepth examination of these ideological 'fragments', typically reveals that there is very little by way of a cogent overall theory guiding them, that would serve as an enduring base for some sort of ideological unity amongst advocates. This gap, while innocent enough at the level of the apparent goals held up for people's lives, is much more worrisome when examined from the point of view of actual social policy and operational practice. For instance, person centred planning is hardly an antidote to political disadvantage, supportive living can easily distort into social abandonment, and 'choice' has transparently been used to justify the most appalling of outcomes for people. Many seem to think of individualised funding as constituting some sort of deliverance and place all their hopes on it. Even a casual examination of how these notions actually get implemented would show that this is no panacea.

Obviously, much more explicit and compelling theory is needed if the field is not to confuse these relatively superficial pieties with the (let us hope) rigorous conceptual and theoretical roadmap it needs to assure that life in the community lives up to its promise. This is most evident in the relatively poor progress that has been achieved with social inclusion. Despite decades of the promotion of this goal, it is striking how little attention has been given to what actually makes the most difference by way of achieving this goal. It hardly seems surprising that progress has been muted given that the state of the underlying theory of 'social inclusion' is so primitive.

This is not intended to be taken as a quarrel with the goal of 'social inclusion', so much as it is a suggestion that remaining fixated on trumpeting the goal, while leaving the means amorphous, does not pass muster as either good theory or a sound guide to social policy. For advocates, there is not much choice but to enter the quagmire of relevant values, ideology and theory, as it is in these realms that the key questions of vision will eventually be resolved.

Leadership

It is inevitable to wonder whether the US advocacy scene will pass its perhaps most strenuous and possibly historically most significant test of its relevance. This concern centres on whether it will serve as a decisive catalyst for positive change by being a key force in ensuring that conditions on the ground either improve or decline. This is a societal question, in that a catalyst cannot mobilise what the populace does not possess. Nevertheless, if capacity intrinsically exists within the US population and culture for some measure of moral, social and political advancement, then it is realistic to ask whether the advocates have heightened this tendency or not. Naturally, all such matters seem clearer when looking backward. However, looking forward it is a much more difficult question, since one faces a plethora of potentials that have not as yet been discounted by events.

It is with such a question that the distinction between informal and formal advocacy becomes important. If one looks at the state of affairs in what might be thought of as 'institutionalised' or largely funded formal advocacy, one is hard pressed to identify it as a sufficient force of radicalism, at least in recent decades. While it has, as a collective institution, progressive leanings, it has largely acted to uphold people's already established rights and entitlements more than it has helped new, unprecedented and possibly even revolutionary advances in societal functioning. In many ways, a case could be made that it is better at defending ground that has already been gained rather than being the creator of new ground. One is hard pressed, for instance, to identify instances where the federal Protection and Advocacy system has directly expanded the scope of what is now culturally possible within American civil society. In this respect, institutionalised US advocacy acts more in the mode of a protective service than as a source of fundamental rethinking of American society itself.

Its advocacy of community living as opposed to institutions might have been a legitimate claim in this regard were it the 1970s, but by the beginning of the twenty-first century it can now be largely taken for granted that the oppression of persons with disabilities will for the most part occur in community settings. What is striking is that it seems as paralysed in its vision for improved community life as does the broad centre of the field. In this way it does not appear to advance the thinking in the field, though it could be expected to eventually cooperate with such ideological progress once others have done the pioneering work. More ominously, it has no vision of what the possible decline and decadence of the field would look like and thus does not offer much of a safeguard against the field's otherwise worthy ideals becoming distorted into wantonly perverse shadows of what they could have been. This is, of course, the pitfall of any social institution that conservatively does not stray very far from non-controversial and low risk orthodoxies.

It is just this tendency to foment a re-examination that ensures progress and the increased human capacity to call into question whatever status quo has captured the field. Not unsurprisingly, the leadership for this sort of vastly more significant form of advocacy leadership will hardly arise from the ranks of even workmanlike and solid daily advocacy and representation, as it requires the more elusive abilities to look beyond what is there today, to what *ought* and *might* someday become commonplace. However one may conceive of this element, it means a capacity to step outside the safety of conventions and to take on the power and might of that which is already established and in control.

This kind of leadership can come from within established social institutions, particularly if the times endorse such experimentalism and innovation. The test tends to come more when the price of undertaking change becomes unattractive to the majority of otherwise moral and decent people. During such inhospitable periods they massively tend to seek the sanctuary of the status quo and may, in their fearfulness, timidity and willingness to cooperate with authority, essentially strengthen the mandate of those who currently prosper from conventionality. If this continues for any period of time, then it is predictable that the field will stagnate and may even become hypocritical and cynical as to its faithfulness to its alleged ideals. This descent into perversity, unless reversed, cannot help but result in actual destructive decline, irrespective of how well the realities are camouflaged to appear respectable.

Thus for the US advocacy scene, as well as that of many other nations, the crux of the leadership for moral social progress will rest with whether there exist people who are not subservient, in either their minds or institutionally, to the great engines of orthodoxy that control all societies to a far greater degree than is ever acknowledged. It is always people such as these, who have not relinquished their free agency, their capacity to dissent, and their moral and values coherency, in order to get along better with the world and its ways that offer us the best hope for leadership. It is simply not conceivable that social change, of any significant measure, can come from people who cannot put the interests of the most disadvantaged party ahead of the interests of social institutions.

People such as those described are much more likely to be the habitués of the volatile and restive ranks of the more informal advocacy world where discontent with the world holds greater sway than accommodation to it. This occurs in the countless networks that exist at the fringes of fields, where people's thinking does not begin and end where official permission stops, and where the unspeakable can be voiced, and the sacred cows sent along to their pastures. These are rarely the sorts of social forces that arise because the world works as it claims, but rather arises from those who have come to see that things are not as they have been portrayed. More importantly, social movements such as these arise because a vision of something better persuades those who need a better and different world.

It is this realm that the USA perennially continues to produce and recruit usually small numbers of innovators and often solitary moral actors and leaders. It does this not because of its social institutions, which can at times and in their way be as oppressive and perverse as any, but rather because of its culture. American culture simply does not support the kind of conformity that would silence all critics, dissidents and free thinkers. Its pluralism, emphasis on singular human conduct, romantic views of human potential, and traditions of public tolerance of the expression of opposing views, is largely inconsistent with a scenario in which progress stills entirely. Also significant is the apparently enduring American capacity for recognising, rewarding and giving support to at least some people who come from outside of the normal pathways of legitimate power and privilege. This frequently comes at the cost of social stability for its social institutions but with great benefit to their eventual renewal and revitalisation.

Thus the astute observer of the American scene, particularly one familiar with its social history, would not be at all surprised to see the USA periodically explore even the extremes of depravity when it comes to how badly its people may be treated. Yet, it is also true that one can be equally sure that even in the face of these conceivable atrocities, often carried out under public sanction, people would appear who oppose such travesties. Many of these would undoubtedly be persons of great imagination and creativity, but perhaps more significantly, they often would be persons of estimable morals and coherent values. Such persons exist, and are the ones who initiate and lead social movements for both good and bad.

This recognition of the creative and resilient powers that may exist near the margins of society in no way assures that the society will not experience many of the evils that occur elsewhere. Even a brief perusal of the American experience of growing up with a disability confirms that the USA has much to answer for by way of lost lives. Nevertheless, this should not blind the fair-minded observer from recognising that in direct response to these formidable shortcomings has arisen an impressive array of change-oriented figures. Thus great evils can often spawn great good. Still, the link is by no means automatic and the prudent course for advocacy leadership is to proactively provide for the rise of this element before it is too late. It is amazing how quickly new perversities can install themselves particularly when a field is full of itself.

The challenge for the US advocacy world is to match the rapid decline of the field with the renewing, moralising and hope-building influence of emergent social movements which are unimpressed with the field's progress, principally because people with disabilities are still not doing well. Change will not come from those who believe that what is now in place is good enough, it will come from a much more sceptical quarter. To the extent that new alliances can be established, then the institutionalised advocacy world might thrive for a little longer. To the extent that such change fails to happen then the quality of the lives of persons with disabilities will be a lot less than they might have been.

CHAPTER THIRTEEN

Better and Worse

Overview Of Formal Advocacy for People with Intellectual Disabilities in Australia

Dimity Peter

Betterer and betterer
Worser and worser
Faster and faster

Introduction

A healthy 57-year-old man with Down Syndrome who has lived with his mother all of his life is placed in a locked ward of a nursing home for people with dementia because his mother has broken her hip and can no longer look after herself and her son. A 5-year-old girl is denied entry to the same school as her sisters. A mother finds that the only option for her son when he leaves school will be to attend the local sheltered workshop. Institutionalisation, discrimination and lack of opportunity are just some of the many injustices confronting people with intellectual disability in Australia.

This chapter attempts to depict the complex and interwoven issues that represent both the fragility and the robustness of advocacy for people with intellectual disabilities in Australia. However, it is difficult to capture the diversity and dynamic nature of advocacy in a country as large as Australia. The chapter has attempted to draw out some common threads and issues although it is important to acknowledge the limitations of such an attempt, which favours the big picture.

History and background

Advocacy, where one person speaks up on behalf of a vulnerable other, is an ancient practice. However, the development of formalised advocacy programmes is a relatively new phenomenon in the Australian sociopolitical context. Following a long process of consultation with people with disabilities and their families, the Federal government established the Disability Services Act 1986, which provided for the funding of a variety of specific advocacy organisations across Australia, although a small number of formal advocacy initiatives had occurred prior to this time. Arguably such legislation is consistent with the Australian ethos of a 'fair go' and the social justice mandate that the government of the time held.

The ensuing guidelines commensurate with the Disability Services Act 1986 provided for four forms of advocacy: self-advocacy, citizen advocacy, parent advocacy and group advocacy. These are described by Cocks and Duffy (1993):

> self-advocacy services assist people with disabilities to develop and maintain the personal skills and self confidence necessary to enable them to represent their own interests in and become a recognised part of the community
>
> citizen advocacy services facilitate people in the community to assist people with disabilities to represent their own interests and establish themselves in the community
>
> parent advocacy services assist families of people with disabilities to represent their interests in the community
>
> group advocacy services facilitate community organisations to represent the interests of groups of people with disabilities...and where necessary to bring about changes in existing systems and services. (Cocks and Duffy 1993, pp.49–51)

However, J. Cross and Zeni (1993) have noted that these classifications have not reflected the on-going development in advocacy practices. In particular, there has been an emergence of advocacy on behalf of individuals (other than citizen advocacy). These advocacy forms are complemented by more generic advocacy services that are not specifically for people with intellectual disability but represent a range of marginalised groups. Such advocacy forms include some legal advocacy services and offices of the 'Public Advocate' which are state government entities. Furthermore, there exists a strong network of informal advocacy, where individuals have come together to lobby for better lives for people with disabilities. As noted by A. Cross (2001, p.4): 'One of the most encouraging features of our state [Queensland] is that there are many, many people involved in many small scale and large efforts to change the realities for people with disabilities and their families'.

The legislative framework for Australian citizens is very different from the United States. Australia does not have a Bill of Rights for any of its citizens, including people with disabilities. As noted by Bruggeman (2000):

> There are very few rights vouchsafed by the constitution, legislation or common law. Most of our rights are legal rights – we cannot be imprisoned without a trial, we have redress in law to right wrongs. We have very few rights to services… Many would claim that we are seeing two of these entitlements – unemployment benefits and free education – under challenge. (Bruggeman 2000, p.5)

Bruggeman (2000) goes on to argue that there is no right or entitlement to services for people with disabilities, only that the government be required to pay regard to the limit of resources available and to take into account equity and merit. He argues further: 'the pursuit of happiness is not enshrined in the Australian Constitution, we have common law freedom to determine our own lives…there is no requirement on government to assist in that process'. (Bruggeman 2000, p.5)

In this context it is therefore not surprising that legal advocacy has not flourished in Australia in the same way as it has in some other countries. However, social justice has long been part of the Australian consciousness and advocacy is certainly consistent with this objective.

The future of formal advocacy programmes in Australia is uncertain. Since the mid-1980s, the formal advocacy effort for people with intellectual disabilities in Australia has both succeeded and fallen short of its possibilities. This chapter examines in depth some of those factors that have sustained and threatened the viability of formal advocacy programmes in Australia over the long term and will continue to do so. This chapter does not include an examination of advocacy conducted by government departments (such as the Office of the Public Advocate), legal advocacy or the informal advocacy networks, but rather, examines advocacy by independent organisations that are government funded specifically for people with intellectual disabilities.

Threats to formal advocacy in Australia

The notion that advocacy itself is vulnerable is not new (Breedlove 1979; Cocks and Duffy 1993). When a person or organisation advocates for the interest of another it is likely, at some point, to lead to confrontation with others. However, it is interesting to note that many of the threats to advocacy in Australia appear to come from within the advocacy movement, rather than from the more well documented external sources.

The want of a collective vision

The disability field is diverse. Even if we narrow the scope to intellectual disability, it is a field divided with competing interests, philosophies and visions of what is to be achieved and what methods are best employed to address the issues. It is therefore not surprising that advocacy for people with intellectual disabilities is similarly disparate. Although unqualified unification on these issues would be unrealistic, the other extreme of disunification has implications that are explored below.

Byrne (2001) noted:

> one of the things that really screams at me every time I get together with anyone else from another advocacy agency is...that they are actually having a very different experience. They are fighting for different things and I am struggling to even have a conversation, use the same words...there are really basic differences philosophically. There is a huge range of practice and a whole lot of different things advocacy might be fighting for. (Byrne 2001, p.1)

An example cited by Byrne of the difficulties encountered from such differences is where one advocacy organisation is lobbying the government for a 20-bed group home or mini-institution. Another advocacy organisation is advocating against this precedent.

What is advocacy and what is it not?

Cross and Zeni (1993, p.iv) note that 'one of the most significant difficulties facing independent advocacy is that it is not well understood'. This lack of understanding extends not only to the Australian public but to many services, the funders and (many would argue) to people within the advocacy movement itself. Millier (2001) and Byrne (2001) note that there has been a resistance to a tight definition of advocacy.

A recurring definition of advocacy in the Australian literature is that advanced by Wolfensberger (1992):

> Social advocacy is functioning (speaking, acting, writing) with minimal conflict of interest on behalf of the sincerely perceived interests of a person or group, in order to promote, protect and defend the welfare of, and justice for, either individuals or groups, in a fashion which strives to be empathic'.

Cocks and Duffy (1993) have subsequently proposed five principles of advocacy:

> advocacy is on the side of the disadvantaged person
>
> advocacy is concerned with genuine life needs
>
> advocacy strives to minimise conflicts of interest
>
> advocacy engages in vigorous action
>
> advocacy has fidelity to disadvantaged people.

However, these principles are not universally accepted within the advocacy movement (Cross and Zeni 1993). Banks and Kayness (1998) believe this model of advocacy 'reinforces the stigma of difference experienced by people with impairments' and although the point is not developed further, it would appear the primary objections are the fact that such principles fail to consider the social model of disability and that advocacy for people with intellectual disability has had a disproportionate influence on advocacy in Australia, at the cost of recognising the needs of people with physical impairments. Others object to some of the principles. Ellis (2001) has drawn attention to the fact that there is no consensus that advocacy should be on the side of the most vulnerable person, the person with a disability. An example she draws on is the confusion about the needs of parents and families. As a parent herself, she believes that the most vulnerable person is the person with the disability and this distinction has major implications for how advocacy is carried out. To illustrate her point she describes the transformation of one organisation from 'advocating for families' to 'strengthening families to become powerful advocates for their family member with a disability, and for people with developmental disability more broadly'. The work of the organisation changed dramatically.

Advocacy is often confused with other worthwhile activities or organisations that have a vital role in seeking change for people with disabilities but which are not advocacy. Such activities include information and resource services, education and training, complaints services, case coordination and case management, or disability agency safeguards (Cross and Zeni 1993).

What are we advocating for?

Each advocacy group needs to have a vision of what society should look like if there is to be true justice for people with disabilities. It does not make sense for movements for societal change not to have a view as to how things should be different. Advocacy groups need to be clear about the vision they have of what needs to change in our society for people with disabilities. They need to have a vision, a direction, something they are standing and striving for, and it is this that should guide the actions of the group.

The good life

Many Australians have access to what could be described as the 'good life'. They have jobs, are able to purchase a home, have a partner and possibly a family of their own, they often make a contribution not only through their work and the support they provide to their family but also to the broader society through voluntary work with schools, charities or service clubs. Many Australians also have the freedom to choose their own lifestyle and have access to services such as health care, public transport and education. The 'good life' enables a person's needs to be met. Not just the basic needs of adequate food and shelter but also the need for personal security and safety, the need for friendship and love, the need to contribute, the need to be recognised as an individual and the need to make choices and decisions about one's life. All of these needs are arguably pivotal to one's emotional and physical well-being.

However, the 'good life' is not available to all Australians (Parsons 1994). If you are a person with a disability (or perhaps a member of another marginalised group) the chances are that you will have less access to the 'good life'. If you are an Australian with an intellectual disability, it is likely that you will be unemployed (and receiving a pension), will not be able to purchase your own home, are not likely to marry or live in an intimate relationship with another person, will have very few opportunities to make a contribution to society (and in fact, you are more likely to be the object of a charity) and you will have far fewer opportunities to make important decisions about your life.

Many Australian citizens have their needs met in the context of ordinary and everyday life through participation in the 'good life'. However, for an Australian with an intellectual disability the implications of not having access to the 'good life' are that it is difficult to have many of your needs met. Human services have had to develop to respond to the needs of people with disabilities, because of the failure of communities and the broader societal framework to offer the 'good life' to all its citizens. People with intellectual disabilities therefore frequently rely on their parents or formal human services to have their needs met. Often the needs of people with an intellectual disability are disregarded.

One area of dissension between advocacy groups is around the organisations' mission or philosophy regarding what represents a 'good life' for people with disabilities? Herbert (1997) describes in depth the notion of citizenship for people with disabilities, 'like other citizens, people with disability...seek dignity, responsibilities, opportunities to make contributions, to be productive and enjoy relationships'. O'Brien and Lyle (2001) discuss the significance of belonging, choosing, being respected, sharing ordinary places and making a contribution.

This 'vision' has a counterpoint. Some common life experiences of people with disabilities are congregation, segregation, social isolation, denial of choices, few opportunities, low expectations for achievement and subjection to negative stereotypes (Annison 1996). These experiences are not uncommon for people with disabilities who are supported by an array of support services. It is therefore arguable that advocacy for more services for people with disabilities may not necessarily achieve participation in the 'good life' described above.

Parsons (1994) uses a social justice and equity discourse to promote an advocacy paradigm in Australia. Although the words might be different, the vision he depicts is not dissimilar to the vision discussed above. Parsons's principles of advocacy include building a 'more inclusive society,' 'empowerment' and 'giving people a place'. Parsons's vision about the 'good life' is consistent with the one depicted above. He also notes that for good advocacy to occur it is critical to develop clarity of principles and purposes.

However, Millier (2001) and Byrne (2001) both express reservations about a purely 'reactive' model of advocacy where the focus is simply on the expressed desire of the person with a disability, without reference to the vulnerabilities of the person. These reservations stem from the knowledge that many people with intellectual disabilities have had different life experiences from people who are not marginalised. People with disabilities lack information, options and possibly have a limited understanding of the implications of any decision. Therefore, for an advocate to merely act on an expressed wish, without knowledge of the context, may not facilitate the outcome the person with a disability desires. Millier (2001) argues that in order not to increase the vulnerability of the person with an intellectual disability it is important to understand the context of the request, to understand the person's perspective and to provide information so he or she can then make an informed decision that best fits his or her needs. On the other hand, Banks and Kayness (1998) would argue that 'best interest' should unwaveringly be defined by the person with a disability, and not to do so is to divorce the individual from his or her right to self-determination. These positions are not necessarily mutually exclusive.

The arguments for having a clarity of vision are compelling. An alertness to some of the vulnerabilities of people with an intellectual disability may also prevent advocates from doing greater harm. The lack of clarity regarding a 'vision' of what an advocacy organisation is aiming to achieve can explain why one advocacy organisation might be lobbying for a 20-bed mini-institution and another might be lobbying against such a proposal. Not only is the power of advocacy dissipated through disparate goals, but also the credibility of advocacy is seriously undermined.

For more services or better services?

It is increasingly evident that there are insufficient resources to adequately support people with intellectual disabilities in Australia to lead full and interesting lives (Cocks 1998). However, as noted above, the addition of further support services may not improve the situation.

Much of the advocacy in Australia has been for more services, which is scarcely surprising given the many individuals who have few or no options. However, clearly, the quality of service being advocated for will have a profound impact on the quality of life of the individual. For example, to advocate for the closing of an institution will not in itself ensure better lifestyle outcomes for the residents. Advocacy has a role in describing what the outcome might look like: will it be a smaller institution or a real home?

There are many services that have met some of the real needs of people with disabilities and have facilitated the movement toward participation in the 'good life'. A real job, a home, a sense of belonging in a community organisation, these outcomes can liberate a person from a life of dependency and isolation. Conversely, services can subjugate people through congregation, segregation and a failure to provide choices and opportunities for participation. As a movement, advocacy in Australia has failed to unite in a clear voice to support the development of emancipatory services.

Regardless of the quality of services, a 'service' response to the need of people with disabilities does not address the basic social inequalities underpinning our social structures. It is therefore important that advocacy seeks something broader than simply 'more services.' Services, even the best services, cannot meet some of the real needs of people with disabilities, such as the need for friendship, love and intimacy. Furthermore, there are many problems that services cannot readily solve such as turnover of staff and the power dynamic between staff and people with disabilities, which heavily favour staff. As noted earlier, not infrequently services create as many problems as they solve, injustices still occur in services – abuse, over medication and denial of basic human rights – such as dignity and privacy.

McKnight (1995) has rejected the 'ultimate liberty' being just the right to services. The 'ultimate liberty', he argues, is full citizenship in our communities.

McKnight (1995) warns against what he describes as an 'advocacy vision' and contrasts it with a 'community vision'. He argues that an 'advocacy vision' is essentially against something and it leads to the creation of a defensive wall of people around the person with a disability. It results in a world in which people with disabilities are guarded by advocates, support people, job developers, housing locaters and so forth. A 'community vision' provides a context where people with disabilities are incorporated into the community, where their contributions, capacities, gifts and fallibilities will allow the development of a network of relationships involving work, recreation, friendship support, and the political power of being a citizen.

Finally, it is often difficult to distinguish between advocacy and casework, when the process of advocacy involves linking people with disabilities with services. Parsons (1994) suggests that 'casework is the process of planning, organising or providing direct services for people with disabilities.' Using such a definition the possible overlap between activities becomes evident. Ideally, advocacy is about facilitating casework not doing casework but it is acknowledged that in some circumstances this may be impractical. When advocates are doing the work of human services, two implications become evident:

> there is no incentive for human services to fulfil this role, as it is already being undertaken by an advocate, so the status quo remains

> in a community and services where advocacy is not understood, misunderstandings of the purpose of advocacy will occur.

On the other hand, Banks and Kayness (1998) argue that separating advocacy from service delivery negates the opportunity for the 'development of a strong and professional advocacy sector'. Their primary concern here is the issue of accountability outside of the human services, however, accountability is possible without a closer identification with services.

Without clarity of vision, well-defined principles and an understanding of the contradictions of human services, the potential for long-term change for people with disabilities is diminished. Advocacy for services presents a minefield of dilemmas and issues that are difficult to resolve without clear principles and direction.

Adversaries or allies?

There is an urgent and pressing need for the issues relating to people with disabilities to be on the social agenda. The Australian advocacy movement has a clear mandate; however, the potential for the advocacy to provide leadership in this regard has not been fulfilled.

Because of the philosophical divides discussed earlier, alliances have been slow to form. Many organisations work in isolation and as government funding becomes tighter, instead of greater cooperation and collegiality, there is a growing competitiveness between advocacy groups. So for example, the government defunds one advocacy organisation and some of the money saved is promised to other advocacy organisations. The demise of one organisation is seen as a bonus for others. Competition between organisations is heightened and the likelihood of trust and alliances developing is undermined.

The impact of such a lack of cohesiveness is immense. If individual advocacy organisations are fighting for a different vision and share no common ideals it is likely nothing will be achieved and, as noted earlier, the credibility of advocacy is seriously undermined. The real loss here is to people with disabilities who need a strong, loud and unified voice to articulate their current circumstances and the importance of creating a better life.

Having noted the lack of unification in the advocacy movement there have been successful coalitions, which are discussed later in the chapter.

Funding

The question of funding is an ongoing issue for advocacy. The Federal Disability Services Act 1986 serves as the primary funding framework for advocacy organisations, although state governments also make a contribution in some states. Most advocacy organisations are also supported by the unpaid efforts of board members and sometimes advocates.

Who shapes advocacy?

As a funder, the Federal government clearly has the power to control and mould advocacy in whatever direction it sees fit. This represents a large threat to the range of advocacy programmes and the independence of advocacy in Australia. The diversity of advocacy types (citizen advocacy; individual advocacy; self-advocacy; systemic advocacy and so forth) is seen as a safeguard because no single advocacy group can address the range of issues confronting people with disabilities.

However, such an array of services may be seen by the Federal government as unwieldy, with the result that the government is tempted to tender for larger and efficient 'one-stop-shops'. This viewpoint has been on the conservative political agenda for some time and such a perception continues to be a threat to advocacy in the long term. The increasing adoption by government of market ideologies (O'Connor 1999) has led advocacy away from clear principles towards concerns with efficiency, outcomes, numbers and turnover. This prompts the question as to who is shaping advocacy in Australia.

The Federal government is the primary funder. Cocks and Duffy (1993) therefore see a key role for the government to facilitate policy development and planning in the advocacy arena. This should be a participatory process with the agenda set by people with intellectual disabilities, supported by their allies and advocates. The role of government should be to foster and maintain advocacy not control it. Ultimately, it is to people with disabilities that advocacy must be accountable.

Shrinking funds

Government interest and support for advocacy in its current forms is diminishing. Many advocacy organisations have discussed the notion of developing multiple sources of funding rather than relying exclusively on government grants, as this is seen as increasing the long-term financial viability of the organisation (O'Brien and Wolfensberger 1980). Some advocacy organisations have attempted fund-raising programmes but the fact is that in Australia few of these attempts have been successful.

There exists a widespread belief that government has a pivotal role in supporting advocacy:

> Through taxation and shared responsibility I think government has an absolute duty to fund advocacy not because it meets the needs of government or not because it meets the government of the day's objectives for smoothing out the rough edges of service delivery but because the state has a responsibility to the most vulnerable members of the community. To support the voice…for people with disabilities who are disenfranchised. (Feigan 2001, p.13)

This view is echoed by Cross and Zeni (1993).

There also appears to be an assumption that fundraising is unrealistic, at least in the Australian context:

> Maybe it's a failure of imagination on my part but I just don't know where we get two hundred thousand dollars per annum. A million dollars every five years.

I don't know where that kind of money comes out of except the collective responsibility through our formal taxation system. (Feigan 2000, p.14)

However, the reality remains that with just a single funding source, advocacy remains very vulnerable to the whims of government policy.

What does/will sustain advocacy in Australia?

Although the threats to advocacy outlined above are real, advocacy in Australia is alive, vibrant and making a substantial difference in the lives of people with intellectual disabilities.

The common adversary: the oppression of people with disabilities

There is almost universal acknowledgment within the advocacy movement that people with intellectual disabilities are extremely vulnerable to abuse, discrimination and other forms of devaluation. Advocacy is seen as an important response to this reality. In 1993 an Australia-wide consultation noted:

At the heart of our consultations lay an absolute recognition of the oppression, devaluation and vulnerability of people with disabilities and their families. While we continue to have an unresponsive community and many unresponsive human services people with disabilities will continue to need advocacy...people with disabilities still experience:

> threats to life itself
>
> the threat of physical, emotional, sexual and imposed drug abuse
>
> the threat of congregation and segregation
>
> a lack of meaningful relationships
>
> no real home of their own
>
> disconnection from the life and heart of community and the relationships this means for others. (Cross and Zeni 1993, p.11)

These issues have been reiterated by O'Brien and Lyle (2001), who noted the widespread powerlessness and lifelong disadvantage experienced by people with intellectual disability. Isolation, abuse, congregation and segregation were common themes.

Nor is the need for advocacy seen to be diminishing. Australian society is increasingly being influenced by the notion of economic rationalism where cost efficiency, contribution to productivity and the corporate realm are becoming the dominant community values (Cocks and Duffy 1993). There is also a growing gap between the rich and the poor and an increasing sense of alienation and pow-erlessness felt by many Australians (Chenoweth 1999). This point is nicely captured by Ward (1999):

> The need for advocacy is increasing. The issues are getting tougher and more life threatening, the allegations of neglect and abuse seem ever more widespread. Also significant elements of society appear less welcoming to those who are marginalised... Economic rationalism and competition policies are placing small, responsive services under threat and managerialism is resulting in failure of leadership within our bureaucracies. (Ward 1999, p.169)

Many Australians are 'called to advocacy' because they believe in a more inclusive and just society and there is a sense of societal obligation. They believe in the notion of a 'fair go' that characterised the early years of their federation. As noted by Millier (2001), Australians are a nation of volunteers.

The power of advocacy

Individual stories can capture the impact that advocacy can have on the lives of people with intellectual disability. Many of these stories are inspirational and of course are often best told by people with disabilities and their advocates. The restoration of people's autonomy and dignity is intrinscally rewarding and advocates frequently note how such a liberatory process has benefited them, as well as the person with a disability. The achievements of advocates provide a strong foundation for advocacy in the future. The outcomes of advocacy are building more equitable, more cohesive and more inclusive communities.

> William is a healthy, outgoing 57-year-old man with Down Syndrome who has lived with his mother all of his life. He was placed in a locked ward of a nursing home for people with dementia because his mother had broken her hip and could no longer look after herself and her son. William became very passive, uncommunicative and withdrawn. He lost interest in food and had to be medicated at night because he couldn't sleep. The local citizen advocacy project became involved because William was the only male in the ward and was much younger and more competent than his fellow 'patients'. The citizen advocacy programme located a widow, Mary, to be William's advocate. Mary had known William to 'say hello to' for many years as they had lived on the same street. The advocacy programme talked to Mary about how vulnerable William was to permanently losing his home, his skills and contact with his mother. Mary began to visit William and believed that William might be depressed, so she sought assistance from the social worker and local general practitioner. She arranged for William to visit his mother

regularly in another hospital. William's behaviour began to change. He started to eat, to dress himself and to speak. He wanted to go home. Mary organised for the social worker to look for supports so that William could go home. After some months, everything was in place; meals on wheels, home help for some cleaning, link to an emergency service and so forth. William is currently managing at home, and although some issues have arisen, Mary has been there to work with William to sort them out. She has also involved some of the other neighbours. It is uncertain if William's mother will come home but it is likely that whatever the outcome, William can continue to live in his own home.

Faith and Robert have a 17-year-old son, Michael, who is nearing the completion of his schooling. Michael is physically strong, enjoys the outdoors and helps his mother around the house. He has a moderate intellectual disability. The family live in a medium-sized rural town. Michael attended the local school and Faith, Robert and Michael were very disappointed when Michael began to do work experience placements from school at the local sheltered workshop. Michael wanted to work outdoors. The family had assumed that he would have choices of where he would work. Faith started to voice her concerns and was invited to the city to attend a parent advocacy workshop. She was very inspired by some of the stories she heard and many of the dreams she heard other parents talk about were the same dreams she had for Michael. With training and support from the city-based programme, Faith has been lobbying for community-based employment opportunities to be established in the town for people with intellectual disabilities. Michael has left school and is currently doing some voluntary work, but Faith is confident that support will be forthcoming for the following year.

Rebecca, her parents and her three older sisters live in an ordinary street in an ordinary neighbourhood. Rebecca's three elder sisters had attended the local primary school and Pat, her mother, was taken aback when the principal refused to enrol her when she turned 5. Rebecca is a lovely looking child with a label of moderate/severe intellectual disability; she also needs a wheelchair for mobility and communicates using different sounds. The principal referred Rebecca and her mother to the special school a 25-minute taxi ride away which he said had the facilities and curriculum that Rebecca needed. When she visited the special school, Pat noticed that the students spent much of their time lying on mats and waiting to be 'toiletted'. Pat felt that Rebecca would find it far more stimulating to be around other children who were mobile and could talk and that the curriculum could be adapted to suit Rebecca's needs. The education department and Pat could come to no agreement so Pat resorted to the Human Rights Commission which oversees the Disability Discrimination Act. The education department employed a flurry of lawyers including a Queen's Counsel to defend its case. Pat was able to find some financial and emotional support from the local independent advocacy programme and the local legal service...it came to pass the Rebecca was able to attend her local school.

Although clearly hard to measure, Ward (1999) has noted some of the advocacy outcomes: fewer people with disabilities living in large institutions; more children with disabilities in regular schools; and the fact that there is a clearer and stronger voice on the side of people with disabilities. Ellis (2001) has noted that since the mid-1990s the number of children being supported by regular classes in the state of New South Wales has grown from about 5600 to 14,000. She believes that advocacy has had a key role in this achievement.

Principles of advocacy

Although it was noted earlier that the advocacy movement as a whole lacked a common vision, there are many programmes in Australia that have a clearly artic-ulated vision and set of principles against which they measure their performance.

Most citizen advocacy projects in Australia adhere to the set of principles outlined by O'Brien and Wolfensberger (1979). Similarly, there are many advocacy organisations that have developed principles against which they can measure their performance. For example, Feigan (2001) whose organisation advocates on behalf of people with high support needs has noted:

> We are very clear about what advocacy is...acting in the sincerely perceived interest of people with disabilities...the people we support...are at the centre of our advocacy...we spend time to develop that relationship...so that out efforts are not misguided or misplaced...we have supervision built into our practice, we have peer review. (Feigan 2001, p.5)

Accountability

Related to the notion of principled advocacy is the strong and pervasive ethos of accountability, although evaluating the quality of advocacy programmes is not a simple task. The standards set by the Federal government are not considered by many organisations to be sufficient. Many citizen advocacy programmes have undergone a specific citizen advocacy evaluation using such tools as the Citizen Advocacy Program Evaluation tool (O'Brien and Wolfensberger 1980) or the Learning from Citizen Advocacy tool (O'Brien 1987). Such instruments focus on the process as well as the outcomes. Ward (1999) has observed that:

the process of advocating can often be as important as a tangible outcome achieved. Indeed, because advocacy is about influencing an outcome which is in the power of others, the measure of advocacy cannot be by its outcomes alone. The quality of advocacy should be measured against advocacy principles and the definition and elements of advocacy, rather than by reference to tangible outcomes only. (Ward 1999, p.169)

An undue focus on outcomes is likely to direct advocacy efforts away from complex long-term issues towards issues that are a quick fix. Clearly a balance is needed which takes account of both process and outcome. Unfortunately, evaluation tools that address the range of advocacy types have yet to be developed.

There is a prevailing ethos – although it waxes and wanes – that advocacy needs to be of good quality and that constructive scrutiny of it by a range of stakeholders can be advantageous. Feigan (2001) has discussed accountability in terms of ownership. He distinguishes between different types of accountability: legal owners (members of the organisation); moral owners (the people with a disability for whom the advocacy action was enacted); and the other stakeholders (taxpayer, government and community). Parsons (1994) has particularly stressed the importance of advocacy being accountable to the people with disabilities for whom it is being carried out. A number of programmes have people with disabilities on their boards.

The general acknowledgment of the importance of accountability is a significant foundation from which to move forward.

The power of networks

The reader would be mistaken to conclude from the earlier section in this chapter that advocacy is characterised by division. These divisions exist but so do many powerful networks. The citizen advocacy network has strong ties within states (where more than one programme exists), between states and internationally.

The State of Queensland has a strong advocacy network embracing different advocacy types (individual, parent and systemic) which developed when the service system in that state was weak. Advocacy effort in Queensland has been centred around individuals and families but has also impacted significantly on service policy and practice (Millier 2001). Ellis (2001) has discussed the alliances that have been made around common goals in the State of New South Wales, where coalitions have developed around key issues. These networks have been very successful in facilitating change and providing the foundation for advocacy in the future.

Conclusion

In uncertain times, advocacy has an uncertain future. Advocacy is a powerful force in the lives of many Australians with disabilities. Although there is much work to do to strengthen advocacy efforts, there already exists a good foundation from which to move forward. Looking to the future, Banks and Kayness (1998) have noted:

> Advocacy services seem to be poised on the edge of change. Advocates can choose whether to allow advocacy practice to become irrelevant...or to take the opportunity to ensure a focus that enshrines a common goal of fundamental social change, within a coherent framework of principles. (Banks and Kayness 1998, p.166)

References

Annison, J. (1996) 'The experience of disability.' In J. Annison, J. Jenkinson, W. Sparrow and E. Bethune (eds) *Disability: A Guide for Health Professionals.* Melbourne: Thomas Nelson Australia.

Banks, R. and Kayness, R. (1998) 'Disability advocacy: too much talk and not enough action.' In M. Hauritz, C. Sampford and S. Blencowe (eds) *Justice for People with Disabilities: Legal and Institutional Issues.* Sydney: Federation Press.

Breedlove, L. (1979) 'The vulnerability of advocacy', unpublished work.

Bruggeman, R. (2000) *Between Two Rocks.* North Adelaide, SA: Intellectual Disability Services Council.

Byrne, R. (2001) Interview transcript, Independent Advocacy, South Australia.

Chenoweth, L. (1999) 'Protecting the gains of the decade: contemporary threats to the humanity of people with disabilities.' In A. Cross, J. Sherwin, P. Collins and M. Rodgers (eds) *Gathering the Wisdom: Changing Realities in the Lives of People with Disabilities.* Brisbane: Community Resource Unit (CRU).

Cocks, E. (1998) 'Vision, values and strategies for the future: time to return to the basics.' Paper presented to Council of Intellectual Disability Agencies (CIDA) Conference, Caulfield, 7–8 May.

Cocks, E. and Duffy, G. (1993) *The Nature and Purpose of Advocacy for People with Disabilities.* Perth, WA: Edith Cowan University.

Cross, A. (2001) *Training and Evaluation for Change Inc Newsletter,* March. Adelaide, SA: Training for Evaluation and Change Inc.

Cross, J. (1992) *An Examination of Disability Related Advocacy in South Australia.* Adelaide, SA: Disability Advocacy Working Group.

Cross, J. and Zeni, L. (1993) *Safeguarding Advocacy for People with Disabilities in Australia.* Canberra: Disability Advisory Council of Australia.

Ellis, J. (2001) Interview transcript, Family Advocacy, Sydney.

Feigan, M. (2001) Interview transcript, Disability Justice Advocacy, Melbourne.

Herbert, A. (1997) *The Missing Dimension of Citizenship: An Exploration of the Current Issues for People with Disabilities and the Role of Advocacy.* Adelaide, SA: Disability Action.

McKnight, J. (1995) *The Careless Society: Community and its Counterfeits.* New York: Basic Books.

Millier, P. (2001) Interview transcript, Training for Evaluation and Change Inc., South Australia.

O'Brien, J. (1987) *Learning from Citizen Advocacy.* Atlanta, GA: Georgia Advocacy Office.

O'Brien, J. and Lyle, C. (2001) Inclusive Lives Workshop on Advocacy, Advocacy Action Inc., Australian Capital Territory, 28 February.

O'Brien, J. and Wolfensberger, W. (1979) *Citizen Advocacy Program Evaluation.* Toronto: Canadian Association for the Mentally Retarded.

O'Connor, M. (1999) 'Replacement of positive ideology and vision by market ideology.' In A. Cross, J. Sherwin, P. Collins, B. Funnell and M. Rodgers (eds) *Gathering the Wisdom: Changing Realities in the Lives of People with Disabilities. Brisbane: CRU.*

Parsons, I. (1994) *Oliver Twist has Asked for More: The Politics and Practice of Getting Justice for People with Disabilities.* Geelong: Villamanta.

Ward, J. (1999) 'The importance of advocacy and advocacy development.' In A. Cross, J. Sherwin, P. Collins, B. Funnell and M. Rodgers (eds) *Gathering the Wisdom: Changing Realities in the Lives of People with Disabilities.* Brisbane: CRU.

Wolfensberger, W. (1992) Workshop on Social Advocacies on Behalf of Devalued and Disadvantaged People, Adelaide, South Australia, September.

CHAPTER FOURTEEN

Advocacy

The Last Frontier in Special Education?

Colleen Brown

Parents who do not have the stamina and resources won't cope.
(Marcus and Leanne, parents of Martin)

Introduction

I write this chapter as the parent of Travers (aged 20) who has special educational needs. I quickly became politicised when I realised that society had very different expectations for Travers than it had for our other three children. For 18 years I have acted as a volunteer education advocate for families who have children with special needs. During that time I have lectured and written about special education and its impact on families both here in New Zealand and overseas.

This chapter draws on the many interviews I have conducted with parents since 1995. It examines the deficits inherent in the 'parent professional partnership' espoused in the special education policy currently being implemented in New Zealand. The chapter explores why parents need advocacy and uses the research carried out by me for the Family Advocacy Charitable Trust (FACT) in 1997. A number of parent interviews conducted for FACT were followed up in 2000 and the results are included in this chapter. I trust the voices of the parents interviewed carry an international message for all readers.

Advocacy

There is no centralised advocacy support service for parents of children with special needs which is available as of right in New Zealand. In 1991, the one-year-old Parent Advocacy Council was disestablished under the newly elected National government. Since 1991 the prevailing view of governments has been that for government to provide advocacy support for parents as of right, would result in driving up the demand for resources (interview with Wyatt Creech, former Minister of Education, 2 June 2000).

In New Zealand, the service organisations involved in the voluntary sector, supporting people with disabilities, intellectual handicap, physical disability and sensory impairments, rely on a mix of government funding and donations to meet their operational costs. Advocacy that is too strident or effective in its criticism of government activity in any area of service provision, including special education, may well jeopardise the continuity of state funding to the particular service and the disability sector that it supports. Certainly, senior ministers of the crown have stated their negative views to me about volunteer organisations that cross the line in advocating against government special education policy.

In the Auckland region, it is often left to volunteer advocates like myself to endeavour to fulfil the advocacy requirements of parents. The types of advocacy asked for by parents often occur during a crisis, and range across the education spectrum from entry into school, attendance at individual education plans (IEP) meetings, Section 10 Appeals, and expulsion meetings. I contend that the present state of affairs offers little dignity or accountability to the parents of children with disabilities. The Ministry of Education appears caught between implementing current education ideologies, appeasing the powerful political forces of teacher unions and principal groups and caught in the middle are parents who have minimal power despite the fact that it is their children who are the pawns in the game.

The current Labour Alliance Coalition government has promised an advocacy centre to parents; however, from data recently collected it appears that the advocates will be little more than advisers at the end of a telephone in the Office for the Commissioner of Children and of a type not able to provide the in-depth, shoulder-to-shoulder advocacy so desperately required by parents of children with special needs. The Purchasing Agreement between the Ministry of Education and the Office for the Commissioner for Children for the provision of such advocacy services does not mention children with special needs at all. There is no reference to how the Ministry of Education might use information from any data collected by the Commissioner to create a more accountable environment for families who are struggling with the educational sector. The budget allocated for advocacy is extremely limited.

For those parents who have lobbied vigorously for years for a dedicated advocacy centre to serve families who have a child with a disability this most recent development is a severe disappointment.

Special education provision in New Zealand

In New Zealand, education was made free, secular and compulsory with the passing into law of the Education Act 1877 but it was not until 1989 that children with special needs were given the same right to be educated alongside their peers. The fourth Labour government changed the education provision for children with disabilities and special needs when it passed the Education Act 1989, enabling all children to enrol and attend their local school, where that was their parents' wish. The Education Act 1989 not only confirmed students' rights but also endorsed parental choice in their child's educational placement.

This Act above all others signalled a move towards a 'rights' approach in educating people with special needs. The recognition by the fourth Labour government of student with special needs' rights was in contrast with much of the neo-liberal policies enacted by Labour during its two terms as government (1984–1990). During this period, the policies of the 50-year-old New Zealand welfare state were systematically dismantled and the ideology of the marketplace imposed on virtually all sectors of government policy.

David Lange, Prime Minister and Minister of Education at that time, spoke of pride in the passing of the 1989 legislation enabling children with disabilities the same rights as their peers.

> I think it is sort of gilding the lily a bit to say that everyone stood up and cheered. One of the good things about the Labour caucus was that it had a residual sense of its conscience or guilt hanging over it from the days of the free spending socially intervening party which had become, through necessity or something else, converted to the party of efficiency and enterprise and international competitiveness. This was one area of life where they could actually say, 'Look we are Labour' and they did. (personal interview, July 1992, in Brown 1994, p.110)

After the implementation of the new Section 8 policy which supported children to attend their local schools, parents were briefly supported by the Parent Advocacy Council (disestablished 1991), but otherwise there were few areas of accountability for schools and the boards of trustees (that governed them). The intention of the state may well have been to legitimise the parent voice in special education by changing the law, and creating greater balance of power between the educational institutions and parent choice. However, that was not necessarily the outcome. There was no advocacy as of right for parents. Ministry of Education officials had limited powers in enforcing the law and parents were often left to battle for their child's right of entry to school with board of trustees members. Effectively parents were abandoned by the state in having their new-founded choices supported and upheld. For many parents it heralded the age of 'paper choice' rather than real choice.

During the 1980s many parent groups had a greater understanding of the workings of the education system through their involvement by educationalists in all aspects of special education policy development. Accompanying that knowledge was an expectation that the new policy would actively promote and support the idea of parents as partners in the process of educating their children.

Since 1989, inevitably, there has been a clash of ideologies. There were those, parents and educators, who viewed professionals as legitimately holding the power, particularly over the placement of a child within the education system. In contrast there were those who viewed the parents as now having a legitimate place within the schooling system, and deserving to be a partner in the relations that existed within that system.

Special Education 2000

In 1995 the New Zealand government announced its policy Special Education 2000. It was to be implemented incrementally over a three-year period, with NZ$55 million new money voted by cabinet to implement the policy.

> The aim of Special Education 2000 was: to achieve over the next decade, a world class inclusive education system that provides learning opportunities of equal quality to all students. (Ministry of Education 1996a, p.3)

The policy had two major components: support for stakeholders and additional funding. The support for the stakeholders was a critical component for families in determining the success of the new policy. Information, education and specialist support were to be provided to assist families, schools and teachers achieve the best possible learning environment for all students with special education needs.

Key elements of this support were:

availability of appropriate information for parents

meetings for principals, staff and boards of trustees

advice on school-wide approaches to include all students

continuation of attached units and teachers supported through enrolments

>choice of regular school or special school where possible

>coordination and provision of advisory and support services through government's contract with specialist agency or agencies.

The Special Education 2000 (SE2000) policy is made up of seven components designed to address the needs of learners in the early childhood and compulsory sectors of the education system. These are:

>severe behaviour (Behaviour Education Support Team – BEST)

>ongoing and resourcing scheme (ORS), for high and very high need students

>speech language

>sensory, physical and health

>special education grant (SEG), for moderate needs

>resource teachers of learning and behaviour (RTLBs)

>early intervention.

The components are resourced in a variety of ways, from centralised management of assessment for entry into a targeted resourcing scheme (ORS) to the bulk-funding to schools on a population-based formula (SEG).

Parents were especially interested in the elements of the policy that contained ongoing and assured resourcing for their children with special needs. Much of the policy implied that efforts would be made to create inclusive educational settings for children with special needs, through additional training for professionals. From the introduction of the policy parents voiced concern as to how they would be supported in understanding and participating in the evolving policy. At the last count a total of 38 documents advising special education policy or guidelines had been released into the educational sector over the three-year period 1996–1999.

Parents also assumed that the hitherto informal 'partnership' that parents had with schools would now be formalised through the publishing of the *Special Education Policy Guidelines* (Ministry of Education 1995).

Whilst the targeted funding was welcomed by parents and the voluntary sector alike, concerns were voiced at how schools would be held accountable for the money bulk-funded into them for the moderate needs children enrolled at the school.

An evolving special education policy meant that for parents to fully understand the implications of the policy on their children, they needed to access clear, on-time information. The rhetoric of the policy implementers underscored the move away from central government accountability to schools making the critical decisions.

The policy also highlighted the importance of the family's involvement in the policy: 'It is the family which is critical to the child's educational achievement' and 'it is the family which has long term responsibility for the child and knows the child best. It is therefore the family which will make the most important decisions on the child's behalf' (Ministry of Education 1996a, p.10).

The policy promised parents that it would 'promote greater understanding of the rights of parents to choose their child's school' and 'make schools aware of the responsibility they have to *all* of the students in their communities' (Ministry of Education 1996a, p.11).

In June 1996 statements were made reinforcing the importance of the partnership between schools and parents/caregivers in order to use special education resources as effectively as possible for the learner. The document also reinforced the legal and regulatory obligations of school boards of trustees. In 1998 the notion of partnership was underscored by the slogan *Getting it Right, Together*.

Under the heading of 'Educators and parents/caregivers – the key relationship', the Ministry of Education (1998a) stated:

> For this new policy to work, it is vital that early childhood centres, schools and families decide together how the special education needs of individual students should be met.

and

> Funding is now provided directly to schools for students with moderate special education needs rather than allocated centrally because it is believed that those closest to the student – schools educators and parents/caregivers – together are best able to make funding decisions about these students. (Ministry of Education 1998a, p.5)

Many parents were left to their own devices as to how they would manage the relationship with their school.

The meaning of 'partnership' for parents

This partnership between parents and professionals was seen by many parents as the core of the Special Education 2000 policy, and the essential component for the policy's ultimate success. It is well established in law that if a term is not defined in a statute, then that term takes on its normal and natural meaning. Bastiani (1993, p.104) states that 'partnership' is 'a term widely used throughout the education service, to cover a range of situations and circumstances. Its use, or overuse, is more often than not uncritical, implying that it is highly desirable, unproblematic and easily attainable'.

The sentiments behind the term 'partnership' may be something everyone thinks they understand, but as Bastiani (1993) states:

> Partnership is one of the most dominant and widely used images of our times, not only in education but also elsewhere. Any attempt, however, to examine it as a set of ideas or practices, quickly reveals its complex and elusive nature. (Bastiani 1993, p.113)

While Wolfendale (1989) comments on the core elements of effective partnership:

> The elements or building blocks of partnership are perceived by various writers to be equality in decision-making, power-sharing, equal rights in self expression and the exercise of mutual responsibility and accountability by all parties to each other and to others outside the specific enterprise. (Wolfendale 1989, p.108)

Parents interviewed appeared to hold similar views to Wolfendale (1989) describing the ideal 'partnership' variously as:

> When they share information with you, they ask you if you have any concerns and display open communication. I never feel as though it is us and them. We're in it together making joint decisions about Simon. (Karly)

> It's about respect, that they respect me for the information I bring to the situation about my child. It has got to be open and honest. (Mere)

> We all sit down with our son Samuel and have a fair deal to say on how the money is going to be spent on him at school. We have regular meetings. We see the principal on a regular basis. (Jane, Samuel's mother)

> It's about finding together how to make things happen for Luke. We need to set goals together in order to own them. (Margaret)

There appears to have been very little consideration given as to how any kind of 'partnership' was going to work between parents and schools, given that the state education system is hierarchical, autocratic and bureaucratic by nature.

Ministry guidelines to the concept of 'partnership'

Having determined that Special Education 2000 was to be implemented around the central notion of 'partnership', the Ministry of Education has expected schools and boards of trustees to determine how that 'partnership' was to be achieved. In many cases parents' expectations exceeded what was being delivered in practice by schools and boards of trustees. For many parents there is a lack of clarity in the information provided by the Ministry of Education (MoE) concerning its role in relation to professionals and board of trustees members. When the 'policy' itself is scrutinised there is a clear message as to where the power in the 'partnership' is to lie (see Table 14.1). The policy slogan of *Getting it Right, Together* appears fundamentally flawed and limited when the respective powers of the three main players are compared.

Table 14.1 Levels of participation and control in implementing SE2000		
Ministry of Education	School/boards of trustees	Parents and child

National policy and funding
National contracts for
    training
    resources
    research
    facilitators
    verifiers
Controls all communication about policy to schools and parents
Controls the membership of external reference groups and advisory groups for SE2000
Negotiates the Document of Accountability with the SES
Enters into contracts with schools as fundholders
	Create local policies
	Fill in ORS application
	Employ teacher aides
	Control SEG
	Can elect to be a fundholder
	Belong to a cluster group of schools
	May employ RTLBs
	Will refer students to RTLB services
		Vote for board of trustees
		Candidate for board of trustees
		May help complete ORS application if asked
		Attend IEP meeting
		May be consulted over use of SEG funds

Parents and partnership with schools

> Everyone's in favour of home–school partnership – whatever it is! But because it's a buzzword, there also tends to be a conspiracy to avoid looking at it too critically in case it falls apart or disagreements break out! (Bastiani 1993, p.113)

Without definite guidelines the stakeholders had to create their own. Often the outcome has been in the form of ad hoc and informal responses to individual requests from parents. This is often a painful process for all concerned. The Ministry of Education has taken a Pontius Pilate stance, effectively removing itself from the debate and insisting that schools and parents sort their concerns out by themselves. Most parents have not had the backing of independent advocates and have been left to battle out their concerns with the school alone.

All the parents interviewed understood clearly that they had to maintain a vigilant attitude toward the school regardless of how well their child was progressing. While all the parents voiced what the desirable elements of 'partnership' were, their reluctance to discuss the concept with the school possibly stemmed from a fear of what attitudes might be revealed if they examined the beliefs of the teachers in detail.

Only one parent, Mere (a Maori parent), had formally raised the question of what form a partnership might take with the school, and with the teachers responsible for educating her son.

Some schools have used the professional discourse to limit the participation of parents, setting the parameters of their involvement and stating that it is non-negotiable, as in the case of Mere and Margaret.

> At a recent teacher parent interview all they did was to tell me what they were going to do for my son. It was like they were making the IEP process obsolete. I don't have a partnership with my school. They think partnership is about parents coming to sports day. Everything is on their terms. (Mere)

Margaret was effectively disenfranchised from having her views accepted as a valid and knowledgeable partner with the school when her son was turned down for ORS funding.

> I was asked to sign the Ongoing Resource Application before the school had filled it in. I refused and that really caused conflict. Eventually they agreed to allowing me to write some information about Luke but it was on a separate piece of paper which they attached to the application. (Margaret)

For a number of parents typified by Martha, the educational professionals became part of the system controlling and limiting their participation through SE2000s pecking order of funding via the severity of disability and thereby further disempowering her as a parent.

> Partnership meant nothing – we got struck off the beneficiary list (because we didn't get Ongoing Resourcing). We thought SE2000 would improve our situation, I read it with a great deal of hope in my heart. But we are a lot worse off than before. It's not that anyone was that down right awful to us, but there was this bureaucratic system that just chewed us up and spat us out. (Martha)

The experience of some parents was typified by this comment made by Allan:

> I've been on the board of trustees for 11 years now. I am determined to stay until Simon has finished primary school. I have kept an eye on the board for Simon's sake and I got onto the selection committee for the new principal. Our new principal is great, she has vision and focus.

Resourcing is critical

Initially the SE2000 policy document stated that the ongoing resourcing scheme (where a student's needs were formally verified and resourcing set in place for a period of three years) would cover 2 per cent of students who would be funded under the categories 'high' and 'very high' needs. As implemented, the situation is very different. Only 1 per cent of such children are resourced in that category. Another 1 per cent of students are resourced separately under the Behaviour Initiative.

By accessing ORS funding the student with special needs has an entry into the 'world of resources' and by association the parent has the right to claim some form of 'partnership' with the school based on the now 'verified' special educational need of their child. With ORS funding for their child, the parent has 'status' and is a legitimate partner in the process, not just someone with an opinion. In contrast to this, the shift in the role of the teacher and special educational professional, who have become 'gatekeepers' of the resource provided by the fundholder, has now become the critical determinant to the success of the policy.

> When we didn't get any resources that was the end of any idea of 'partnership'. The school had the power and the control. They kept Luke on in the unit without any funding through the 'goodness of their heart'. I was beholden to them because Luke didn't have any resources. What did I have to bargain with? (Margaret)

Where resources and attitudes of the professionals are positive, parents are usually happy and see the benefits of the policy as it works for their child.

> SE2000 has been great for us. Simon has all the resources he needs. The school is not stressed. The teacher time is spent increasing his reading and hand writing skills. Combined with the resources we have a school where the teachers have excellent attitudes. (Karly)

The MoE officials developing SE2000 have designed the policy to ensure that in managing the special education resourcing, including SEG, the school would make decisions at the point closest to delivery of that support. This was intended to reflect the views of the family. However, many parent experiences as expressed to the author, would indicate otherwise.

In summary many of the parents interviewed regarding their experiences under the SE2000 policy stated that:

> they had not had any IEP meetings with the educational professionals at the school their child attended

> the number of professionals invited often limited their contribution to any meeting

> they were confused about how their child was resourced

> many of the children who were previously resourced through Special Education Discretionary Assistance, which had used the IEP process for planning and review, no longer were gaining that same level of resourcing under the current policy

> parents had no input into how the SEG (bulk) funding to schools would be used for their child, i.e. they had no option but to leave it to the school and para-professionals to decide what to do with the resources

> in one case the parent didn't know their child was in a unit

> there was little if any communication between the parent and the school.

These responses occurred despite the instruction to principals on the use of SEG (bulk) funding in the New Zealand Educational Institute publication *The Principal's Kit* (1999, p.77) which required that 'parents should be consulted on the work to be done with their children' and 'the board must have policy guidelines on how the SEG is to be used'.

In commenting on these points of difficulty, Armstrong (1995) noted that:

once 'special education needs' were defined in terms of the additional resources that ought to be made available, professionals were thrust into the role of gate-keepers and the possibility of genuine partnerships with parents was undermined. (Armstrong 1995, p.22)

Thus, without independent advocacy support many parents feel that they are unable to be true partners in their child's education. In many cases parents will go unaccompanied to meetings, not understanding the subtleties of the policy and come away feeling a junior member of a 'partnership' where they are supposed to have a key role in determining their child's educational future. This is due in part to poor information, no training and the lack of guidance by the Ministry of Education on the responsibilities of the school in the process. There is virtually zero accountability for schools in how their 'partnership' role with parents is executed.

External support in the form of advocacy is seen as one means of redressing this situation so that the chance of partnership becomes more attainable.

Policy information and dissemination

For many parents the intricacies of the MoE communication system defeats any idea they may have of obtaining sound information about what to do and where to go in order to achieve support and resourcing for their child. The system is just too complex and baffling.

In June 1998 an *Information for Families* kit was produced for parents and care-givers (Ministry of Education 1998b). Despite assurances by the MoE to the contrary, in the final event, there was no leaflet produced on rights for parents, apart from the inclusion of specific references restating the sections of the Education Act 1989 that gave children with special needs access to school, and the section detailing the appeal process to follow via arbitration. For a number of parents typified by Martha, the educational professionals became part of the system controlling and limiting their participation through SE2000s pecking order of funding via the severity of disability and thereby further disempowering her as a parent.

> The school never told us anything. Nobody ever told us we could do an arbitration. To do a Section 10 [arbitration] you have to be educated and wealthy. No solo mother from Otara [a low socio-economic area] is going to get through it. It seemed there were endless toll calls to Wellington to make – the 0800 number didn't get you through to those people who were in charge of Section 10s in Wellington. Then you really needed an advocate to help you out. I would say that thousands will have given up on getting resources for their children. (Martha)

Consistently MoE officials were telling parents that the SE2000 policy 'is a very large, complex education programme', but there was no training for parents to understand the intricacies of the policy.

Whilst the Ministry of Education has published a number of special education updates since 1998, to be distributed mainly by schools, many parents have found these publications difficult to understand, if they have received them at all. The updates are printed only in English, despite there being a large number of parents using special education services for whom English is a second language.

The MoE officials established a communication link with many of the national organisations in the voluntary sector. Some of these organisations have tried to fill the gaps the process created, by the production and dissemination of information. The smaller parent support groups working at the grassroots level often were unable to be of any real assistance to parents as they tended to be left out of the information loop.

Through the special education updates parents were also informed that professional development was critical because it would enable schools to take greater responsibility for all the students with special education needs. However, the professional development is not compulsory for teachers, principals or boards of trustees. When Mere challenged Ewan's teacher as to whether she had read the *Special Education Policy Guidelines*, the teacher defensively replied that 'she was too busy to do so'. Yet this teacher has virtually total power and say in Ewan's teaching programme and the use of his resources.

Mere, experiencing high levels of frustration and tension with the staff at her son's school, concluded:

> It seems to me we have a culture of teachers who are uninformed about Special Education 2000. I took in a pile of resources, chapters from books, ideas and nothing has changed. How could they tell me they had read all that and not changed at all? They didn't even discuss it. I can't believe I have to feel this way. It's like we are being punished. (Mere)

Attitudes

The attitude of educational professionals to students with special needs remains the biggest stumbling block for parents. Where parents have challenged the school or educational professionals there have often been paybacks.

When Mere challenged the teacher's attitude to her desire to be a more active partner in her son's education, there emerged a number of consequences.

Recently, in a letter home, the school outlined its view of the relationship with Mere as follows:

> We work collaboratively with parents but as the professionals it is for us to decide what a good education is for Ewan and how we use the resources available.

and

> It must be realised however that the communication between the school and parent can only be as it is for the other 500 children in the school. This is the agreed premise behind mainstreaming.

When Mere and the advocate decided to ask a facilitator to intervene with the school as the relationship had deteriorated so much, the school wrote a communication guideline to be followed by Mere as follows:

> she was allowed to speak with one teacher aide at 8.55 a.m. on Monday to 'discuss [the] week, needs and concerns'.

> the second teacher aide was available for Mere to speak with at 2.50 p.m. on Thursday

> any other issues that have caused concern outside the normal daily routine would be discussed by Mere with the teacher either before or after school.

The proposed communication plan was implemented before Mere could agree to it or ask for any modifications. She was expected to rubber stamp the plan.

In 1997, research data for the Family Advocacy Charitable Trust was collected via a questionnaire to parents of children with special education needs, asking about their advocacy requirements. The research was undertaken in the Greater Auckland Metropolitan area (1.2 million people); 899 questionnaires were distributed to schools with mainstreamed students with special educational needs and principals were asked to distribute them to the families of the children. A follow-up of 50 per cent of the schools was conducted. This showed that less than half of the questionnaires were forwarded to the target group of recipients by the school principals. The action of the principals in this situation reinforced the prevailing view held by many parents that professionals deliberately act as 'gatekeepers of information'.

The research carried out by FACT was undertaken concurrent with the introduction of the Special Education 2000 policy. The concerns noted in 1997, over the attitude of educational professionals to students with special needs, remained after its introduction and persist to the present day. Parents wanted advocacy support for their children regardless of what year their child was in the education system or in what setting. Parents interviewed for the 1997 FACT research and re-interviewed by me for this chapter on the whole reiterated their concerns about professional attitudes to their children and the difficulties arising for parents from the lack of advocacy support.

> I have been trying for five years to get agencies to establish a plan for my son. We were told with help, he would achieve. SES identified him as needing special schooling. Since then we have battled for help, support and information, and received very little. 'He's not bad enough,' they say. My son is slowly slipping further behind, I guess he'll soon be bad enough! Frustration levels are high. (Rachel, mother of Howard, 1997)

> The support person told us recently: 'If he gets suicidal, let us know, then we can do something about it.' We have known about this since he was 4 years old. (Rachel, mother of Howard, 2000)

Many of what are essentially routine processes under the SE2000 policy implementation carry high emotional costs for parents. The reality for one mother was shared in this way:

> IEPs are a major nightmare. They secretly stack the odds against me. I no longer go to IEPs alone. I feel that it [the school administration] is really patronising and condescending. They say: 'Now listen very carefully and I'll repeat that one more time.' I don't deal with it well. I don't mind being punished but I do object to my son being punished. Frequently, I must confess, I give in. It is a feeling of total disempowerment. (Margaret, mother of Luke, 1997)

Schools are very aware of parents' responses and feelings. On some occasions the school would use them to support the school's position on special education issues, on others parents were left isolated and vulnerable.

> Everything was about power and control. I didn't get offered any SEG money for Luke. The teachers said to me that they would give him some teacher aide time, but they also said to me: 'You realise we don't have to don't you?' I had to be very grateful. It was ironic, when the taxi service was threatened they couldn't wait to get my support. But they certainly didn't want you asking questions about things they wanted to keep to themselves. I took two different support people to IEPs. One was a workmate, the other the school counsellor. I can tell you they [the school's professionals] watched what they said then. (Margaret, mother of Luke, 2000)

With the support of two advocates Margaret had found the strength to proceed, but this had still not addressed the deficiencies in the parent's working relationship with the school.

Where the policy has been implemented with a balance between resources, attitudes and practice change can occur. When first interviewed in 1997, Jane had the following experience.

> At an IEP meeting the teacher appointed by the school to attend the meeting had little knowledge or involvement with special education. The teacher stayed 20 minutes then walked out as she had another meeting to attend. Jane said:
>
>> I asked her to stay but she wouldn't. I had an advocate there, the SES and an adviser from Homai [a special school for students who are vision impaired or blind]. The school would not let Samuel leave the school to do his lifeskills, which involved him working in different places. Both the advocate and SES said this was wrong and it could be done. The meeting got very hot. (Jane, mother of Samuel, 1997)

Subsequent to the 1997 interview, Jane changed Samuel's school and achieved the desired balance:

> The last two years have been a wonderful experience for us. Samuel does his own shopping. He goes all by himself. The other school would not dream of letting him do this. The school absolutely respects us. The principal shows leadership, and the school immerses the students with special needs in everything it does. The SES is the fundholder. The last meeting was great. The SES worker had loads of ideas and she was up to date with everything. (Jane, mother of Samuel, 2000)

The FACT Report, 1998

The research carried out by the Family Advocacy Charitable Trust in 1997 revealed that only 37 per cent of respondents belonged to a support group (Brown and Browning 1998, p.42). The research also showed that over 50 per cent of those parents who belonged to a support group had a child 7 years of age or younger (Brown and Browning 1998, p.21). In the study, those parents who belonged to a support group were identified as being more likely to be European, earn over NZ$40,000 and hold tertiary qualifications, and have a child with an identified disability (Brown and Browning 1998, p.19). Whilst there is validity in the assumption that support groups can assist parents in making decisions about their child with disabilities, it must be accepted that over 60 per cent of parents in the Greater Auckland region do not receive support from any such formal group. Coupling this with the known over-representation of Maori and Pacific Island children using special education services, and their under-representation in support group membership in the FACT survey, it would appear that the MoE's strategy in communicating with parents on SE2000 policy matters via support groups is potentially flawed.

In October 1999 (prior to the change of government) a Ministry of Education statement accompanying the Budget announcement on education expenditure advised that facilitators were to be appointed to resolve difficulties in the family–school partnerships for students with special needs. That statement read:

> A core role for the Ministry is to build effective relationships with education providers and communities so they can achieve the best possible education outcomes for students. Fundamental to this premise is that where difficult situations exist, the support should go to develop and enable a working partnership to be maintained rather than pitting one group against another. There has been a strong lobby from the Family Advocacy Charitable Trust (FACT), the Commissioner for Children, IHC, NZCCS and the Quality Public Education Coalition (QPEC) *et al.* for a Parent Advocacy body. *Whilst parents are strong in their lobby for advocacy, representatives from the school sector question the size and nature of the problem. They also state that they receive unreasonable expectations from parents of students with special needs in requests for provision of service and accountability.* (Ministry of Education 1999, p.1, added emphasis)

The Ministry of Education statement is interesting in that it ignores the quantitative and qualitative data collated by the FACT research, and other approaches by lobby groups from the early 1990s, yet appears to give greater credence to what can only be viewed as anecdotal evidence contributed by the schools' sector.

Accountability and appeal: the Ministry of Education

It appears that good will and the desire to build a relationship between the key stakeholders have prevailed over the development of any formal accountability structures centred on the child and family.

There is no accountability for parents despite the Ministry of Education stating that they will act when advised that schools are not fulfilling their obligations. There is no prescriptive requirement in the implementation of Special Education 2000, and no policy for MoE intervention in school administration. It appears that at best the MoE liaison person will 'have a chat' with the school. In all probability the parent would be advised by the MoE to write to the board of trustees and get them to act. The situation for parents becomes more precarious when the school is also the fundholder.

The Special Education 2000 policy may involve a process of verification of individual children's needs. Parents are able to appeal under Section 10 of the Education Act 1989 if their child is not verified with resources appropriate to his or her needs. There is no advocate allocated to the parent to assist them in the appeal. After an appeal by a parent using this provision was successful; the MoE changed the procedure for its use to disallow the introduction of any new material to challenge the decision of the verifiers. As a consequence the need for accurate and complete appraisal at the time of completing an application on the child's behalf has become even more crucial.

The MoE does not have the formal power to enforce accountability in the relationships with the other parties that they rely upon, such as boards of trustees and schools, to implement the policy and deliver services to students with special educational needs.

Conclusions

The foundations of the Special Education 2000 policy were established in the belief of the parent's right to enrol their child with special educational needs in the school setting of their choice. It assumed that:

> parents and professionals would work cooperatively to obtain the best outcome for children with special education needs

> schools' administrators, and boards of trustees were competent and willing to implement the policy fairly in the interests of those children

> support for parents was not necessary to ensure a fair and equitable delivery of services under this policy.

Having reviewed the implementation of the policy since 1998 a parent's conclusions might well be:

> despite the best intentions the imbalance of power between parents and professionals at a local level remains a major impediment to the successful implementation of a policy based on partnership; without a balance of power no partnership can in fact exist

> despite a demonstrated need (at least in the minds of the parents) for effective advocacy support to assist parents in dealing with professionals, there appears to exist a deliberate strategy in government not to fund such support, as to do so would inevitably mobilise pressure for increased resources

> the edict of 'those that hold the funds hold the power' as ever applies to the delivery of special education services. However, sufficient

expertise will often not exist within schools or their administrations to resource their special education needs effectively.

Until formal lines of accountability are created, and fully funded advocacy centres are established to safeguard students' rights, this special education policy and any variations on it will inevitably fail.

References

Armstrong, D. (1995) *Power and Partnership in Education: Parents, Children and Special Educational Needs.* London: Routledge.

Bastiani, J. (1993) 'Parents as partners: genuine progress or empty rhetoric?' In, P. Munn (ed) *Parents and Schools: Customers, Managers or Partners?* London: Routledge.

Brown, C. (1994) 'Special education policies of the fourth Labour government, 1984–1990: an interpretive analysis', unpublished thesis, Massey University, Auckland.

Brown, C. and Browning, H. (1998) *Students with Special Needs: The Case for Advocacy.* Auckland: Family Advocacy Charitable Trust.

Ministry of Education (MoE) (1995) *Special Education Policy Guidelines.* Wellington: Education Gazette.

Ministry of Education (1996a) *Special Education 2000.* Wellington: MoE.

Ministry of Education (1996b) *Special Education 2000: The Special Education Grant.* Wellington: MoE.

Ministry of Education (1998a) *Special Education 2000: Getting It Right Together.* Wellington: MoE.

Ministry of Education (1998b) *Information for Families.* Wellington: MoE.

Ministry of Education (1999) *Budget Statement: Liaison Positions to Facilitate the Development of Family School Partnerships where there are Students with Special Needs.* Wellington: MoE.

New Zealand Education Institute (1999) *The Principal's Kit.* Wellington: MoE.

Wolfendale, S. (1989) 'Parental involvement and power-sharing in special needs.' In S. Wolfendale (ed) *Parental Involvement: Developing Networks between School, Home and Community.* London: Cassell.

The Contributors

Dorothy Atkinson is a Senior Lecturer with The Open University

Deborah Baillie is a Lecturer in Social Work Law with The Open University

Colleen Brown is a Senior Lecturer in Communication at Manukau Institute of Technology, Auckland, New Zealand

Rohhss Chapman is a Volunteer and Co-researcher, Carlisle People First

Tim Clement is a doctoral student with The Open University

Andy Docherty is Project Director, Carlisle People First

Colin Goble is a Lecturer in Disability Studies, King Alfred's College, Winchester

Barry Gray is Head of the Applied Social Studies Department, King Alfred's College, Winchester

Elizabeth Harkness is a Training Group member and Co-researcher, Carlisle People First

Robin Jackson is Development and Training Coordinator, Camphill Scotland

Michael Kendrick is an independent consultant with Kendrick Consulting Services, Holyoke, Massachusetts, USA

Janet Larcher is an independent speech and language consultant, Surrey

Niall McNulty is a member, Carlisle People First

Dimity Peter is Senior Lecturer in the School of Special Education and Disability Studies, Flinders University of South Australia

Nick Pike is Service Manager for Children's Services, Annie Lawson School, Norwood/Ravenswood, Berkshire

Mike Pochin is Coordinator, Dorset Advocacy

Janet Scott is Coordinator, Scottish Centre of Technology for the Communication Impaired, Southern General Hospital, Glasgow

Fred Spedding is Director, Carlisle People First

Veronica M. Strachan is a Senior Lecturer in Law, Robert Gordon University, Aberdeen

Louise Townson is Administrator and Co-researcher, Carlisle People First

Jan Walmsley is Dean of the School of Health and Social Welfare, The Open University

Author index

Subject index